SHIFT!

SHIFT!

Moving From the Natural to the Supernatural

KEN AND JEANNE HARRINGTON

DESTINY IMAGE® PUBLISHERS, INC.

P.O. Box 310, Shippensburg, PA 17257-0310

"Speaking to the Purposes of God for this Generation and for the Generations to Come."

This book and all other Destiny Image, Revival Press, MercyPlace, Fresh Bread, Destiny Image Fiction, and Treasure House books are available at Christian bookstores and distributors worldwide.

For a U.S. bookstore nearest you, call 1-800-722-6774.

For more information on foreign distributors, call 717-532-3040.

Or reach us on the Internet: www.destinyimage.com

ISBN 10: 0-7684-3098-4

ISBN 13: 978-0-7684-3098-1

For Worldwide Distribution, Printed in the U.S.A.

1 2 3 4 5 6 7 8 9 10 11 / 13 12 11 10 09

ACKNOWLEDGMENTS

KEN and JEANNE would like to thank Brenda G. Smith for the marvelous job she did on the initial edit of this book. Her insights and suggestions greatly improved the flow from the choppy original manner in which it was written.

We also thank the women of Spruce Grove Community Church for transcribing the original handwritten manuscripts. Without their help, this project would have taken months longer to complete. Thanks first to Myrna Muckli, who organized and did the lion's share of the work. Thanks also to all the others who transcribed: Tangy Shields, Teresa Hunter, Suzanne Harrington, Laverne Kundert, Cheri Mitchell, and Shara-Rae Mitchell. Thanks also to Lauri MacKinnon for her photography.

We would also like to thank Destiny Image for pushing us to get this book ready. Special thanks to Don Nori Jr. for his vote of confidence to write this second book even before a single copy of the first one had been sold. Thanks also to Ronda Ranalli for her enthusiasm and persistence in keeping us in synch with our deadlines. Thanks to Dean Drawbaugh for his oversight of the editing and efforts to get the book into print and shipped. Also thanks to Jeff Gerke and

Donna Scuderi, whose editorial comments prompted me to make this a better book than it was when they first read it.

Most of all, we acknowledge the inspiration of the Holy Spirit and honor Him as the true author of this book. Ken received the entire outline for this book and *Designer Genes* in a 45-minute period as He downloaded some of the Holy Spirit's wisdom into his own spirit. The Spirit's divine revelation and the recalling of Scriptures to our minds made this book a joy to write.

ENDORSEMENTS

All I can say is: "Wow!" It is so refreshing to see how the two of you, together, ingeniously reveal the heart and mind of God. When I grow up I want to write as clearly and accurately as you do. Truly, anyone who reads this book will undoubtedly be lifted up into a fresh new realm of excellence.

—Michael Danforth
Founder, Mountain Top International
Yakima, Washington

Ken and Jeanne's writings are charged with wisdom and insight from above. The many real-life stories and their practical applications help make this book an excellent resource for drawing upon the power of God and sanctifying the entire soul.

—Lorne and Rita Silverstein
Directors, Every Home for Jesus
Edmonton, Alberta

This sequel to Ken's first book, *Designer Genes,* really gives all Christians something that is so necessary and vital to lead a quality, fruitful life. Character building and fruit production are what a Christian life should be about; this book will help everyone in both areas. This practical book greatly assists the Kingdom of God and those in it to fulfill their calling.

—Kim Weiler
President, Fe Viva World Missions
Guatemala

The Harringtons share from their personal encounters how the Lord is moving supernaturally through their lives. This book should encourage believers in their walk with the Lord as they are led by Him to experience His ever-surprising ways.

—David Demian
Director, Watchmen for the Nations
Vancouver, British Columbia

Ken and Jeanne's newest book is filled with the same poignant and piercing truth as Ken's first one, *Designer Genes*. This makes *Shift!* a must-read for all believers. Aside from this obvious treasure, there is an impartation of faith that can take you places you never thought possible. Great grace is about to be poured out on the generation that will receive it—and this book carries a significant measure of that grace.

—Marc Brisebois
Senior Pastor, Spruce Grove Community Church
Director, Watchman on the Wall
Spruce Grove, Alberta

Ken and Jeanne are God's faithful servants. They are filled with the Holy Spirit and have been building the basis of spiritual revolution through their prophetic lives. Their new book, *Shift! Moving From the Natural to the Supernatural,* will change your spiritual paradigm. It will clarify your identity as a child of God and His inheritor. This powerful shift of your sight will carry the revolution in your life.

—David Kim
International Director, Jesus Ministries International
Seoul

CONTENTS

FOREWORD

IF we are going to walk with God, we must be willing to change our way of thinking. When God called him to leave Haran and venture into the unknowns of Canaan, Abram had to shift his thoughts about home and family. He had to shift again when God promised him a son and changed his name to Abraham.

Likewise, Jacob had to reexamine his methods of obtaining his heart's desires as God's dealings changed his *striving* to *receiving*. Jacob's grasping nature dictated his entire walk in life, which God changed when He changed his name to Israel (meaning "prince with God").

Finally, Joseph's tranquil, favored view of life was altered dramatically as he was shifted into a place of power. Israel had to shift out of a slave mentality in order to operate in the freedom God purchased for them. Had they been able to make one more shift—out of their grasshopper mentality to that of conqueror—they would have been able to enter into the Promised Land and experience all the fullness of their destiny.

Shift! is a book that examines this need to change not just the things we do but the way we think—the way we think about God, ourselves, and our words. Each chapter challenges another aspect of the mind-sets that we have erected to define "our world." Ken and Jeanne expose their own fears, sins, and misconceptions that hindered them on their journey out of the natural realm into the supernatural.

This book is a prophetic call for the Church to be aroused from its slumber, shake off the old thought patterns, and shift to where God is going.

Because God is moving, the whole earth is shaking. Economies and political structures are shaking. Everything that is not founded in Him is shaking. This is not punishment or judgment; this is just what happens when God touches the earth. He puts His finger on every idea that opposes the establishment of His Kingdom and our abilities to move into the fullness of our destinies. God orchestrates these changes in our thinking by first pulling His grace back to expose our true natures. With no grace to empower our performances and no illusions of righteousness to hide behind, we are forced to examine our heart motives. Most of us look at this process as a step backward in our Christian walk. We may question our faith and our commitment, thinking we have grown cold and betrayed God.

Peter felt this way when he denied Christ. The truth was that he had always been that way; he just didn't know it. Jesus did: He prophesied Peter's denial, but added: *"I have prayed for thee, that thy faith fail not: and when thou art converted* [when you change your mind], *strengthen thy brethren"* (Luke 22:32).

Until God lifted His grace off of Peter's self-reliance and reckless nature, Peter had trusted who he was and what he thought, so much that he even tried to rebuke Christ (see Mark 8:32). Peter was fearless in the face of a whole company of armed men and single-handedly started to attack them (see John 18:3-10). Once the grace was gone, he couldn't even face down a servant girl (see Luke 22:56-57). Jesus was not trying to expose Peter to anyone but himself and had only one purpose in shaking his self-confidence: to bring Peter to his destiny in the Kingdom. Peter recognized his calling, but was unaware that he could not function in that calling without changing the way he thought.

Casual Christianity will not keep us where God intends to take us. He is setting off the fire alarms in our lives to warn us to get ready. Ken and Jeanne have discovered in their own lives how to get results by shifting from natural to supernatural thinking. *Shift!* calls the Church to come up higher, above the plane of reason to the plane of faith. It teaches us how to apply godly principles in our ordinary lives to get extraordinary results. It reminds us that idolatry is trusting in our thoughts and our efforts—faith is trusting in God's words and His grace. As the Bible tells us, *"this is the victory that overcometh the world, even our faith"* (1 John 5:4).

It is with great pleasure that I recommend the Harringtons' book, *Shift!* If you apply the principles laid out in this great book, your life will move from the natural to the supernatural. Life on earth will never be the same!

—Stacey Campbell, Prophet
Co-founder and Director, RevivalNOW! Ministries,
Be A HERO, and Praying the Bible International
Founder and Facilitator, Canadian Prophetic Council
Kelowna, British Columbia
www.revivalnow.com
www.beahero.org

FOREWORD

I am always amazed at how certain passages of Scripture can lift us out of the mundane and give us a prophetic window into what is possible. The following are a few of my favorite passages:

> [God] ...*is able to do exceedingly abundantly above all that we ask or think, according to the power that works in us...* (Ephesians 3:20 NKJV).

> ...*Eye has not seen, nor ear heard, nor have entered in to the heart of man the things which God has prepared for those who love Him. But God has revealed them to us through His Spirit....* (1 Corinthians 2:9-10 NKJV).

> ...*the works that I do shall he do also; and greater works than these shall he do; because I go unto My Father"* (John 14:12).

> ...*for with God all things are possible* (Mark 10:27).

And yet the questions remain: Why aren't we seeing more of the greater works? Where are the signs and wonders that Jesus said would follow the believers? How can I participate in seeing "all things" become possible?

In order to address these issues, I would first like to tell you a true story from my childhood.

Growing up in our small town in Southern Ontario was idyllic. It was during the 1950s and 1960s, when life was simple. Dads went to work, moms were home with the kids, and families were largely intact. Our lives were not unlike the black and white TV shows we watched such as *The Andy Griffith Show* or *Leave It to Beaver*. The biggest events of our year were the first day of school in September, the last day of school in June, the County Fair in October, and the annual December lighting of our Christmas display in the park.

From my perspective, our neighborhood was the best. Large maple trees lined both sides of the quiet street where older, middle-class homes and manicured yards provided the backdrop for our lives. All the kids would regularly gather on the front porch of our next-door neighbor, Mrs. Potts, the kindest of elderly widows who kept us in treats, lemonade, and stories of the good ol' days. From her porch there on the hill, we could survey both ends of our street—our domain—and make sure all was well.

Then, suddenly, the news came. The town planners had chosen our street to become the new four-lane artery conveying traffic to the center of our town. Within months, the maple trees were cut down; the road widened substantially; and our neighborhood changed forever.

Part of the change included the demolition of the house directly across the street from ours where our town's own version of Eddy Haskell lived. The house next to his (a house owned by the Winslows), was going to be uprooted and relocated to another part of town!

Finally, moving day arrived. With crews assembled, a police escort in place, power lines severed, and old plumbing disconnected, the drama was about to begin. Like the aging matriarch of a family, the large, two-story home was ready for her move. It would be more than a mile to her new lot; she would soon sit on a hill overlooking a park, with a panoramic view of the town (certainly a promotion for her in her senior years). As she inched across town, the streets were lined with more spectators than we usually had for our Santa Claus parade. And as she approached the lot which would become her new resting place—there it was—a brand-new, state-of-the-art, never-been-used-before, rock-solid foundation waiting just for her!

Within a few days, she was securely founded, wired, and plumbed, ready for the family to move back in and enjoy. She still sits atop that hill some 45 years later; and has been a gracious home to several families during that time.

But what is the point of my story? Just this: There are so many wonderful things that God wants to do in our lives! Things beyond anything we could ask or think! Greater things! But He can't! Why not? *Because our lives are on old foundations that are weak and crumbling, decaying, and passing away.* If He were to build what He desires on that old foundation, it would surely collapse—and the new structure with it.

God is too wise for that. So He lays a new foundation (with the help of apostles and prophets), and then ever so lovingly invites us to rebuild our lives on a rock that cannot be moved.

Which brings us to this book—*Shift!* Ken and Jeanne Harrington have masterfully laid a foundation from the Word of God that is unshakable and immovable. Then with personal experiences from their own journey, they illustrate the principles with very clear life lessons that cannot be denied.

Peter Wagner says that, as of 2001, we have entered into the greatest reformation since the days of Martin Luther! He calls this the "New Apostolic Reformation."[1] This is not "church as usual." God is building a super-highway! He is preparing for global harvest! Old foundations and old structures will not be able to contain the greater things that God will do!! Some must be torn down and others must make the "shift" to higher ground.

If your plan is to live your life your way on a quiet little street while sipping lemonade, then this book is not for you! But if you can say "I am ready for God to build something awesome in my life—not my dream, not my will; but His dream and His will!—something abundantly above anything I could conceive; then this book is for you! The foundational truths contained in these pages will go a long way to equip you to do what you never knew you could do...and greater!

Hats off to the Harringtons for sharing this exciting journey with us! And seatbelts on for those about to embark on it!

—Dennis Wiedrick
President, Wiedrick and Associates
Apostolic Ministries
Oshawa, Ontario

ENDNOTE

1. C. Peter Wagner, *Dominion: How Kingdom Action Can Change the World* (Grand Rapids: Chosen Books, 2008), 22, 34.

PREFACE

THIS book was originally part of a larger work, the first part of which was published as *Designer Genes*. The manuscript was too large and, because it covered two topics, it was later divided.

Designer Genes covered the various aspects of character and how these affected our destinies. *Shift! Moving from the Natural to the Supernatural* focuses more on aspects of the beliefs, attitudes, and subsequent actions that also affect our destinies. Since both books were originally part of a single volume, we have included parts of the original Preface as part of this work.

The purpose and methodology of *Shift!* remain the same as for the original work and warrant explanation to you, today's reader. The book has two main purposes:

1. To illustrate in a practical way how attitudes and actions permit an individual to walk in real authority.

2. To get the principles *and* Word of God into people's spirits so they can be empowered, not only by knowledge, but also by revelation.

To accomplish this, many Scripture quotes are woven into the text as part of the "conversation" rather than as standalone passages.

This approach enhances the uninterrupted flow of ideas and encourages readers to take in the Scriptures rather than skip over them. While principles are important, only the Word of God has the power to impart life.

Jesus, the Word, said, *"All power is given unto Me in heaven and in earth"* (Matt. 28:18). The Greek word for "power" here is *exousia*, which implies authority[1,2] both the right and the might to perform an act.[3] Jesus wants to delegate that authority to His people on the earth. We have not understood that His authority comes out of His nature, not by force of our will. This misunderstanding has created a situation in which we have allowed *might* to masquerade as *authority*.

To walk successfully in the true authority of the Spirit, we must recognize that there is a "latent power of the soul"[4] opposing that authority. Jesus did not attempt to access anything from His soul to accomplish the will of God, choosing rather to *"do nothing of Himself, but what He sees the Father do..."* (John 5:19 NKJV). Our challenge is to refuse to use the power we may have in our souls and rely totally on the Spirit instead.

This book is based on the supposition that authority (from the same Latin root (*auctor*)[5] as the English word *author*) rests in the Author or Creator of this world. His authority will be manifested in us as we allow Him to be the rightful author of our thoughts and actions.

Through scriptural and personal examples and insights, this book will lead readers into a paradigm shift in the way they perceive and access the authority in which God has destined them to walk.

ENDNOTES

1. Berry, George Ricker. *Interlinear Greek-English New Testament* (Grand Rapids: Zondervan, 1973), Matt. 28:18, s.v., "exousia."

2. Zodhaites, Spiros. *The Complete Word Study Dictionary:*

New Testament (Chattanooga: AMG Publishers, 1992), s.v., 1849.

3. 1849, www.blueletterbible.org/search/lexiconc

4. Nee, Watchman. *The Latent Power of the Soul* (Manassas, VA: Christian Literature Crusade Publishers, 1972).

5. Merriam-Webster Online Dictionary. Merriam-Webster Online 2009, s.v. "author," http://www.merriam-webster.com/dictionary/author (accessed: May 21, 2009).

INTRODUCTION

THERE is a shift in our natural world. It is seen in an aggressive movement by individuals and governments to find alternative sources of energy designed to alleviate our dependence on traditional supplies.

In the transportation realm, this initiative includes the development of vehicles that run on propane, natural gas, and hydrogen. Where the generation of electricity is concerned, wind, wave, and solar power are touted as possible alternatives.

All of these new sources are in the experimental or developmental stages, even though some of them have been around, in one form or another, for centuries.

Now, faced with the "next" energy crisis, ideas are being retooled and huge sums of research and development monies are being poured into the quest. The hope is to find more economical and efficient methods of deriving much-needed power out of previously ignored or under-developed sources.

But technology changes fast. The tech world moves so fast that it sometimes seems economical to skip over the "current" innovation (which will soon be obsolete) and wait until the "next" technological improvement arrives.

Our parents lived through the obsolescence of the gramophone, the record player, the eight-track, and the cassette deck. We had to junk our Beta player when VHS won the video war, only to repeat the process when DVDs took over. Now it looks like déjà vu with the arrival of Blu-ray. The lesson is that we must be flexible. Change will come, and always with a cost.

Christians, likewise, need to embrace change in the Kingdom of God. We need to resurrect previously ignored or underdeveloped sources of power *and* find new, untapped sources if we are going to overcome our spiritual power crisis. These shifts must be made; and always, there will be costs associated with making them.

ISRAEL'S COMPROMISED KING

King Saul had been anointed by God to rule, but could not overcome his own fears. Thus, he was unable to trust and obey God's instructions. God would have *"established* [Saul's] *kingdom upon Israel for ever"* (1 Sam. 13:13), but Saul's good and godly intentions were nullified by his soulish actions.

This prompted God to shift His authority from Saul to David. Jonathan knew that God had assigned the kingdom to David. Even though Jonathan was heir apparent to the throne, he was willing to step aside because he understood what God was doing. He even prophesied that he would occupy a place right next to David and made a covenant with him (see 1 Sam. 23:17-18).

Not many people could give up their legal place of authority and joyfully submit to the one who would supplant them; but Jonathan loved David and was committed to him (see 1 Sam. 18:1).

The problem was that Jonathan was also committed to his father. He would vacillate in his loyalty: He would stand with David for a time and then go back to Saul's camp; he would strategize with David and then get back in collaboration with Saul.

Jonathan was torn between the soul tie that involved honoring his father and the spiritual tie that supported his role in the new kingdom being established by God through David. In the end, Jonathan's inability to sever his ties to the old structure (which God had established, but which was now dying) and fully embrace the new, would cost him.

The price was high; wavering between the two cost Jonathan his life and the destiny of his family (see 2 Sam. 1:23-27).

KINGDOM SHIFTS

Power structures always seem to be fixed. In reality, they are fluid. When God shifts structures, our shifting with Him is not a sign of our disloyalty to the old structures or the people within them; rather, it is a validation of our loyalty to our King.

The Church has, in an attempt to be relevant, stepped into a Gospel that is more designed to meet man's needs than it is to manifest God's glory. The Church has vacillated between meeting the people's needs and occupying her primary, heavenly calling as the Bride of Christ.

Jesus chastised the church at Ephesus, even though they were doing great works. They had left their "first love," which was Him. They were in danger of losing their light (their relevancy) if they didn't repent (see Rev. 2:2-5). Jesus said that the destiny of those who overcame was to "...*eat of the tree of life...*" (Rev. 2:7). The life in them was vital if they were ever to impart life to the world.

Jonathan tried to save his father's kingdom by fighting all the enemies of the realm. The problem was that God had ordained the death of that manifestation of His Kingdom in order to establish the next phase under David. Jonathan's only solution was not in resistance to opposing forces, but in relinquishment.

We, as a Church, have been trying to save and heal a wounded world by ministering to them where they hurt: in sickness, broken relationships, poverty, and hopelessness. We have been trying to resist all the evil that results from the sinful nature. Jesus says that we are to "*...resist not evil...*" (Matt. 5:39); instead, we should only *...resist the devil...* (James 4:7) and his subtle lies. We must shift our emphasis from trying to mitigate the damage to mastering the problem.

The world's redemption is not tied to our ability to solve their problems; it is dependent on our ability to be "*...a well of water springing up into everlasting life*" (John 4:14). We, the Church, are to be the Bride who is married to the power source: Jesus.

THE POWER SOURCE

Unfortunately, we as people, have descended into methodologies *"having a form of godliness, but denying the power thereof..."* (2 Tim. 3:5a). The world has obeyed the next and final portion of this verse and has *"from such* [turned] *away"* (2 Tim. 3:5b). The Church has resisted this transition. Its structures, doctrines, methodology, and actions have not, except in rare circumstances, demonstrated that we are connected to the source of power.

This is born out in the parable of the sower and the seed (see Matt. 13:3-23). In every place where the seed was sown there should have been growth because there was life in the seed. The condition of the soil (the hearts in which the Word was sown) was the only variable affecting yield (see Matt. 13:19-23). The sower sowed seed on the path, among the rocks, in the weeds, and in good soil. No fruit was produced in the first three cases (three quarters of the ground that was sown!). Even the good soil varied greatly in its productivity, yielding 30-, 60-, and 100-fold.

God, the sower, has predicted dramatic increase in the last days, saying, *"The earth shall be filled with the knowledge of the glory of the Lord, as the waters cover the sea"* (Hab. 2:14). It will take good soil (in us) and tremendous power (His) to produce this kind of result.

This "good soil" is not a natural, earthly soil. Natural soil cannot produce the supernatural fruit described in Habakkuk 2:14. To produce supernatural fruit, our hearts must shift to God's point of view.

Just as knowledge is increasing at an accelerated rate in the world's energy and communications sectors, so is the knowledge and manifestation of the power of the Lord increasing. God says in the last days *"...I will put My law in their inward parts, and write it in their hearts....And...they shall all know Me..."* (Jer. 31:33-34).

"Knowledge is power."[1] It is not our knowing about God, but our knowing God, the source of all knowledge, which will allow us to enter the halls of power. Our shift into this phase will come because God gave us *"...power to become the sons of God,...born, not of blood, nor of the will of the flesh, nor of the will of man, but of God"* (John 1:12-13).

If we are not operating in power then we are not operating in the Spirit or in the Kingdom! *"For the kingdom of God is not in word, but in power"* (1 Cor. 4:20). Our lack of legitimate power indicates that we are stuck in a grid powered by thoughts that come, not from the Spirit, but from the realm of the soul.

God wants us to shift to His way of thinking, seeing, and speaking. He declares: *"My thoughts are not your thoughts, neither are your ways My ways..."* (Isa. 55:8). We must be honest with ourselves and acknowledge that, if our thoughts are not aligned with His, our ways will not look like His, either.

Richard Feynman said,

"The first principle is that you must not fool yourself—and you are the easiest person to fool."[2]

Join us on our journey as we invite God to invade our minds with His thoughts...and then allow Him to shift our trajectories to match His. To enter God's Kingdom in this way will require us to venture beyond the structures that we have erected to protect ourselves.

We will not be able to build a boat big enough to navigate the storms that are coming. The only safe place will be in the supernatural realm, walking on the water with Jesus. What that will look like, we can only imagine.

"WE ARE HERE"

Before you can shift your trajectory from the natural to the supernatural, you have to find the *x* that marks the spot where you are now, the place on the map that says: *You are here.*

If we're to embark on this journey together, you'll also need to know a little about us. Jeanne and I are pastoral elders in our church. We own a construction company, have been married 40 years, and have been joined to the Lord longer than that.

Our passion is to see the body of Christ rise to the level of its full potential and reestablish the authority of the Kingdom that has been lost over the centuries. God has been restoring many of His "forgotten" truths, but we as a people have been unable to apprehend them. The social, religious, and political structures that influence our thoughts have obstructed our rightful supernatural viewpoint.

That is about to change. God is pulling back the veil and allowing His body to see true spiritual realities. More people are having visions, visitations, and revelations as that veil gets thinner. As He imparts His wisdom, we need to shift our thoughts into agreement with His so that we, too, can walk in the supernatural realm.

Shift! was written to highlight vital truths and promote the corresponding actions that will facilitate our passage through the spiritual "gates" God desires to open to us. He longs to flood the earth with His grace, power, and glory. As we cooperate with His ways, we will hasten the widening of those gates and experience the momentous shift that awaits us.

These pages are filled with biblical perspective and practical examples of the outworking of these biblical truths (from our lives and the lives of those to whom we minister). We have tried to be as transparent as possible; therefore, you will encounter not only the victories, but also the defeats. Both will provide pertinent wisdom as you shift your perspective from the natural to the supernatural.

Love,
—Ken and Jeanne Harrington

ENDNOTES

1. Bacon, Francis. "Of Heresies," in *Religious Meditations* (1597), quoted in The Quotations Page, http://www.quotationspage.com/subjects/knowledge/ (accessed May 17, 2009).

2. Feynman, Richard P., "Cargo Cult Science" (commencement address, California Institute of Technology, 1974) http://calteches.library.caltech.edu/51/2/CargoCult.pdf (accessed May 18, 2009) and adapted in Richard P. Feynman and Ralph Leighton, "Cargo Cult Science," in *Surely You're Joking, Mr. Feynman!* (New York: W.W. Norton & Co., 1985), 342.

Chapter 1

DON'T WASTE YOUR SORROWS

God Uses All of Our Circumstances to Heal Us

SOMETIMES, when we are hurt or wounded, we don't think anybody cares about us—not even God.

Nothing could be further from the truth. God says:

> *When you pass through the waters, I will be with you; and through the rivers, they shall not overflow you. When you walk through the fire, you shall not be burned, nor shall the flame scorch you. For I am the Lord your God...* (Isa. 43:2-3 NKJV).

To shift from the natural (and any current circumstances that hinder us) to the supernatural (and a life of destiny fulfillment in God's plan) , we must examine our thoughts, attitudes, responses, and hidden wounds. To do this, we need to trust that God is always watching—*whatever* we go through—and is never caught off guard the way we are.

I (Ken) was at home painting a car when a phone call came. I was enjoying my days off, but the call was from work. "They must want me to come in for some overtime," I thought. But I was wrong!

"We need you to come in and clean out your

locker. You have been laid off."

"Laid off," I shot back "Why?"

"We have eliminated your position," was the curt reply. "We need you out by tomorrow."

That ended my short, four-year career as a maintenance mechanic. It had been a well-paying job and I was home every night. That had been part of my reason for taking the job in the first place. Now it was over, and I was mad.

I (Jeanne) sensed that God would use this situation for good and I encouraged Ken to trust Him. This was a blow to Ken's ego; he was not about to let go and let God straighten it out.

I (Ken) teamed up with the ironworker on the opposite shift who was also laid off. We had both lost our pensions because we were a year shy of being vested. We decided to fight our layoffs and not just roll over for this obvious "abuse."

The strip-miners' union, however, had always considered us outsiders. They would not fight for us or grieve our layoffs. We could have bid out, gotten lesser jobs at the mine, and worked another year to get vested; personally, I was too mad to do that. Though I wouldn't admit it, my pride was wounded. I was hurt and felt betrayed.

As I seethed in anger, I was ignorant of the fact that God had other plans. A month before my layoff, I had been offered a job back in construction, running a crew of ironworkers. I had agreed to give my answer on October 1, but had already decided I couldn't justify leaving my position at the mine.

Meanwhile, I got laid off on September 28. God made up my mind for me. On October 1, I restarted my career as an ironworker. I would now have to shift my thinking about how my life was to be played out.

I soon recognized that this was God's hand operating on me. I had seen it happen several times before; I was learning in God's "school of medicine" how to get both wounded and healed. The hand of God doesn't always manifest in the kindest and gentlest manner because He allows hard and insensitive people to do His work.

Positions and possessions that I had longed for and seemed to have obtained were often snatched from my hands. My first major loss was the family farm; that took me years to get over. Then there was a job lost overseas; that disappointment lasted about a year. Because I was learning to trust more in God's provision for my life, this newest layoff at the mine only affected me for a month or so.

We are always in the process of learning to trust God more. He never fails us. He is good whatever is going on in our lives. At the time of my "newest" layoff, I was learning that God only wants to bless and that trust is the key to His blessing.

The outcome of this layoff was that I earned twice the wage as an ironworker that I had earned as a maintenance mechanic. I was now able to be at church every week instead of every other one, as my shift work had dictated. I came out of my dry time with the Lord. Suddenly, I had more joy.

This move was obviously God-ordained. I forgave everybody concerned with the layoff, repented of my own anger and feelings of rejection, and threw myself into this new role.

In other words, I *shifted*.

RESPONSES MATTER

Events don't shape our lives; if they did, we would be subject to the whims of fate or chance. Instead, our responses to life events are what God uses to mold us.

These responses are not random; our thoughts dictate our actions. But how do thoughts form? The answer is that thoughts spring from our perceptions. When we understand how our perceptions are framed, we also understand the things that may be preventing us from moving into God's realm.

Several natural things can frame our perceptions, experiences, traditions, and fears. The thought patterns that develop then express themselves as individual or group tendencies. (Groups can be religious, national, ethnic, etc.) These tendencies create actions which, when repeated, become habits. Habitual actions then form our characteristics.

God has chosen to speak not through the natural, but through the Spirit to counteract the cumulative effect of these influences. If we are ever to change our actions and, ultimately, our characters, we must learn to shift our affections away from the natural voices to the supernatural voice of the Spirit.

Jesus is always our example of how to act. He was falsely accused, arrested, and abandoned by His friends; He was beaten, lied about, denied justice, laughed at, abused, and finally nailed to a cross. Yet, His response was not one of anger or retaliation. Instead, as He hung from the cross, He said, *"Father forgive them, for they do not know what they are doing"* (Luke 23:34 NIV).

Why would He say that—especially since He had the power to stop the injustice? The whole scenario had been building for years. The plans and schemes of the enemy (of which Jesus was fully aware) had come to fruition. His opposers were laughing; He was dying. Yet He didn't react.

If we are going to follow Jesus to the cross, as He says we must to be His disciples (see Luke 9:23), then we must understand the simplicity of His secret: *Don't stay wounded!*

Wounds will happen. *"...Offences will come..."* (Luke 17:1). People will hurt us. What will be our reaction? Jesus was able to resist the hook with which satan was trying to snag Him because satan had *"...nothing in* [Him]*"* (John 14:30). There was nothing onto which satan's hook could catch: no offenses, no wounds, no hurts. Of course, Jesus had been hurt; He had been offended; He had been wounded. But as soon as those events occurred, He dealt with them and was healed. *"...He learned obedience by the things which He suffered..."* (Heb. 5:8 NKJV).

Jesus submitted Himself because He trusted His Father. He was committed to God's plan no matter where that plan took Him. David prophesied that Jesus would *"delight to do* [God's] *will..."* (Ps. 40:8). We can be like Jesus; He is the *"author and finisher of our faith; who for the joy that was set before Him endured the cross..."* (Heb. 12:2).

This kind of delight and joy is the attitude of a true worshiper. It is also the attitude required to get and stay healed. *"A merry heart doeth good like a medicine..."* (Prov. 17:22). In other words, a merry heart causes good and makes one well.[1]

RECEIVING RESTORATION

The Kingdom of God was never meant to be a dull, sullen place. It is to be a place of *"...righteousness, and peace, and joy..."* (Rom. 14:17). If there is no joy, we are likely operating in the wrong kingdom and the wrong spirit. When Jesus' disciples wanted to call down fire from Heaven, Jesus said that they were operating in the wrong spirit (see Luke 9:54-55). They couldn't think like He did because they were operating on a different grid, viewing events from a different reference point. They needed to get out of their soulish "box" and see things from Jesus' point of view.

We shouldn't react defensively when our lives are not all sunshine and roses. We are in a war; there will be wounds and pain. God sees all we go through. In fact, He keeps a record of our wanderings; He saves our tears in His bottle (see Ps. 56:8). God sees and cares. He is a God of justice. Everything is recorded in a *"book of remembrance"* (Mal. 3:16).

God is going to bring a *"...restoration of all things..."* (Acts 3:21 NKJV). God comes to restore; satan comes to *"steal and to kill, and to destroy..."* (John 10:10). Our suffering is not in vain. But we need faith to believe that and to allow God to restore us.

How do we get back (restore) what has been stolen? We must catch the thief! *"...But if* [a thief is] *found, he shall restore sevenfold; he shall give all the substance of his house..."* (Prov. 6:31).

We are engaged in a legal battle in which God is the judge; Jesus is our advocate (defense lawyer); and satan is our accuser (the prosecuting attorney). (See 1 John 2:1 and Rev. 12:10.)

Although he is the biggest thief and murderer of all, satan tries to use the law to demonstrate *our* guilt. However, we are not at his mercy. As judge, God is committed to justice. And for His part, Jesus intercedes for us (see Rom. 8:34) and has already paid our fine with His blood.

If we have applied that payment to cover our sin debt, God is free to demand that satan repay what he has stolen. That is why we must not waste our sorrows. They are the very evidence God will use to demand, not only that we have restored to us what was stolen, but that we are recompensed sevenfold out of satan's kingdom.

Receiving this recompense requires that we shift. How? By learning to fight from our spirits rather than from our souls.

RESTORATION, FIRSTHAND

I (Ken) have lived this principle and seen it work in my life. Several years ago, I was contracted to superintend the building of the world's largest dragline at a mine west of Edmonton, Alberta. I was hired out of the company's head office in Toronto. Unbeknownst to me, the regional office in Calgary wanted to control the job.

Something seemed strange to me from the first day I went to sign on with the company. I was given keys to a truck, two boxes of company procedures and forms, and was sent on my way to run the $85,000,000 job. There was no briefing, no meeting, and no guidance offered. Other problems were brewing: the project had been grossly underbid and the hours designated for each task were woefully short.

I was being set up to fail. The people in the Calgary office assumed that if I messed up the job, they would be called in to rescue the situation, which was exactly what they wanted.

For the next six months I poured myself into the project. The construction went well, but the hours went over budget. During this time, the struggle continued higher up as Calgary sought to wrest control.

Then, when my general foreman quit and I was told to wait and not hire a replacement, I knew something was up. Sure enough, within a couple of days, a delegation from the Calgary office showed up to say they were replacing me.

God (being God) has a habit of overruling where and when He wants to (see Dan. 4:17). The owner of the mine and the dragline supplier were furious with Calgary's decision to remove me from the project because I was the one they trusted. The company invoked a clause in the contract concerning its final approval of all supervision on the job. The mine owner refused site access to the team from Calgary until the matter was settled.

For the next four days, I went about doing my regular duties as these four guys cooled their heels in my office, unable to come on site. During this time, although I felt agitated and betrayed, God started to speak to me about submitting without fighting and leaving the consequences to Him. As God spoke, a sense of peace concerning the whole situation settled on my spirit. I moved out of my soulish funk into a spiritual rest, submitting to God's strategy.

In the end, God triumphed. I still lost my position and was demoted to general foreman, but in the process, my pay structure changed. I went from receiving a monthly salary (with a bonus that had to be paid out) to earning an hourly wage. Because of the hours we needed to work and the fact that I now had to cross over shifts, I actually made $25,000 more than I would have as superintendent.

I still was in charge of the physical running of the job, but had fewer meetings and less paperwork. It was the best demotion I ever received! God repaid me and more, just as the Word promised.

Since that time, our own company has been hired to do maintenance on all the draglines at three different mines in the area. That contract has been worth hundreds of thousands of dollars to us.

If we submit to God's plan, satan has to pay when he tries to steal from us. However, God cannot intercede for us unless we shift our thinking and let Him do things His way.

SOWING AND REAPING

The whole universe operates on the laws that God has set up. These laws are designed to bring in blessing and life. Once sin entered the world, those same laws enabled destruction and death to flourish.

One of those laws on which everything in the universe operates is the law of sowing and reaping. This law is described by the world with this common expression: "What goes around comes around."

Words are the primary seed source in sowing and reaping. The Bible says, *The seed is the word of God"* (Luke 8:11). Here's how it works: we hear God's Word; we plant it in our hearts (we believe); we declare the Word into our situations; and it produces blessing. *"...[We] shall have whatsoever [we] saith"* (Mark 11:23).

The reality is that, all too often, we hear satan's words (his lies); we plant those lies in our hearts (we believe); and we declare them into our situations (we curse our situations by grumbling and complaining or judging). Those lie-based words are potent seeds that produce destruction and death.

There is always a time period between when we sow and when we reap. If I sow wheat, I will reap wheat 90 to 100 days later. If I sow acorns, it may be 20 years or more before I can harvest acorns from an oak tree.

Sometimes, the time of our reaping is so far removed from the time of our sowing that we cannot connect the dots. Instead of realizing the origin of the harvest, we assume a random disaster has struck. Not so! If there is bad fruit in our lives—whether sickness, relational problems, or financial problems, for example—somewhere there is a bad root from which it grew.

Jesus understood sowing and reaping. That is why He was never sick. Jesus never had financial problems. He did have relational problems, not because of an evil root within Himself, but because He chose to challenge the archetypes (the demonic mind-sets over a region) of the Jewish leaders.

Jesus was pushing their buttons on purpose, knowing they would kill Him. Even His disciples were confused and upset with His actions. They didn't want to arouse opposition; they asked Jesus: *"Do You know that the Pharisees were offended when they heard* [what You said]*?"* (Matt. 15:12 NKJV). The disciples seldom operated from the same mind-set as Jesus did.

Jesus also understood the law of increase, which runs parallel to the law of sowing and reaping. He knew that a small offense, like a small seed, would grow into a huge offense over time. Left unhealed, anger grows to hatred (see 1 John 3:15) and eventually to death. Even a minor offense will grow into mistrust and eventually break a relationship if left to grow unchecked.

God is the most purposeful being in the universe. Every action and word has a purpose and is designed to produce a desired result. Jesus also was purposeful in His actions. He knew that every action of His would grow and multiply to fulfill prophecies concerning Himself. Thus, His action of driving out the moneychangers with *"a scourge of small cords"* (John 2:15) eventually increased into His own extensive whipping from the Romans. He relied on this law of increase to fulfill the prophetic word which said, *"...they shall look upon Me whom they have pierced..."* (Zech. 12:10). His strange request for swords, on the night He was betrayed (see Luke 22:36), caused the violence against Him to increase, until the Romans pierced Him with a spear, though He was already dead (see John 19:33-34).

These principles of sowing and reaping and increase are the foundational principles governing sin and salvation in the Bible.

They started functioning with Adam and were completed in Christ; both principles are demonstrated in the statement: *"By one man's disobedience many were made sinners, so by the obedience of one shall many be made righteous"* (Rom. 5:19). Our ignorance of these laws has robbed us of our ability to shift from the natural to the supernatural and operate these laws for our benefit.

REPLACING LIES WITH TRUTH

God is working to restore our authority. To do this, the Spirit needs to first remove from within us the roots of any lies we have believed; then the lies must be replaced with truth.

This process can be frightening. These lies are embedded in our thought processes (the foundations of the way we think) via neural pathways, most of which are in place by age three,[2] long before most of us encountered God. Our thought patterns are thus not godly. In order to dismantle these structures, we have to trust God.

God says *"...I kill, and I make alive; I wound, and I heal..."* (Deut. 32:39). In this Scripture, God sounds hard and cruel. The truth is, He is hard and cruel if we think He is! Our thoughts and words dictate how God can relate to us. Jesus said, *"Out of your own mouth* [by your own words] *I will judge you..."* (Luke 19:22 NKJV).

This truth has taught me (Jeanne) to declare that my God is good. He is gracious to me and I trust Him. Once I was making a good, healthy, homemade soup for my family, using a pressure cooker. The last thing I did was to add some lentils to the pot.

As the pressure cooker began to sputter and build up steam, I sensed that something was wrong. A lentil must have lodged in the vent. The wise solution would have been to take the pressure cooker off the heat and allow it cool. Then, with the pressure dissipated, I could have safely released the lid.

Ken was driving home from work and I felt as though I couldn't wait for the pot to cool down. Foolishly, I began to open the lid without releasing the pressure. In an instant, the pot blew up. The lid hit the ceiling and scalding soup exploded over the left side of my face and neck. The pain was unbearable.

Ken wasn't home yet; the kids were scared to see Mommy crying. I raced to the bathroom. We lived in the country, far from help. The only thing I could do was douse my burns in cold water. As long as I kept the water on my face and neck, the pain was somewhat eased.

When Ken arrived home, it was clear that the whole side of my face and neck were scalded. He rushed me to the hospital. I was in total agony all the way there.

"Lord help me get through this," was all I could pray. At the hospital, they gave me painkillers and bandaged my face. I was told that I had second- and third-degree burns; I would need my bandages changed daily for the next few weeks.

As soon as he heard the news, our pastor came over and prayed for my healing. Every day, I would go to the hospital and get my bandages changed. One day, the doctor cut some skin off my neck. After examining the wound, he said it was infected. He also said I would be scarred for a long time.

The skin on the left side of my face and neck became brown and scaly like fruit leather. I no longer looked like the pretty young woman I had been before the accident. I was in a great deal of pain and could only pray that the pain would stop and that I would be healed. This went on for a long time.

One day while I was at home just before my appointment at the hospital, I relinquished my healing to the Lord. I prayed, "Lord, if this is how You want me to look, I will accept it."

Suddenly, I felt the Holy Spirit prompting me to get a cotton ball and start rubbing it over my face. Slowly and carefully, I rubbed and watched myself in the mirror. It was as though scales were falling off the burned areas. I rubbed until healthy, light skin appeared from underneath the leathery surface.

God had truly healed me! There wasn't even any redness in the new skin. I went to the doctor's appointment and no one there recognized me. I said, "I'm the lady with the burns on my face and neck." They could not believe what had happened.

People suggested that perhaps I heal faster than most, but that was not the case. About a month later, I took some cookies out of the oven and accidentally burned my arm. The wound wasn't nearly as severe as the burns on my face and it only hurt a fraction as much. Yet, it took a year for that scar to heal. For a whole year, that little scar served to remind me how wonderfully Jesus heals.

Having the mind-set that God is in control and loves me is what released Him to work the miraculous. But He not only healed my burns; He also "operated" on my thought processes.

In Deuteronomy 32:39, God did not say that He makes us sick. He said, *"I wound."* A surgeon wounds us when he operates, but he is not trying to hurt us; he is trying to heal us. If you have a broken bone that has not set right, the doctor may have to re-break the bone to align it properly. Likewise, God wounds us so we can be restored.

Just as we need to pay attention to the outward signs (fruits) that there is something wrong in our physical bodies, we must also remain alert to signs of spiritual ills that may be hidden in our minds and hearts.

OPEN EYES

Jeanne and I ministered with Dennis Wiedrick at a citywide conference in which several churches were represented. Dennis has an apostolic ministry and wrote one of the forewords to this book. At the end of the conference, we were doing personal prophetic ministry. A lady in her forties and her daughter, who was in her twenties, came up. The mother was a very dignified woman. Her daughter was visibly upset and did most of the talking. She revealed their story; it involved betrayal, a harsh husband, and a hurtful father.

I had compassion for them, sensing that the mother's gentle spirit had been crushed. So many people were awaiting ministry that Jeanne and I had split up to handle the crowd more efficiently. So I prayed a simple prayer for this woman's healing and interceded (stood in the gap) for her husband. I was also led to do a visual act to demonstrate God's response to her betrayal.

I said to the mother, "I am going to do a prophetic act. Figuratively speaking, I will pull this knife of betrayal out of your back." I reached between her shoulder blades and made the motion of pulling out a knife. The next thing I knew this elegant, sweet, proper woman was screaming and writhing on the floor.

She cried out, "My back! My back!"

By this time, I was well out of my comfort zone. (In our ministry, I am the teacher; my wife, Jeanne, is the "wacky prophet.") Under my breath I whispered, "Jeanne, where are you?"

I was in a panic, trying to figure out what had just happened. I thought, "It can't be the knife of betrayal, I just pulled that out."

I fired off one of those desperate prayers: "God, help!"

The daughter was pleading with me to help her mother; the crowd was reacting in fear and curiosity. Meanwhile, Jeanne, busy with her own prayer line, was saying, "Oh, he gets all the good ones."

I stood there drawing a complete blank. Just then God dropped a hint in my mind: "There is a second knife of betrayal." I gently got down beside the woman, who was still in agony. I gingerly helped her to sit up.

I said, "Your father betrayed you, too, didn't he?"

"Yes," she winced. "He fired at me with a shotgun and once boarded me up in my room."

I got her to do a quick forgiveness of her father then prophetically pulled out the second knife. Immediately, the color came back into her face and she smiled at me saying, "The pain is gone."

Her daughter and I helped her onto her feet. She then composed herself, but just as I hugged her, she began to sob. When she was done sobbing, she looked at her daughter and said, "All my depression is gone."

The original betrayal from the father had been reaped in the husband. The release didn't come with forgiving her husband; that action merely released the pain of the former wounding. She needed to forgive both her father and her husband. In doing so, a cloud of depression lifted and she was healed.

So, apart from the fact that a marvelous healing took place, why do I share this particular testimony? It has to do with the need to shift—in this case, out of a comfort zone. To see this emotional wound healed, I needed to shift out of my teacher mode and get into the Spirit. When I did, the schemes of the enemy were defeated.

QUALIFIED OR DISQUALIFIED FOR SERVICE

Under the Old Covenant, blemishes (defects) and unhealed wounds disqualify us from ministering to God. In the Old Testament, priests were forbidden to *"go near the veil or approach the altar* [if they had] *a defect..."* (Lev. 21:23 NKJV). However, under the New Covenant, the Lord clearly says that *"...by* [His] *stripes* [or wounds] *you were healed"* (1 Pet. 2:24 NKJV). Even before His whipping, Jesus healed by divine exchange when He *"...took our infirmities, and bare our sickness"* (Matt 8:17). This was an action that God alone could institute, but Jesus declared that we could, if we believed, do ... *"greater works than these"* (John 14:12).

These greater works are not manifest in us because we have power but, rather, because Christ dwells in us. We are to be His body, literally! Isaiah prophesied that *"...when* (we) *make His soul an offering for sin, He shall see His seed He shall prolong His days ..."* (Isa. 53:10). He lives in us and we become the *"...body of Christ, and members in particular"* (1 Cor. 12:27). As an extension of Him, *"...we have this treasure in earthen vessels that, the excellency of the power may be of God, and not of us.* (2 Cor. 4:7).

But it is not only the power but also the wounding that we are privileged to bear. Paul went on to say that we are *"...always bearing about in the body the dying of the Lord Jesus, that the life also of Jesus might be made manifest in our body. ...so then death worketh in us but life in you"* (2 Cor. 4:10,12). Our wounds, emotionally, physically, and spiritually, are designed, through Jesus, to bring life to those we minister to.

Paul emphasized this point when he said, *"...that we may be able to comfort them which are in any trouble , by the comfort wherewith we ourselves are comforted of God. ...whether we be afflicted, it is for your consolation and salvation* [or health][3] *...or whether we be comforted, it is for your consolation and salvation* (health) (2 Cor. 1:4,6).

Unhealed wounds disqualify us; healed (resurrected) wounds give us authority, through Christ, to heal others.

Don't waste your sorrows. Instead, change the way you think about your wounds and hurts. Believe the best, *"...confidence...hath great recompense of reward"* (Heb. 10:35). True intercession always requires the one standing in the gap to be part of the group that is being interceded for. That is why Jesus took on the form of a man because *"...both He that sanctifieth and they who are sanctified are all of one..."* (Heb. 2:11). So we, who have been wounded and healed are able to identify with those who have been wounded as Jesus was (see Heb. 4:15).

Without healing, we have no life of Christ, in that area, to offer. We are just *"...blind leaders of the blind"* (Matt. 15:14). Use your brokenness to bring healing, your former poverty to bring wealth, your former sickness to bring health. Whatever has been lost, God wants to restore and heal.

BE HEALED

Truly, it is God's will to heal! This is part of the atonement package. Jesus has "*...borne our griefs (sicknesses, weaknesses, and distresses) and carried our sorrows and pains....He was wounded for our transgressions, He was bruised for our guilt and iniquities...and with the stripes [that wounded] Him we are healed and made whole*" (Isa. 53:4-5 AMP).

When dealing with the Syrophenician woman (see Mark 7:25-29), Jesus declared that healing—freedom from demonic oppression and disease—is *"the children's bread"* (Mark 7:27). In other words, healing belongs to covenant people.

In Matthew 8:2, a leper told Jesus that if it was His will, the man could be cured. Jesus replied, *"I am willing; be cleansed by being cured"* (Matt. 8:3 AMP, emphasis added).

Jesus' willingness to heal seems clear enough. But, if it is God's will to heal and restore, and if we are praying according to His will, why are our results inconsistent?

Some have suggested that God answers prayers three ways: "Yes," "No," or "Wait awhile." This view is based on individual experiences with God and with parents standing in their place of authority.

However, our individual outcomes are not the standard by which we can accurately judge healing. Instead, we must base our doctrine on the Word of God. We can be confident in the Word, which says *"...Jesus Christ...was not yea and nay.... For all the promises of God in Him are yea, and in Him Amen..."* (2 Cor. 1:19-20). In other words, we can rely on whatever promises God has made.

Our parents are not God, even though as little children, we tend to elevate them to that position. We don't realize that our parents are imperfect. Then we formulate our thinking based on their imperfect performances. This distorted view clouds our ability to see God in the proper light.

I (Ken) once went forward at church to get prayer for more power. God responded to my prayer by saying, "I am not like your father. I am faithful." I started to cry at this revelation. God repeatedly said, "I am not like your father. I am faithful. I am not like your father. I am faithful."

I was shocked at God's response to my prayer. It forced me to realize that I had assumed that God was just like my dad. This misconception short-circuited my power. I had to repent and fix my thinking.

My dad was a good father, but he wasn't a Christian until a year before his death. My experiences with my earthly dad taught me that I would have to look after myself. We were raised to be rugged individuals, making our way in a hard, uncaring world. The often-used statement in our house was that "God helps those who help themselves."

That became my creed. Until I repented of that unbiblical mind-set, I could not enter into the provision of God. My past wounds prevented me from believing that God would look after me and give me power.

I believed in a lie called *independence*. My dad was independent and taught me to be the same way. Now I had to learn in God's school how to be dependent upon Him. I had to shift my thinking until I believed in God's faithfulness and utter trustworthiness.

MINEFIELDS IN OUR MIND FIELDS

A Vietnam veteran told me about how the troops used to clear away the jungle from their base camps. If any enemy approached that "free fire zone," he would have no place to hide.

However, during battles over that open space, mortars and bombshells would pockmark the ground, providing the enemy new places to hide and launch fire. So, every now and then, the base camp would send out a bulldozer to flatten the ground and fill in the depressions.

We must do the same thing in the "battlefields" in our minds. Even after we have cleared out all the cares and worries and lies that choke our minds, we must deal with the wounds (bomb holes) that mar our thinking. When those wounds (holes) are healed (filled in), we gain an advantage over our enemy. If the holes are not fixed, they give the enemy an advantage over us.

These battlefields are important, but we must also remember that they are only part of the greater spiritual war being waged. Often, when things fail to go as we'd hoped, we assume that we are not making progress. Yet, the Word reminds us that God "...*is not slow about His promise...but is patient...not wishing for any to perish...*" (2 Pet. 3:9 NASB).

God answers our prayers right away, but He still has to line up all the circumstances involved. This takes time. Our prayers are not His only considerations. The whole universe may be affected by His response.

Consider Abraham, the father of faith. He had to wait 25 years for his son Isaac to be born. It would take another 430 years for the children of Israel to come out of bondage and yet another 400 years for David to capture the stronghold at Zion from which God said He would rule. Was God slow? No, Israel was. They were not ready to manifest God before then.

There are many reasons why answers to prayer take time. When Daniel prayed, an angel was dispatched right away. Yet, demonic activity delayed the angel's arrival for three weeks (see Dan. 10:12-13). Faith always receives now, just not yet. The sending of the answer is immediate; the manifestation of the answer can take time.

The struggles and sorrows we go through are part of our preparation to rule and reign with God but "*your iniquities...and your sins have hid His face...that He will not hear*" (Isa. 59:2). Our wounds cause us to doubt; our doubt becomes unbelief; our unbelief is sin and separates us from our source of healing.

THE PRICE OF SPIRITUAL POWER

As painful as it might be, we must be willing to let God heal us. We must be like the proverbial clay in the Potter's hands. If we are marred by "hard" spots and sin, can we not trust the Potter, the master craftsman, to smash us down and re-form us? Or will we instead ask Him, "What do You think You are making?" (see Isa. 45:9).

The fiery trials we experience are not strange, isolated events (see 1 Pet. 4:12). They are for our testing. Every man and woman of God has endured them, including many of those we know and admire, including Elijah.

Many of us dream of walking in tremendous power, as Elijah did. But, he didn't get that way without lots of trials and sorrows. Yes, Elijah operated in power and authority over the weather, over provision, over death, over demonic forces, and over the laws of nature. He also had to deal with fear, depression, hopelessness, and pride. As James said, Elijah was *"a man with a nature like ours..."* (James 5:17 NKJV).

Yet, Elijah had power and authority. How did he get it? Elijah allowed God to deal with his wounds—his "stuff." The question then becomes: how much do we want to be like Elijah, whose spiritual influence has carried on for two and a half millennia (and isn't finished yet)?

If we are willing to be healed, we, too, can have power. But we can't waste our sorrows; we have to shift our thinking about them. They hold the key to our power and authority. We can take *"...the prophets...for an example of suffering affliction, and of patience....We count them* [blessed and empowered] *which endure...."* (James 5:10-11).

We can endure if we are healed. Our wounds may be in our emotions or our wills. They may have broken our spirits and even affected our bodies. All of these can be healed; but we need to pull up the roots to remove their effects from our lives.

It's important to realize that the good fruit in our lives grows alongside the bad. In the parable of the sower, Jesus told the angels to let the tares, or bad fruit, grow with the wheat until the harvest (see Matt. 13:30).

We, then, should do the same. We should deal with our wounds when they "ripen" or become obvious in our memories and actions. That way, when we pull out the roots, there will be no damage done to the good fruit that is coming up.

Pulling out roots will likely require the wounded to forgive those who caused their injuries; it will also require forgiveness to be received when it is offered. If either party cannot or will not cooperate in this process, we can through intercession (standing in the gap), accomplish the same healing without them.

We may be holding judgments toward the "perpetrators" in our lives or toward those who now occupy a previous perpetrator's position. We may even hold judgments against God and ourselves. In order to be healed and walk in power, we must release these judgments. Then our wounds will be excised.

As with any "surgery," there will be pain. "...*Weeping may endure for a night, but joy cometh in the morning*" (Ps. 30:5). Don't waste your sorrows; instead, "...*rend your heart, and not your garments, and turn unto the Lord...*" (Joel 2:13). The power that is released in healing is worth it!

SHIFT INTO PRAYER

Throughout this book, we will invite you to pray simple but effective prayers like this:

Lord, I trust You to take all of our pains and sorrows and turn them into trophies of Your faithfulness and love. I believe Your Word, which says that "...*all things work together for good to them that love God, to them who are the called according to His purpose*" (Rom. 8:28).

ENDNOTES

1. Zodhaites, Spiros. *The Complete Word Study Dictionary: Old Testament* (Chattanooga: AMG Publishers, 1994), s.v., 3190.

2. Paterson, Robert. "Vulnerable Children—A Research Project," *Robert Paterson's Radio Weblog,* http://radio.weblogs.com/0107127/stories/2003/05/24/vulnerableChildrenAResearchProject.html (accessed May 18, 2009).

3. Zodhaites, Spiros. *The Complete Word Study Dictionary: New Testament* (Chattanooga: AMG Publishers, 1992), s.v., 4991.

Chapter 2

THIS FAR AND NO FARTHER

Positions and Spheres of Authority

WHEN a football team lines up over the ball, each player assumes a specific position. The linemen on the defensive side of the ball take a stance that will allow them to explode forward at the snap of the ball. The linebackers assume a stance that facilitates movement in any direction. The backs set up to respond to the receiver they are going to cover.

On the offensive side, the linemen must maintain a more balanced stance so as to disguise which way the play is going. The quarterback sets up so he can backpedal as soon as the ball is snapped, to get out of reach of the defense.

Everyone on the field is playing the same game. Yet, each player must take a stance that is specifically designed to accommodate the reactions dictated by his game responsibilities.

Likewise, the stance or posture we are to assume in the Body of Christ is dictated by the position we occupy. That position is our function; it is not our ranking in a hierarchy, or our level on the proverbial ladder.

Our function, or our responsibilities, could be described as our realm of authority. Just as in a football game there are different responsibilities, so in our lives we function in different realms or circles of influence. These circles are like the ripples on a pond: each one expanding further out, but with decreasing amplitude.

FROM CIRCLE TO CIRCLE

The smallest but most absolute realm of authority is our personal life. In our own lives, we are the absolute monarchs. Nobody can tell us what to think or what we should feel. I determine whether I like neon plaid, bell-bottomed dress pants. I can prefer bubblegum ice cream over vanilla and not have to defend my preference. I can decide whether I raise my hands in worship or close my eyes and meditate. I can also choose to repent or forgive.

These thoughts, decisions, and preferences are all within my realm of authority. I have final say. Yet, satan will try to usurp my authority and gain access to that realm—whether by force or by fear.

Unlike satan, God will never try to intrude uninvited. He is the perfect gentleman who will go only as far as to *"…stand at the door* [of our hearts] *and knock; if anyone hears…and opens the door,* [He] *will come in…and dine with him…"* (Rev. 3:20 NKJV).

The next realm, in order of size, is the family. Here we operate in a larger realm with more people, but less absolute authority. The man is the head of this realm, but co-leads with his wife. They set the rules of the house and train the children to comply so the family can function in harmony. Every family is different and will operate differently. There is no right and wrong way to function, as long as love is the motivating force.

Even in the family realm, individuals have their own personal realms, which cannot be usurped by the corporate realm. Any decision to subjugate someone's personal realm for the family's sake should be voluntary and not coerced. Likewise, our personal realms should not protrude into another's authority without their consent.

This give and take in the family is the training ground God uses to prepare us for larger corporate expressions in society. It is here that we first learn conflict resolution which, in a healthy environment, is effected (as much as possible) through consensus. Although the father has the final say in the family setting, any control exercised at this level amounts to manipulation, which is a form of abuse.

Beyond the family, there is the ecclesiastical or church realm, which is larger still in its influence but operates with an even shallower depth of authority. Cults will reveal themselves at this level when they demand authority over the individuals or the families involved. Control at this level is coercion.

Above the ecclesiastical or church level we have the government realm, which includes local and national governments and the authority structures at our places of employment. This realm is larger still and offers individuals a smaller voice and decreased influence over others. Control at this level is oppressive domination.

Last of all, there is the Kingdom realm, which includes all of creation. Individually, each of us has a very small role in this realm. Yet, because the realm is so vast, our impact can be far greater. Control at this level is evidence of demonic intimidation.

RECOGNIZE REALMS AND ROLES

To properly respond to the situations we encounter in each realm, we must be aware of the sphere in which we are operating and understand where our own authority and begins and ends.

Paul said *"…we will not boast of things* [beyond] *our measure, but according to the measure of the rule which God hath distributed to us…"* (2 Cor. 10:13). In the church that we attend, there have been prophetic words that the church's influence in the spirit realm extends to a radius of 150 miles. We send teams and ministries all around the world to help others, but the weight of our responsibilities is limited to that designated area.

It is much like a family situation. In my personal life I have absolute authority and I am responsible to carry the weight of all the decisions I make. In our family I am still the head, but my authority only deals with the corporate aspects of our family; each individual member has his or her own realm for which each will have to answer to God.

Ideally, to move into another area that God has not designated as ours, we should come under the covering of the spiritual authority in that area. The ideal situation is seldom present, and in those situations we need a direct word from God on whether we can go in or not. Paul was *"...forbidden of the Holy Ghost to preach the Word in Asia"* (Acts 16:6).

In the Bible, Joshua was given authority to occupy the designated area God had promised to Abraham's descendants. The Promised Land was an actual physical location. But, to accomplish the task of occupying that land, Joshua had to shift his thinking beyond its boundaries. He had to move past his limited natural thinking and limited governmental realm and draw on a higher authority to influence a much larger arena: the Kingdom.

Therefore, when Joshua commanded: *"Sun, stand thou still"* (Josh. 10:12) he was emboldened to speak into the heavenly realms—not because he had authority there, but because he had seen God throw *"great stones from heaven"* (Josh. 10:11) upon Israel's enemies. This interjection of power from the Kingdom realm increased Joshua's faith. He had heard, in his spirit, the declaration that Jesus would later utter: *"...I give you power ....over all the power of the enemy: and nothing shall by any means hurt you"* (Luke 10:19). He had discovered that God was willing to fight for him (see Matt. 8:2,3). That knowledge enabled him to believe that he, too, could call down whatever was needed from that realm.

The prophetess Deborah also shifted beyond the natural realm and was granted celestial help in her battle against Sisera, who was subjugating Israel. She later sang that *"they fought from heaven; the stars in their courses fought against Sisera"* (Judg. 5:20).

Both of these leaders were allowed to draw power from the heavens at God's pleasure. Normally, those realms were beyond the boundaries that God had set up for them to function in, but God had stirred up their faith to reach further. Since Jesus has given us authority to sit in the heavenly realm (see Eph. 2:6), we, too, have access through faith to the power that flows from its fount.

GOD'S BOUNDARIES

God has always set up boundaries and designations in His creation. He set a boundary for the sea and declared: *"This far you may come, but no farther..."* (Job 38:11 NKJV).

Even in the spirit realm there are territories laid out along specific geopolitical lines. The Scriptures talk about the prince of Persia (see Dan. 10:13) withstanding the angel and the prince of Greece (see Dan. 10:20) that would come later and fight also.

These princes aren't men; men can't hold back angels. They are ruling spirits with a defined territory; satan always attempts to model his kingdom after God's standard, which has defined borders for every territory.

God not only assigned territories; He also denied access to certain lands. He granted territory saying: "...*I have given* Mount Seir *unto Esau for a possession....*[and] *I have given* Ar *unto the children of Lot for a possession*" (Deut. 2:5,9, emphasis added).

But He said to Israel, "...*I will not give* thee of the land of the children of Ammon any possession..." (Deut. 2:19, emphasis added). We must understand not only our territories but also our boundaries if we are going to be able to function within them by faith.

God has ordained limits to the exercising of authority in the physical and spirit realms. Even *"the angels which kept not their first estate* [principalities], *but left their own habitation, He hath reserved... unto the judgment..."* (Jude 6). Spheres of authority are territorial in scope; they are also functional in nature.

For example, the Kingdom of God operates with two main functionary divisions: kings and priests. Kings occupy the ruling and governmental areas, while priests have authority in the humanitarian and spiritual areas. When Naaman the Syrian was sent to the king of Israel to receive his healing, the king was at a loss of what to do and thought the request was a ploy to start a war. Only Elisha the prophet had authority to intervene and heal him (see 2 Kings 5:1-14). Conversely, when King Uzziah was elevated politically, he decided that he could operate in the priestly realm and was smitten with leprosy for his presumption (see 2 Chron. 26:16-21).

When Miriam challenged Moses' exclusive ability to speak for the Lord, she was struck with leprosy (see Num. 12:1-11). Korah's rebellion, attempting to move into "...*the priesthood also*" (Num. 16:10), caused the death of all those who tried to operate in that realm, which was not theirs.

Like all spheres, only the designated authority has a legitimate right to rule there. Any other operation in that realm would constitute illegitimate authority, which is always accompanied by demonic activity.

When civil authorities attempt to move into spiritual realms and attempt to exert control from those realms, disaster always occurs. The human tragedies in the communist states of Russia and China, as well as in Nazi Germany, are good examples. Their attempts to dictate thoughts in moral and ethical areas resulted in millions being destroyed.

When the Church moves into governmental areas (as it did in the Middle Ages and during the Inquisition), the results are even more devastating. It was estimated that 17,000,000[1] people died as a result of the priestly class attempting to rule in governmental realms during those times. It wasn't merely a matter of evil, sadistic men dominating through illegal infringements of authority; they themselves were dominated by demonic influences.

We cannot nullify God's edicts or laws; only confirm them. God's laws operate in the spirit realm equally as in the physical realm. We can chose to ignore them, but cannot stop their effect. For example, we can choose to ignore the law of gravity but that will only confirm it, not eliminate it. So it is with divisions of labor; if we cross into realms in which we are not ordained to operate, problems occur.

Even today, there is demonic pressure for governments to usurp priestly functions. A demonic structure has been assigned to influence our thinking that allows and even invites illegitimate authorities to operate. Satan attempted to use Jesus to legitimize his claim as god by getting Jesus to worship him (see Luke 4:6-8). Paul states that the world has accepted satan's authority and has been blinded by him to such an extent that he is called *"...the god of this world"* (2 Cor 4:4). But he is illegitimate; for the *"...earth hath He given to the children of men"* (Ps 115:16).

A culture (i.e., a set of corporate thought patterns) of entitlement has dominated Western thinking for years. We, as the Church no longer want responsibility for or even believe in the operation of the priestly realm. We have institutionalized that anointing instead of operating in it and have assigned it to a profession instead of releasing its authority into the broader body of Christ.

Just look at the areas where there seems to be no end to monetary pressures: education, welfare, and health care. These areas are all under a priestly mantle. It will take a major repentance and shift in our thinking to recover these realms for the Kingdom. In the natural, this seems impossible, but we are not designed to operate in the natural; we are assigned to operate in the supernatural.

Worldwide, all the great universities were at one time under religious orders, whether Christian, Muslim, Buddhist, or Hindu. Education has only recently come under government rule with increasingly disastrous results. Hospitals and welfare started with spiritual communities. The care and oversight of the poor and needy is still a priestly function.

The government was designed to rule, not care for its subjects. Governments were created to set regulations and supply army, police, infrastructure, and legal systems. That is their God-ordained realm of authority.

In 1977, there was a blackout in New York City.[2] With the lights out, crime skyrocketed. Many people turned lawless, committing terrible acts of destruction. It was not the civil authorities' responsibility to mold people's consciences so they would be good citizens; that was the Church's ongoing job. However, it was New York's responsibility to keep the lights on.

If each realm had done its job, there would have been no problem. These divisions of labor are functional in every realm of responsibility, right down through the Church, the family, and even into our personal lives. To have legitimate power and authority, we must understand the realm in which we are dealing. Then we can take the appropriate posture and apply the proper resources to the situations we face.

WATCHING AND WAITING

As mentioned earlier, *position* can actually refer to a physical place. This is why Jesus told the disciples to *"not depart from Jerusalem, but wait for the promise of the Father"* (Acts 1:4). Jesus explained that, in Jerusalem, they would *"...receive power, after...the Holy Ghost* [had] *come upon* [them]" (Acts 1:8). Jesus was teaching them, not only to remain in a physical location, but also to wait for a time and a season when things would change.

Why would God make them wait 50 days until the Holy Spirit was poured out? The Scriptures had to be fulfilled concerning the Holy Spirit being released on the day of Pentecost. This was a kairos (fixed or set) moment. It was going to happen whether or not the disciples cooperated. If they wanted to receive the release of power, they had to be at the right place at the right time.

In the parable of the ten virgins, the foolish virgins were at the right place at the right time, but were not prepared to receive the blessing. Those who were ready *"…went in with Him to the marriage: and the door was shut"* (Matt. 25:10).

How sad to have been right at the door and to have missed it! Yet, in the Kingdom, position and timing will often dictate whether we receive available power. Christ is coming for those who are watching and waiting; He is looking for those who have light in them and are looking for Him.

Timing and watching are important in the spiritual *and* the physical realms. The kids and I (Jeanne) were driving back from a visit with my parents. A shiny new tanker truck passed us on the highway just outside of Rocky Mountain House, Alberta.

Suddenly in the ditch, I saw two angels holding up a sign that read "DANGER." I could hardly believe what I was seeing. I had been listening to a teaching tape and just then the speaker had quoted Psalms 103:20, which says, *"…His angels…do His commandments, harkening unto the voice of His word."* The speaker was talking about inviting the angels to come into your situation.

As that word from Psalms was spoken, I called on the angels to come in and protect us as we drove home. The tanker, driving right in front of us slowed down to turn onto Highway 22. This was the same highway that we were taking to get home. About that time, I felt that we should stop in the town and gas up instead of taking Highway 22, even though we didn't need gas. We took our time, even letting out the dog and eating a snack before resuming our drive on Highway 22.

A short way up the road, we encountered a torrential downpour. I could hardly see beyond the windshield. Having been alerted to danger, we slowed down and continued to pray for protection.

Up ahead, I saw flashing lights and emergency vehicles. I realized there had been an accident. We looked out the window as we passed the crash scene and saw the tanker that had passed us earlier. It was flipped on its side, covering one lane of the highway. Had we continued to follow that truck, we would have been at the wrong place at the wrong time and could very well have been involved in the accident.

We need to shift our thoughts to realize that position and timing are important.

WHERE ARE YOU POSITIONED?

In a war, battles are fought along the borders of each army's sphere of influence or *kingdom*.

Being in the center of God's will positions us away from the battle lines. Jerusalem symbolizes the center of the kingdom of Israel and the center of His will.

There are also positions known as *high places*; these are the specific spots God has chosen for release of authority. Satan understands this principle. That is why he tries to occupy those positions at all levels of authority, from the personal to the kingdom realms.

The stronghold of Zion is a good example of this principle: The Jebusites were occupying the stronghold of Zion in the center of Jerusalem. David finally drove them out, more than 400 years after Joshua first invaded the land. (See Second Samuel 5:6-7.)

The Jebusites were confident in their ability to occupy the place God had ordained as His seat of power. Zion was to be God's temple site. Even today, there is a battle over the temple site in Jerusalem.

Satan's tactics seldom change, whether at the kingdom level or in our personal issues. A stronghold is any position in which the enemy becomes entrenched and tries to deny our rightful occupation.

In our own lives, satan defends his strongholds by capitalizing on our woundedness. In order to operate in our rightful power and authority, we must cooperate with God's healing (and defend that healing), refuse ungodly thoughts, and kick out the enemy, as David did. David knew that Zion was part of what belonged to him and to Israel. He had faith to remove the Jebusites because they were trying to occupy his inheritance. For David, it was more than a territorial conflict—it was a spiritual issue.

The power to change the nations won't come because we evangelize more, pray more, or work more. It will happen because God said, *"Ask of Me, and I will give You the nations for Your inheritance..."* (Ps. 2:8 NKJV).

Therefore, we must shift our thinking and posture ourselves as sons and daughters who possess an inheritance. We aren't hirelings who receive wages; we are children with an inheritance. For a son or daughter is *"...no longer a slave but...an heir of God..."* (Gal. 4:7 NKJV). *"...It is your Father's good pleasure to give you the kingdom"* (Luke 12:32).

It is our position in Christ as children of God that gives us the authority to receive nations. We come into this position as sons and daughters because we are *"...dead, and* [our] *life is hid with Christ in God"* (Col. 3:3).

When God sought to cover Adam and Eve's sin, He sacrificed animals (the first animal sacrifice) and wrapped His fallen children in the animal skins (see Gen. 3:21). God saw Adam and Eve as being literally "dead" in those animals. He no longer saw them, but the sacrifice that was made for them.

Likewise, if we are positioned in Christ, God no longer sees us, but Christ. That position of being hidden under Christ's blood is vital. The Passover was an Old Testament demonstration of how to come under the blood. The Jews were to kill the Passover lamb and put its blood on the doorpost and lintel (door header).

Jesus is called *"our Passover lamb"* (1 Cor. 5:7 NIV). So, while the Jews applied the blood by painting it onto their doors, we apply the blood of Christ by faith. We confess its value, demonstrating our trust in what the Word promises that blood will accomplish (see Rev. 12:11). Our words of faith "activate" the blood to overcome the enemy. Therefore, we are protected.

STAY WITH THE BLOOD

All in Egypt who applied the blood to their doors and stayed in their houses under the covering of that blood were spared. It didn't matter who was in the house, Jew or Egyptian…good person or bad. Their trust in the blood protected them.

Many Egyptians followed suit and painted their doors. This is evident because *"a mixed multitude* [which included non-Jews] *went up with them also…"* (Exod. 12:38). Those Egyptians who had taken protection from the plagues would no longer have been welcomed in Egypt. They would have been treated as traitors.

Today, our safety is still found by positioning ourselves under the power and authority of the blood. Think of it as being under an umbrella. Even when a storm rages, there is protection—if you remain under the umbrella.

As the protection of the Spirit moves, we must shift with it. Conversely, we must avoid moving ahead of the Spirit. If we come out from under the "umbrella," the storm that assails will not be the result of judgment, but a consequence of our moving outside of God's protection.

During the Exodus, the covering of the Spirit manifested itself though the pillar of fire by night and the cloud by day. To the Egyptians, *"it was a cloud and darkness…but it gave light by night to* [Israel]…" (Exod. 14:20). The covering of the Spirit is confusion to the enemy, but illumination to us. This is the powerful advantage of being properly positioned.

I (Ken) remember in my early twenties, a situation in which I positioned myself to bring confusion to the enemy's camp. We got a phone call sometime after midnight. The neighbors were having a brawl and the wife was desperate for a mediator.

They were a couple in their fifties. I wondered whether they would even listen to a young pup like me. But, before I left, Jeanne said, "Bind the spirit of contention and strife."

The war was going hot and heavy when I entered the couple's house. They were so busy yelling at one another, I might just as well have been another wall in the room. Nobody was listening to my advice or even cared that I was there. In all the confusion, I had simply forgotten my wife's advice.

Finally, after five minutes of enduring the rising decibel level, I remembered Jeanne's words. Silently, I interceded, asked forgiveness for the argument that was raging, and bound the spirit of contention and strife. Immediately, in mid-sentence, the husband said, "I'm tired. I think I'll go to bed." That was it. There was silence.

The wife didn't comment or fire another volley. There was nothing but silence! With the husband gone and the wife still looking confused, I started to minister to her. In less than five minutes' time, she gave her heart to the Lord and peace entered in. With tears in her eyes, she gave me a farewell hug and I went home.

The intercession I sent up became a cloud of darkness (confusion) to the enemy, but gave light (wisdom) to her. It only depended on my positioning myself and this couple under the supernatural forgiveness offered by the blood.

POSITION AND ORDER

Position is so important that God gave Israel instructions on the correct order for marching and fighting. At the front of the marching line were the *"children of Judah..."* (Num.10:14). In battle the Lord said, *"Judah shall go up first"* (see Judg. 20:18). The name Judah means "praise"; God intended, whether in times of peace or war, that praise would have the preeminent place. Proper positioning denoted a specific place of power. Jesus told the high priest that *"...hereafter you will see the Son of Man sitting at the right hand of the Power"* (Matt 26:64 NKJV). Even John and James's mother recognized the importance of position and asked that her sons *"...may sit ...one on Thy right hand, and the other on the left, in Thy kingdom"* (Matt. 20:21).

Jesus, as a beloved Son, was always in a position that you could see the"…*heaven open, and the angels of God ascending and descending upon the Son…*" (John 1:51). He continually manifested the power of operating under an open heaven: having permanent access into that realm.

The fact is that the heavens are not normally open. Satan's original function was to cover, veil, or guard the throne of God (see Ezek. 28:14). Even in his fallen position, he is able to veil or hide God's glory. He has blinded eyes (see 2 Cor. 4:4) and cast a "…*covering… over all people, and the veil …over all nations*" (Isa. 25:7). Jesus cut through that veil because of his position of intimacy with God, which prevented any separation when He died on the cross (see Matt. 27:51).

Jesus' position under an open Heaven allowed Him to function with power and authority. We, the Church are to operate in the same fashion. Jeanne and I participate with a team in an outreach called the Angel's Booth. The team does prophetic evangelism at trade shows. Our booth is set up like all the other booths at the show. The difference is there is an anointing at our booth that opens the heavens. We minister to Muslims, Hindus, Mormons, Jehovah's Witnesses, and atheists with equal success.

No matter what the theology or lack thereof, the love of God descends on these attendees and hundreds give their lives to God each day. It is amazing! In a ten-day stretch, the Angel's Booth team has led more than 2,400 souls into a relationship with Christ.

Outside the booth, each of us might lead two or three people to God per year. That is the difference positioning under an open Heaven makes. To the natural mind, this doesn't make sense, but God is asking us to shift our viewpoints in order to see things in the Spirit.

OPEN HEAVENS

The first mention of the Church (the house of God) in the Bible uses the same imagery of an open Heaven: "…*behold a ladder set up on the earth, and the top of it reached to heaven: and behold the angels of God ascending and descending on it....this is...the house of God...the gate of heaven"* (Gen. 28:12,17).

The house of God, the Church, is to be positioned under an open Heaven and is to keep that gate or veil open. That is to be our position. To do this we, as the Church must be in the center of God's will. Mount Zion was the center of worship in Israel. Mount Zion is where the ark of God, the presence of God, was located.

The Bible says in various places that out of Zion comes salvation, strength, beauty, rule, blessings, the law, judgments, praise, vengeance, deliverance, and the Word of the Lord. All of these are attributes of dwelling in God's presence. It is from that place that the Church will *"...destroy in this mountain [Zion] the face of the covering cast over all people, and the veil that is spread over all nations"* (Isa. 25:7).

The "going" and "preaching" to the nations will not free them. It is by our dwelling in Zion in the center of God's presence that we, the household of God, can break through the veil. That is how we operate under an open Heaven—and only then will we go to the nations *with power* and set them free.

BATTLES, VICTORIES, AND SUBMISSION

With few exceptions, the Church has not been effective in reshaping nations for many years. Yet, a time is coming when God's cosmic drama will be played out to the finish. This battle is not only for our sakes; also it is for the benefit of all of creation, that they might witness the manifold goodness of God.

I experienced a small-scale example of the type of battles that will be fought from this position within God's will. Our family was driving back from a day in Disneyland. The Los Angeles freeways were crowded and, somehow, in the frantic rush, I managed to infuriate another driver. A full-blown case of road rage exploded right before our eyes. The angry driver started honking and swearing at me and tried to cut us off. Jeanne insisted that I try to lose this man by getting off the freeway. I exited, but he followed right behind us.

On a side street, he swung in front of me and stopped. I expected him to jump out with a gun or a knife, but he just emerged from his car with his anger at full vent. I got out of my vehicle and that seemed to make him even angrier. He came charging at me; then he just stopped. The man seemed confused. He turned around and headed back to his car. Suddenly, he turned back and lunged toward me once more. Again he was stopped.

I was standing there confused myself and expected to get pounded. Yet, all he threw at me were a couple of expletives. He stopped again, but this time he just waved at me in disgust, got in his car and squealed out of there. It wasn't until I got in the car that I learned the rest of the story.

While I went off gallantly to try and appease this guy, Jeanne took on the real enemy—a spirit of rage. Every time the man approached me, she bound the spirit. He would turn away from me; she would pause in relief; and he would charge back. She finally took her full authority, and he left in disgust, likely wondering why he hadn't smoked me. My wife was the true warrior in that situation, fighting the enemy in the spirit realm and teaching our children how to do battle.

It is often in family situations where the true victories will be won. Families are God's primary institution for expressing His love and protection; therefore, they are satan's main targets.

Paul clarified the family relationship saying, *"The husband is the head of the wife, even as Christ is head of the church..."* (Eph. 5:23). This order is a role-play in the natural that mimics the relationship between Christ and His Church in the Kingdom.

Because of this, the positions and stances that husbands and wives take result in bigger consequences than we have imagined. The greatest teaching tool we can offer our children is to model a loving, joyful approach to covering and submission.

Submission is not just important for women to learn; it is a universal character trait that God uses to pour power through His people. God gave my wife the authority to do battle with the demon that had enraged the angry driver.

Through my job, the same God taught me how to operate in submission. I had a particular situation occur three or four times on the job. I would be promoted to the top job only to be demoted to the second-in-command position. This was frustrating to me as it would happen over and over again with no apparent reason or explanation.

God is efficient. He never wastes an opportunity. He was preparing me to function as a Number 2 person in the Kingdom realm. In our church, I operate as the support and helper to Marc Brisebois, our pastor, even though Jeanne and I have our own ministry. Because Marc travels extensively, Jeanne and I occupy the pastoral role in his absence and step back when he is in the house. God simply used the workplace as my training ground. I was OK as Number 1, but I was better at the Number 2 position.

The training I received in the marketplace also served to set me free from untoward personal ambitions in the Kingdom. For leaders, finding a faithful helper who is *not* jockeying for position is often hard to do.

In order to shift from the natural to the supernatural (whether in ministry, business, or family), we must always position ourselves according to where God is currently blessing and moving. We can't camp where the blessings used to be; we must understand where the blessings are coming from now.

In the Old Testament, the Holy Spirit was represented as a pillar of fire. That pillar needed to be followed if the supply of manna and water was to continue. The Israelites had protection, direction, all forms of provision, and health under that cloud. The same Holy Spirit must be followed today if we want our families to remain healthy and don't want our proverbial shoes and clothes to wear out. If we stay where the cloud was before and don't go where it is headed now, we will experience life in the desert.

RED-SEA MIRACLE

Jeanne and I went camping with the kids and decided to do some touring. We drove down an old country road in our V.W. beetle. It had rained a lot. We got stuck axle-deep in the mud. It was a Saturday afternoon; we had no money for a tow truck; and I had to be at work on Monday. To make matters worse, it started to rain again. I was so discouraged, I felt like crying.

We abandoned the car and hitchhiked back to the tent trailer on foot. I started to read the Bible and Jeanne prayed as we pondered our predicament. I was reading in Exodus and came across the story of God drying up the Red Sea with a strong east wind.

In Alberta, an east wind always brings bad weather, but I felt impressed to ask God to intervene on our behalf. We called out to Him and a strong surge of faith came over us. The faith that God imparted shifted our thinking and empowered us to ask for a supernatural intervention. I was confident now that God was going to do something for us.

We had gotten stuck about two miles down a dead-end road. There were no farmhouses on that stretch, but I knew that God could fix anything. All that night, a strong east wind blew, yet it didn't rain.

The next afternoon, we went back to see if we could free our beleaguered car. It was still bogged down in the mud, but we gave it a try by faith anyway. I told Jeanne to drive and I would push. The first time she gunned the car it pulled itself out of the mud! God had dried up our own little Red Sea.

We have to put ourselves into a place of faith so that God can come through for us. We need to shift into the proper position before we will see an impartation of His power.

POSITION AND RELATIONSHIP

Elisha saw the anointing on Elijah and desired to have it imparted to him. Elijah advised Elisha to be in the place where he could receive the anointing. Elijah said, *"...if you see me when I am taken from you, it shall be so for you....And Elisha saw it..."* (2 Kings 2:10,12 NKJV). Because Elisha positioned himself, he inherited Elijah's mantle (see 2 Kings 2:13).

We need to change our thoughts about power and position ourselves, in the Body, to serve those from whom we wish to receive an impartation. Today, most people want the impartation, but they don't want to serve. Elisha was Elijah's servant. He was called the one who *"...poured water on the hands of Elijah"* (2 Kings 3:11).

Unless we posture ourselves as servants, we will never walk in our own power. Jesus said, *"If you have not been faithful in the use of that which is another's, who will give you that which is your own?"* (Luke 16:12 NASB). Are we willing to take the position Jesus describes, or do we just want a position that elevates us?

Jesus' disciples were in a position *"...to know the mysteries of the kingdom of God..."* (Luke 8:10). They received an explanation of the mysteries because of whom they knew: Jesus.

A decade ago, because of a prompting from the Holy Spirit, I (Ken) made a choice to forgo a construction project that would have paid thousands of dollars. I did this in order to hear a speaker, Dennis Wiedrick, teach on intercession.

This teaching about standing in the gap for the sins of others revolutionized the way Jeanne and I pray for people. The impact on the Kingdom was beyond measure. Like the disciples, we need to come under anointed teaching if we are going to operate in anointing and power. We must not *"...think of* [ourselves] *more highly than* [we] *ought to think, but to think soberly, according as God hath dealt...the measure of faith"* (Rom. 12:3).

Even if we are the heads of our families, coming under God's authority requires us to have a right perspective of who we are in relationship to others. God always looks at the family as the primary source of encouragement and love. He demands husbands to "*...dwell with* [their wives] *according to knowledge, giving honor...as being heirs together...that your prayers be not hindered*" (1 Pet. 3:7).

Proper relationships determine blessing and a receptive response from God. I received the best job offer I ever had about eight years ago. It would have paid more than triple what I had been making at that time. The only problem was that I would have to be away from home for two to three weeks at a time and I would have to commit to a two-year contract. Jeanne and I prayed about the job; we both got a "no."

It was hard for me to turn that job down, but I knew we had done the right thing. Two weeks later, Jeanne was diagnosed with colorectal cancer. God knew what He was doing. (Just for your information, God preformed a miracle for us. Today, Jeanne is totally free of any cancer. But at that time, I needed to be there to walk with her through the ordeal.)

TRUST AND TEAM MENTALITY

God allows us to be part of His victories when we are willing to trust Him in the places to which He leads us. Sometimes it seems from our vantage point that there is nothing but disaster all around. When we are under attack, we feel isolated and alone. We need to remember that the view from the foxhole is different from the heavenly view.

God sees where we are at; if we will hold fast our position in faith, He will change the circumstances. While we wait, we become like small cogs on a big gear: we need only remain in place and bear the pressure when it is our turn. As long as the cog holds up, it will turn the whole gear. Eventually, the pressure will ease; others will bear it until our "turn" comes again.

Some of us hide when it is our turn to bear the weight. Then the gear slips, because the Body needs all of its parts to function. The days of "one man's ministry" are over. Even this book is the labor of a dozen people. Bob Jones once prophesied that our church would require 200 intercessors to function in the sphere that God had given us. The mission takes many; we are all a vital part of getting the job done—in the place God has chosen for us.

Do you remember the story portrayed in the movie *Saving Private Ryan*? Shortly after the D-day landing, half a platoon of soldiers went looking for Private Ryan. While they searched, they accomplished nothing for the war effort.

In fact, they were virtually useless—until they became vital. A certain bridge had to be kept from the enemy, and this half platoon happened to be the only ones positioned to keep it.

We need to shift into a similar posture and recognize that, while I may be unimportant in the big scheme of things, I am vital in the place God has put me. God places each one of us in positions no one else can fill; He puts us into contact with people nobody else can reach.

Change your thinking to reflect these truths. Where you are is important even if you can't see the relevance. In those places that don't seem important to the Kingdom—whether it be the workplace, the home, minding the kids, or taking out the trash—God develops character.

While I was studying in university, I worked for the Farm Credit Corporation as a loan officer. I lent money to farmers for land, equipment, and livestock, so I understood what a good loan application looked like.

I applied for a loan myself, to purchase a farm that was located in a remote area. I knew that my education, experience, and financial plan fit the criteria for that loan to be approved. Jeanne and I had one misgiving: the farm was not near a good church. We knew the Scriptures about the children of Israel who stayed on the far side of the Jordan River. That position placed them far from the center of worship in Jerusalem. They were not actually in the Promised

Land, just the conquered land. They went into captivity more than 200 years before Judah did (see 2 Kings 10:32-33).

Knowing this, we prayed that God would shut the door if this farm purchase wasn't His will. Sure enough, despite meeting all the criteria for the loan, it was turned down. God did not want us out there. He wanted us in a place where we could be part of a church that would affect the nations. For us to operate in authority and power, our physical location must match our calling.

DIVINE PRIORITIES

Just as we need to submit to God's sovereignty in location, so we must submit to His delegation of responsibilities. God has a divine order of priorities. The list goes against most human reasoning, but if it is adhered to, God can trust us with His power.

Here is a well-ordered list of five key priorities in our lives:

God

Spouse

Children

Job

Ministry

Let's first establish the fact that the categories *God* and *Ministry* are indeed two separate priorities. Our service to God includes our personal devotion to Him and our obedience to anything He specifically speaks to us.

Our ministry is what we do in the Kingdom. In Israel, the priests ministered to the Lord on one level and ministered to the people on another. Ministry to the Lord had higher qualifications. They could be disqualified from ministering to the Lord, yet serve the people (see Ezek 44:13-14).

We cannot properly function with power in the lower priorities on the list until the top of the list is in proper order. Jesus chided the

Ephesian church for putting work and ministry above their love for God (see Rev. 2:2-4). We can't run off and save the world until our own families are in good order.

I heard a powerful evangelist from Canada relate his battle with this principle. He said that while he was traveling around the country, the glory of God manifested through him, and many people got saved, healed, and delivered. He felt like a powerful man of God, but when he got home, his wife made him take out the trash. The reality was that they had four small children and he needed to be a servant, just as she was. You can be the hero "out there," but first you must be one at home with your wife and kids.

Paul asked, *"If a man does not know how to manage his own household, how will he take care of the church of God?"* (1 Tim. 3:5 NASB). We won't have authority over the large arenas in life until we take care of what is right in front of us. We must be able to take out the trash before we attempt to kick out a demon.

Similarly, God will give us authority over demons before He gives us authority over people. If you mess up with a demon, you've simply made a mistake. If you mess up with people, someone gets hurt. The disciples were casting out demons (see Luke 9:1) before they stopped being competitive, territorial, and cliquish (see Luke 9). In fact, they really didn't even know how to pray until later (see Luke 11:1).

God is a God of order. We must take our place in His order if we want His power to flow down through us to others. The picture Jesus gave of divine life flowing through the vine to the branches illustrates this principle (see John 15:1-8). In addition, Paul said that we were *"...grafted in...and... became...partaker[s] of the root and fatness of the olive tree* [God Himself]*..."* (Rom. 11:17 NKJV). This grafting in allows us to *"...sit together in heavenly places in Christ Jesus"* (Eph. 2:6), *"far above all principality, and power, and might, and dominion..."* (Eph. 1:21).

Satan wants to pull us down from that exalted position because he is unable to assail us there. Just as he taunted Christ to come down from the cross and prove His claims, satan tries to goad us into claiming our rights. The only power satan had in the Garden was the words he spoke to Adam and Eve. In the wilderness, satan attacked Jesus with suggestions, and on the cross he attacked with taunts. He attacks us the same way.

If he can accuse us and tempt us to justify ourselves, then he has won. The seat we have in the heavenlies was not imparted to us because we did something right; neither do we lose it because we've done something wrong. We got it because Jesus did everything right and we trust, believe, and declare His Word.

This is grace. We can only lose our position in Christ if we react to the enemy's accusations by trying to justify our actions and prove that we did everything right. When we do this, we are appealing to the law instead of grace. Then *"Christ is become of no effect unto you… [if] you are justified by the law; ye are fallen from grace"* (Gal. 5:4).

That is where satan wants us to be. It is the only chance he has to defeat us. We must resist him and maintain our position in Christ by faith, believing that God has established for us a specific realm of authority—a place of service.

God wants us to …*be fruitful, and multiply, and replenish the earth and subdue it, and have dominion…* (Gen 1:28). We can increase the boundaries of our influence *"…as* [our] *faith is increased, we shall be greatly enlarged by you in our sphere"* (2 Cor. 10:15 NKJV). You climb to your position up the ladder in the world, sometimes stepping on those you climb over. Paul is saying you are pushed up like the top of a pyramid as you minister to and increase the base (those under you) in the Kingdom.

That is why Jesus said, *"If anyone wants to be first, he shall be last of all and servant of all"* (Mark 9:35 NASB). The Lord Jesus is our head; *"the name of the Lord is a strong tower; the righteous run to it and are safe"* (Prov. 18:10 NKJV).

We are hidden in His righteousness through His name. It is a powerful name. We need to shift the way we think so we can position ourselves under His authority. Then we will be safe and able to function in the authority and power He appoints for us.

SHIFT INTO PRAYER

Lord, help us to realize our realms of authority and take possession of them. Forgive us when we have not believed that our positions are vital in the Kingdom and have abdicated our rightful places there. Lord, cause us to be faithful in whatever sphere of authority You have given us, and help us to be willing to take on a greater capacity as You give us the grace to do so. In Jesus' name.

ENDNOTES

1. http://www.provethebible.net/T2-Objec?G-0101.htm.
2. Tornquist, Cynthia. "After 20 years, New Yorkers recall night the lights went out," *CNN.com*, July 12, 1997, http://www.cnn.com/US/9707/12/blackout/ (accessed May 20, 2009).

Chapter 3

LET YOUR LIGHT SHINE

Repent and Be Converted

*R*EPENTANCE. The word calls up images of barefooted monks whipping themselves and living in mournful silence. Such is the lie satan and our own flesh conjure up to keep us from one of the most powerful, successful, and simple acts we can perform to usher in the presence and power of the Lord.

Repentance is one of the quickest ways to extract ourselves from the spiritual prisons into which we have locked ourselves. Peter said:

> *Repent...and be converted, that your sins may be blotted out, when the times of refreshing shall come from the presence of the Lord* (Acts 3:19).

Peter's description of repentance offers a paradigm shift that takes us from being pitiful to becoming powerful. With a single act, we go from being slaves under sin (dry and weary) to being clean and completely changed, able to draw the presence of the Lord into a situation and be refreshed.

Such is the power of repentance. The modern concept of repentance—the self-flagellating-monk mentality—carries the connotation of having to pay by sacrifice for our wrongdoing. We connect repentance with penance. *Penance* is a "sacramental rite" in some churches. It can also be "an act of self-abasement" in response to sin.[1] Penance often ends with sacrifice; it does not necessarily indicate a change of our minds or a turning of our hearts.

The Hebrew word for repent is *nacham,* meaning to breathe deeply or groan or sigh. It is a display of emotion indicating a change of heart or disposition. The Greek is more of a mental process, as indicated in the word *metanoeo,* meaning to perceive outwardly, thus to have another mind or viewpoint based on hindsight.

Both of these aspects, the emotional and the intellectual, need to be involved for proper repentance to take place. The main ingredient needs to be an understanding of our own wrong concepts, thoughts, attitudes, and actions. Unless we are convicted and believe we have done something wrong, we cannot repent.

Interestingly enough, we can't repent without Jesus' intervention. He said He came *"...to call...sinners to repentance"* (Matt. 9:13). The Holy Spirit is used in this work, for one of His jobs is to *"...convict the world concerning sin...because they do not believe in Me"* (John 16:8-9 NASB).

One of the functions of the individual spirit is to convict us of the things we do wrong. Another is to alert us to our fleshly nature, thereby preventing us from going down a hurtful path. To cooperate with our own spirit, we must agree that our human nature is evil.

This nature fosters unbelief and disagreement with the Word of God. We need Jesus to speak to us and the Holy Spirit to convict us so that we can come out of our unbelief. The ultimate goal of changing our minds (repentance) is to come into agreement with the Word and will of God. Once we know we have the mind of the Lord on a matter, it positions us to walk in new power and authority.

I (Ken) couldn't always see that my thoughts were wrong. I thought that if my actions were righteous, then my thinking was acceptable. This is comparable to a novice driver assuming that, as long as he doesn't drive into a ditch, it doesn't matter which side of the road he is on.

Driving into the ditch can be compared to breaking the law with our actions. But Jesus was clearly focused on heart attitude when He said, *"Whosoever looketh on a woman to lust after her hath committed adultery with her already in his heart"* (Matt. 5:28). Our flesh, whether in thought or action, is continually opposed to God.

Even though Jesus, who was sinless, never had to repent, He demonstrated the necessity of having God's view rather than a fleshly view when He cried, *"...Not My will, but Thine, be done"* (Luke 22:42). Even Jesus did not trust His own will to accomplish God's will!

God's will is to restore us back to the relationship He had with Adam and Eve in the Garden. Unless we recognize that our thoughts are opposed to His and are thus sinful, God cannot fully restore that kind of relationship.

ONE MIND WITH GOD

The story of Jacob and Esau is a powerful representation of God's emphasis on the heart rather than the actions.

The Bible says not to be a *"...profane person, as Esau, who...sold his birthright"* (Heb. 12:16). Esau was the eldest son. As such, he was in line to inherit double the assets and a blessing (empowerment) to carry on the family destiny.

In Esau's mind, this birthright was worth nothing, and that is exactly what he sold it for. God, however, knew what He was going to do through the family line and was furious with Esau. God declared *"Jacob have I loved, but Esau have I hated"* (Rom. 9:13).

God then allowed Jacob to take the blessing from Esau (see Gen. 27:35) and allowed Isaac to invoke a blessing (empowerment) of corn, wine, servants, and lordship over the family. Esau, because of his attitude lost the authority in the family (see Gen. 27:28-29).

Esau was not evil; there are no recorded deeds which caused God to reject him. In fact, Jacob was the one who lied and cheated, not Esau. Esau even married in an effort to please his parents (see Gen. 28:8-9). Yet, Jacob had the same mind as God concerning the blessing and the birthright. God could bless a man that valued what He valued.

Esau couldn't change his mind. He should have received the blessing but "...*he was rejected: for he found no place of repentance, though he sought it carefully with tears*" (Heb. 12:17).

Amazing! On the one hand, Esau's inability to repent removed him from his privileged place in the family—and even God despised him. On the other hand, Jacob, who valued what God valued (even if for the wrong reasons), was loved.

Our place of privilege and power in the Kingdom depends on our willingness to change our minds (repent) about how things should operate. Unwillingness to repent leads to backsliding. Why? Because "[we] *hold fast deceit,* [we] *refuse to return*" (Jer. 8:5). In the Hebrew, the word for "return" points to a turnaround.

God calls our contrary thoughts *deceits*, or *lies*. It is not necessarily that we are lying, but rather, that we believe lies. We need to "*know the truth, and the truth shall make* [us] *free*" (John 8:32). Jeremiah describes one of the effects of repentance saying, "*After...I was turned, I repented; and after that I was instructed...*" (Jer. 31:19). Repentance and turning from our lies allows God to speak to us.

God will not give you the next direction if you are going the wrong way. First, you must repent; then you will get direction for future steps. In the parable of the prodigal son, the father did not stop the prodigal from "doing his own thing" but gave him his inheritance and let him go until he "*... came to himself ...said ...Father, I have sinned against heaven, and in thy sight...*" (Luke 15:17,21).

Our son, Shannon, decided to take off with a bunch of guys, with only one month remaining before he graduated from high school. They were going off to live on their own and, like the prodigal, have a riot. So they left and went to Vancouver Island on the Pacific coast, rented an apartment, and set up shop. Shannon phoned me and asked me to send him the $1500 that I was keeping for him in the bank. I knew what would happen but I sent him the money anyway.

Sure enough, in a matter of a week, I received another call. This time there was a different tone to the conversation. Shannon said that he had gone out and gotten a job, paid the rent, and bought the groceries while the other guys were lounging around and doing drugs.

He asked, "I'm sorry. I made a mistake. What shall I do?"

I said, "Do you have anything of value that you need at the apartment?"

"No".

"Then don't go back. Stick out your thumb and catch a ride home."

God provided him with a Christian judge who drove him right to the door and he was home in 15 hours. Repent, and the Father will take you in, clean you up, and reestablish the relationship.

There is a humorous aside to this story. A few days later, as we were all sitting around talking, the phone rang. It was the police. They had received a missing persons report on a Mr. Shannon Harrington and they were wondering if we had heard from him. It seems when he took off, his buddies had missed their meal ticket and had filed the report, looking for it. The officer laughed with me as I explained the situation. In a matter of weeks, the rest of the gang filtered back home since there was no more money.

"WHAT ARE YOU DOING HERE?"

Elijah's life provides an example of what can happen when you step out of the Spirit and into your flesh.

After his great victory at Mount Carmel (see 1 Kings 18), Elijah followed his feelings rather than God's viewpoint. You can tell he is operating in his feelings, because he experienced a huge mood swing. One minute he was a man of power, outrunning Ahab's chariot to Jezreel. The next, he was fleeing from Jezebel for his life and whimpering *"It is enough; now, O Lord, take away my life..."* (1 Kings 19:4).

God was gracious to Elijah and even gave him angelic empowerment, including supernatural provision and strength, to do his "own thing":

> *And the angel...came again the second time, and touched him.... And* [Elijah] *did eat and drink, and went in the strength of that meat forty days...* (1 Kings 19:7-8).

Finally, when Elijah got to where he wanted to go, God asked him, *"What are you doing here...?"* (1 Kings 19:13 NKJV). Elijah tried to explain his actions, but God replied in First Kings 19:15: *"Go, return on your way...."* (Again, the Hebrew for "return" denotes a turnaround.)

More than one servant of God has been questioned and redirected by Him. We had a pastor friend who was a great man of faith. He and his family went out to minister to a church in a small rural town in the hopes of introducing a stronger Holy Spirit emphasis to a more "traditional" congregation.

As often happens, the people were not ready for change and dissension resulted. The spirit that arose was so divisive that our pastor friend decided to leave rather than split the church.

A short time later, he felt that God was leading him to begin another venture in the area. He started it by faith and God honored him by supplying all the money. God even used him and his wife to effect the healing of a sinus condition that had bothered me (Ken) for 35 years. I assumed that, with all his faith and power, this friend must have been spiritually mature and totally submitted to God.

I was wrong. He and his wife had one rule that put everything else out of order. They were never allowed to speak about anything negative to each other. As a result, they couldn't express their fears or doubts or even bring correction to one another.

God gives husbands and wives to bring balance and speak truth, one to another. I don't want my wife to tell me everything is OK and I'm wonderful when she's mad and I'm acting like a jerk. I need to know the truth, so I can repent.

This couple's code of silence isolated them from each other. Within two years of leaving the church, the husband ran off with a 16-year-old girl they had taken into their home. The man and his wife had several children of their own; some were older than the young girl for whom he left his wife.

I met up with this man 20 years later. He was still lost in the wilderness, still thinking he did the right thing. The lesson is this: If your feelings or thoughts conflict with the Word of God, shift your thinking. You will isolate yourself from God's source of power until you do.

How many of us have done what we wanted, thinking it was the best thing? How often have we misread evidences of power or giftings? Neither power nor giftings ensure us that we are in God's will. Instead, *"let the peace...from Christ rule (act as umpire continually) in your hearts..."* (Col. 3:15 AMP).

Elijah was striving when he ran away; he had no peace and he had no vision. God restored Elijah because he returned to God, submitted, and obeyed.

I (Ken) remember back when I was just graduating from university and had my life all planned out. I wanted to go into farming because I had invested four years of my life completing a Bachelor of Science degree in animal science.

That's all I wanted, but God said, "I don't want you to go back."

"But I want to."

God said, "I don't want you to go."

"But I want to!" I exclaimed.

God said, "OK, but you will be sorry."

You know what? I didn't care. All I knew was that I got what I wanted. But the Word says, *"The blessing of the Lord, it maketh rich, and He addeth no sorrow with it"* (Prov. 10:22). Needless to say, God was right. I was sorry. Everything went wrong. When Jeanne and I left the farm, we were broke and disillusioned. I had to repent.

God doesn't want us to be like *"...the horse, or as the mule, which have no understanding: whose mouth must be held in with bit and bridle..."* (Ps. 32:9). He wants our mouths to be able to repent and come in agreement with Him so that we might draw nearer to Him.

Looking back to our farming days, Jeanne and I realized that there was no strong, healthy church in that area. Had we remained on the farm, we would not have grown in the Lord as we were able to elsewhere.

This is even more important now. Why? Jesus said, *"Repent, for the kingdom of heaven is at hand"* (Matt. 4:17). The principles that govern the Kingdom are different from the ways in which the world works. To function in the Kingdom, we must be aware of how it operates.

> In the world: The greatest rule over the weak.
>
> In the Kingdom: The greatest serve the weak.
>
> In the world: If I have more, you have less.
>
> In the Kingdom: *"...he who gathered much had nothing left over, and he who gathered little had no lack..."* (Exod. 16:18 NKJV). This is infinite abundance.
>
> In the world: First is first; last is last.
>
> In the Kingdom: First is last; last is first.
>
> In the world: Peace is the absence of war.
>
> In the Kingdom: Peace is rest in the midst of war.

In the world: Lust operates; the motivation is what I can get.

In the Kingdom: Love operates; the motivation is what I can give.

It is easy to see why we need to learn to repent. We cannot operate or even believe the principles of the Kingdom with our current mind-sets.

GEARING UP OUR MIND-SETS

We humans function like vehicles equipped with a standard, five-gear transmission. We start in first gear; but once we have reached maximum RPMs in that gear, we have to shift up to access more of the motor's power potential. In fact, we must shift four times to get all of the available power from the engine.

So it is with repentance. If we know there is more power yet to be accessed, we need to repent and change our thinking at least one more time. If we don't shift out of our first-gear and second-gear mind-sets, they will become obstacles preventing us from reaching our full potential

We start developing our thought patterns or structures (which are designed to protect us) in the womb and as newborns. Our spirits, however, come into this life fully mature, as revealed by John the Baptist's response to Jesus while both were still in the womb (see Luke 1:41).

Thought structures or mind-sets either shift or become solidified during early development. The brain incorporates the emotional state of what is learned and will require relearning in a safe emotional context. This all takes place before the age of four.[2] Even the early church recognized fixing thoughts in children at a young age. St. Francis Xavier is quoted as saying, "Give me the children until they are seven and anyone may have them afterwards.[3] I (Ken) was very independent as a child and mature for my age, but that was not an indication of wisdom. I lived on a farm and whenever I needed to get to town for a hockey game I would hitchhike—even though I was only nine years old. Those were different times, but those experiences taught me to be even more independent. The structure I developed enabled me to get to hockey games, but it set up the root for later problems.

This independent spirit eventually made it difficult for me to operate in a corporate setting, either at home or in the church. Remember that, for many of us, the foundations of most of our thought patterns are constructed before we encounter Jesus. Thus, they are unredeemed, fleshly, and usually demonically inspired. They do not allow us to function in the way God intended or to think as He does.

Isaiah said, *"As the heavens are higher than the earth, so are My ways higher than your ways, and My thoughts than your thoughts"* (Isa. 55:9). Left to ourselves, our ways of thinking and doing will not match God's.

This is what Jesus meant when He said, *"No one puts new wine into old wineskins…"* (Luke 5:37 NKJV). The old structures, or thought patterns, must be torn down and replaced with new thought patterns to contain the life of the Holy Spirit. This is not just in individual lives, but also in families, communities, churches, and nations.

Because I had this independent spirit, some of my thinking was twisted. I even developed a martyr complex after I became a Christian. Situations may change, but strongholds like this persist and adapt in future scenarios. Shortly after Jeanne and I got married, that martyr spirit prompted me to warn her that if God were to call me to Africa, I would have to leave her here and go. (Now there's a way to make your new bride feel secure.)

I know what I told Jeanne sounds stupid, but that is the nature of strongholds. You can't argue with them or reason with them; they have to be torn down. This is part of the ministry of the prophetic. God sets prophets *"…over the nations and over* [our own strongholds], *to root out, and to pull down…to destroy…to throw down, to build, and to plant"* (Jer. 1:10).

We need prophetic insight to get at these roots that are buried. If we can't see these roots, we can never even acknowledge that they are there, let alone repent of them. How to identify and remove these roots is beyond the scope of this book, but their removal is the key to lasting repentance.

UPROOT STRONGHOLDS

I (Jeanne) was raised to mistrust. When I was the most fearful and dependent, God brought Ken and me together to help each other get healed. Healing comes as we expose our wounds and hurts to each other and bring them to the Lord.

If I have an open wound or bruise on my arm, I will not be hurt as long as no one touches it. If I allow someone to get close to me and maybe even hug me, chances are they will touch that sore and cause me pain. That is how God exposes our wounds: he brings someone into our life that, through intimacy, we allow to get close to us.

Marriages and churches are designed to be filled with people that love us enough to irritate us—to touch our wounds. Our reaction should not be, "You hurt me; stay away", but rather, "That hurt; I wonder what in me is wounded at that point."

Open yourself to the Word and to Jesus, allowing Him to salve your wounds. Then, through faith, accept your healing. If we repent of our strongholds, God will show us mercy. Over time, I replaced my shield of mistrust and fear with the shield of faith (see Eph. 6:16) and learned to depend on God and not on others for strength.

These strongholds or kingdoms arrayed in our hearts manifest chiefly through the tongue. Jesus said, *"Those things which proceed out of the mouth come forth from the heart…"* (Matt. 15:18). The tongue is designed to do two things: to speak encouragement to the heart (see Ps. 42:5,11) and declare what the heart believes (see Luke 6:45).

The tongue is also the best indicator of what is going on in the heart. Therefore, it follows that *"if any man offend not in word, the same is a perfect man…able also to bridle the whole body"* (James 3:2). In other words, if our words are truly pure, we are able to master our bodies overall.

Yet, the Word also says, *"Out of the same mouth proceed blessing and cursing…"* (James 3:10 NKJV). James goes on to say that a fountain or a tree cannot produce a mixture of good and bad; but the tongue does.

So what is wrong? If the mouth only proclaims what is in the heart, does it mean that certain areas of the heart are saved or renewed and others are unconverted and unrenewed? Are we saved, or aren't we? If my Bible tells me that *"whosoever is born of God doth not commit sin…and he cannot sin…"* (1 John 3:9), why does sin continue after salvation is received?

Allow me to make this personal. First John 3:9 always threw me because, although I was born again, I sinned. A clue is found in what Paul told us: *"…Work out your own salvation with fear and trembling"* (Phil. 2:12). This validates the idea that there are places in us that have not come under the Lordship of Jesus.

In other words, the blood washes us and all our sins are covered, but the demonic structures in our lives continue to operate right in the middle of what should be God's Kingdom.

These structures are just like the Jebusites' stronghold of Zion mentioned in the previous chapter. The Jebusites said to David (a type a Christ) *"…'You shall not come in here; but the blind and lame will repel you,' thinking, 'David* [a type of Christ] *cannot come in here'"* (2 Sam. 5:6 NKJV).

The Jebusites were a tribe that occupied the land before Israel invaded. God had commanded that all the former inhabitants be removed from the land, but the Jebusites remained.

The Jews knew they were there and must have made a pact with them, allowing them to remain in their stronghold. This event took place 400 years after Joshua entered to conquer the land—400 years! That is how long a stronghold can resist the rightful owner.

It was the lame and the blind (the hurt and the wounded) that the Jebusites (the demonic occupiers) claimed would keep David out. It is the same with us. The demonic opposition will use the wounds, hurts, and offenses that we carry in our hearts to guard our strongholds from yielding to Jesus.

Interestingly, once David took the stronghold of Zion, it became the seat of his power, and the lame and blind were not allowed in. When we repent and throw out demonic structures that have mocked us for so long, we must determine never to let those wounds, hurts, or offenses take up residency again.

This approach to strongholds follows the pattern that Jesus laid out when He was wounded for us. It is by His stripes (wounds) that we were healed (see 1 Pet. 2:24). When we are wounded but choose to forgive, when we sin but repent (change our minds) and are healed, we place ourselves in our Zion, the residence of Jesus, and we have authority to heal others just as He did.

DEMOLISH JUDGMENTS

Some of the structures and strongholds that escape demolition are absurd, even bordering on the ridiculous. Yet, they can still trap us.

Several years ago, when Jeanne and I first "discovered" judgmental strongholds, I (Ken) found myself dealing with one concerning my mother and Jeanne. Jeanne is 5'2" and I'm over 6 feet tall. I noticed that I was becoming irritated with her whenever she would ask me to get something that she could not reach.

This was not normal. It was especially odd because I was a workaholic, not prone to sitting or resting. Yet, whenever Jeanne asked me to get something, I would mumble under my breath some sort of complaint for having to help. Understanding how judgments work, I asked the Holy Spirit to help me find the root of this reaction.

in the natural, we plant seeds and expect a particular harvest in a specific time period. It works the same way in the spirit realm. The seeds we sow in the form of judgments against others will, in time, come to fruition in our lives.

We discovered that the timeframe for reaping in the spiritual realm often has to do with the age of the person against whom the judgment was sown. In my case, the Holy Spirit took me back to my teen years. Back when I was about 15, my mother was the same age Jeanne was years later when I first noticed my judgmental reaction.

I pictured in my mind my father sitting on the couch, exhausted, watching TV. My mother, who had lots of energy, was still working and needed some help. "Bob," she called. He roused himself to help her and then eased himself back onto the couch and fell half asleep. In a few minutes "Bob" rang out again, and the scene repeated itself. I then heard my inner self say, "Leave him alone, he's tired. You're going to kill him."

That was the seed. Right then and there, I had made a judgment against my dear mother that she was going to work my father to death. Slowly, that seed of resentment grew, hidden in a dark spot in my heart. Because the judgment started as a lie, there was no problem expanding its influence with more lies.

The truth was that my mother loved my dad. I knew about the Bible's description of the woman as the weaker vessel; yet I also knew that women outlived men by almost eight years. My reasoning went like this: "If women are weaker, but live longer, they must be doing something that kills us men off. I know what it is. They get us to do all the hard things. That's what kills us."

Brilliant deduction, except it was a lie. Once I recognized the root of my reaction to Jeanne's requests for help, I repented of believing the original lie, disavowed my words, and broke off that judgment. I then took the issue to the cross and asked Jesus to reap on His body what I had been sowing. We are literally asking Jesus to take the judgment of my thoughts, words, and deeds onto Himself on the cross: to bear the weight of my sin. Next, I asked God to put to death all the neuro-pathways, thought patterns, and lies that made up this stronghold; I asked Him to give me a new heart to love and help my wife.

Within a few days I could joyfully help Jeanne with anything she needed. I had used repentance and the cross to change the way I thought. That simple act moved me from duty to joy.

I (Jeanne) had a similar situation, which occurred because of harsh verbal treatment I received from my father when I was younger. I am the oldest of seven children. My dad lied about his age and enlisted in the army at the start of the war. Thus, he was only 16 when he began enduring five years of battle. He hardened himself to survive the devastation and death that he saw.

I judged my dad and thus all men as being harsh and hurtful. I ended up being afraid of men. I believed that if I went into a room full of men, one of them would hurt me. My judgment was strong enough, in those situations, to continually defile a particular man and empower my self-fulfilling prophecy. This allowed him to hurt me. When I dealt with the root, forgave my dad, repented, and broke off the lie, that scenario disappeared. Now I am very comfortable with any group, whether men or women.

Our task is to identify those areas of our hearts that are unconverted, hard, or hiding in darkness—those areas that we have not submitted to God's authority or way of thinking. We can see the dark holes in our hearts, but we don't know how deep they are. Until we shine a light into these dark places, we can't tell whether they are surface indentations or perforations that cut right to the core of our beings.

I had a *Star Trek* type of dream where Bones, the doctor, used a tricorder-laser combination. When he set it on the disperse setting, the scattered beam effected some healing in the room and gave some light. As he changed the setting and concentrated the beam, the charge sent the patient reeling, but penetrated right into the problem area inside his body.

The difference was the intensity of the light. This is what God meant when He *"...who commanded light to shine out of darkness... shone* [His light] *in our hearts, to give the light of the knowledge of the glory of God in the face of Jesus Christ"* (2 Cor. 4:6 NKJV).

We need to see our own hearts through revelation in order to see the condition our hearts are in. Otherwise, we will be deceived because *"the heart is deceitful above all things...who can know it?"* (Jer. 17:9).

God says, *"I...search the heart, I try the reins..."* (Jer. 17:10). Unless God reveals our condition, we will remain in darkness and ignorant of what we are really like.

We were cleaning out the large indoor atrium in our newly purchased house when God gave me (Jeanne) a view into my heart. Our atrium held a lot of plants, and at that time the floor was just dirt. The previous owner had left old cans filled with developing fluid and other chemicals under the decking.

The former owners' mess was a prophetic picture for me of all the smelly junk I had allowed to accumulate in my heart over time: bitterness, resentment, and unforgiveness. As we removed the stuff from the atrium, it stirred up the dirt around the plants. This caused the odors to waft through the house. The smells alerted us to the poisons lurking in some of the garbage.

It is the same in our hearts; when the stink arises, God is revealing what is in us. I was devastated with the condition of my heart as, one by one, God started putting His finger on my attitudes. I saw where I was critical, controlling, and negative. I loved Jesus, prayed, and was in the Word, but had not seen myself in God's light.

With agony and tears, I repented before the Lord. I cried for two weeks straight (and for six hours in just one day) as God, in His love, showed me my sin. God was preparing me to be part of advancing His Kingdom, but, before I could go any further, I had to press through this cleansing of my heart.

I (Ken) couldn't see the stuff that was hidden in Jeanne's heart. To me, she seemed far more righteous than I was. The truth is, we all have junk hidden inside. The Holy Spirit knows when it is time to turn on the light so we can properly perceive it.

REMOVE THE ACCUSER

Job had a struggle laying down his perception of God. He said, *"I have heard of Thee by the hearing of the ear: but now mine eye seeth Thee. Wherefore I abhor myself, and repent in dust and ashes"* (Job 42:5-6).

Revelation will cause repentance and bring us power with God. God was not mad at Job because he had misconceptions. He loved Job and was patient as Job worked through his ignorance. Even after all of Job's ranting and complaining to God (which came from his warped perceptions) God desired to promote Job. He spoke to Job's friends and said *"…ye have not spoken of Me the thing which is right, like My servant Job"* (Job 42:8). Earlier in the same verse, God said of Job, *"…him will I accept…"* Acceptance by God is a high honor indeed.

When we are dwelling in a stronghold, any effort to shine in a light or dismantle the house of lies will seem as a direct attack. The very act of our refusing to "go there" is evidence of a stronghold's presence. If we will allow some light to shine into the darkness, instead of perceiving the light as an enemy, that light will become our friend.

The source of the light God chooses to use doesn't matter. God even used satan, not to test Job, but to help him develop his character, by exposing his heart. God was not interested in testing Job; He already knew where Job stood. The test was needed so Job could see his own heart and repent, thus allowing God to promote him. That is why Jesus said *"…Agree with your adversary quickly…lest* [he] *deliver you to the judge…and you be thrown into prison….You will by no means get out of there till you have paid…"* (Matt. 5:25-26 NKJV).

The point here is not whether we are guilty; we *are* guilty. Jesus is saying that if you get before a judge, you will have no defense. The devil is appealing to the law to accuse you. If you appeal to the law (get before the judge) to defend yourself, you will lose. When the law is in play, *"there is none righteous, no, not one"* (Rom. 3:10).

Therefore, when you are accused, don't defend yourself. Agree, even if it is only 1 percent true. That is how you remove an accusation. When the Pharisees accused the woman taken in adultery, Jesus didn't try to defend her; she was guilty. What He did was take away the accusers. He challenged them to go before the court of their own conscience. None of them wanted to stand before that judge; they all left.

Jesus acknowledged the adulterer as a sinner, but because there were no accusers, He could show mercy. Satan *"...accuses* [us] *before our God day and night"* (Rev. 12:10 NASB). But in agreeing with the accusation, repenting, and thereby removing the accuser—therein lies power. When that accusation no longer hangs over us, we experience a freedom and lightness in our spirits.

Repent! It's fun!

AFTER GOD'S OWN HEART

God said of David that he was *"...a man after His own heart..."* (1 Sam. 13:14) because David always took responsibility for his actions and never tried to blame someone else for his failures. He was set up as the plumb line against which the coming kings of Judah would be measured. All the kings were judged by whether they *"...walked in all the ways of* [their] *father David..."* (2 Kings 22:2 NKJV).

David was not the standard because he did everything right; as a father in Israel, he was often a failure. In David's house there was rebellion, murder, incest, jealousies, and neglect, all of which later manifested in his kingdom.

Instead, David's authority came from a heart of repentance and a desire to please God. It is the same with us; God doesn't care if we blow it as long as we repent and humble ourselves under Him when we are corrected.

In the past, I (Ken) have had a hard time repenting. I didn't want anything exposed. To help me, God gave me a dream about a man to whom we were ministering. I was standing beside a garbage can. It had a label on it that said, "Dead Babies." The man lifted the lid and threw something into the can. That was when I woke up.

God was saying to me that this man continually threw his dreams and failures (miscarriages) into this can and just shut the lid on it. I realized this dream also applied to me. The problem was that the junk in the garbage can was still a part of me. These babies were my failed dreams and lost hopes, my bitterness and resentments. Now they were starting to stink because they had never been forgiven or healed.

Men are actually worse than women at stuffing their failures somewhere out of sight. But "stuffing it" never helps. Time does not heal unrepented wounds; it makes the stink even worse.

Dennis Wiedrick says, "Sin does not evaporate." If we have a problem, we will have a problem all our lives; if we have a sin, we can repent and get rid of it today. That is the way to real victory and power. The world encourages you to manage problems and not deal with them as sins. Alcoholics are encouraged to say, "Hi I'm (so and so). I'm an alcoholic." We are not sinners saved by grace; we are the "...*wisdom, and righteousness, and sanctification*" (of God) (1 Cor 1:30) through Jesus Christ.

I remember a time when Jeanne and I were driving home and an argument erupted concerning my inability to express love toward her. I used the excuse, "That's just the way I am." I thought Jeanne just needed to lower her expectations.

I knew I had a problem, but couldn't change myself. I was partially right; but what I had wasn't a problem—it was a sin. It was called *selfishness*. As we drove in silence for a while, God started to talk to me in my spirit.

He said, "When you were first married, did you pursue Jeanne?"

"Yes." I answered.

"Did she respond?"

"Yes," I replied again.

"Why did you pursue her?"

God does not ask questions because He wants to know something. He wants to know if *we* know something. God is also not a prude. He lives in us and is better acquainted with our real thoughts than we are. I thought for a minute and when I realized the point He was getting at, I answered Him truthfully.

"I was motivated partly by my hope that I would get her into bed."

"Use that same pure motivation now and it will work."

I had to repent of not pursuing my wife with my natural sexual desires for her. I can report that the repentance forged that day has brought a lot of joy into both our lives. God always has a strategy; and if we will cooperate and shift our thinking to His perspective it will always work. He designed us so that body, soul, and spirit would be a single unified expression of Him. We just need to see the real issues and repent.

It is a matter of bringing things to the light. We don't do this because "…[we have] *loved darkness rather than light, because* [our] *deeds were evil*" (John 3:19). We love to stuff, hide, and bury things. God says, "*If we walk in the light, as He is in the light, we have fellowship one with another, and the blood of Jesus…cleanseth us from all sin*" (1 John 1:7).

This is the crux of the Gospel message. If you want freedom, walk in the light; don't hide from man or God. We are not bad because we do bad things; we are bad because our nature is evil. If we substitute His nature for our nature, then we are righteous (see 1 Cor. 1:30).

The exposure He brings frees us; it doesn't condemn us. We don't want to live phony lives, always having to perform and pretend. We want to be free to live authentic lives; we want to overcome, or hate, anything that keeps us from God's best. *"Ye that love the Lord, hate evil"* (Ps. 97:10). The easiest way to overcome sin is to hate it.

FREEDOM IN THE LIGHT

When I (Ken) was young, I had a problem with masturbation. Since no sexual sin ever operates in a vacuum, fantasy and pornography entered the picture. When I got married, I figured that sex in marriage would end my masturbation impulse. I was wrong.

Masturbation is about lust. Sexual intercourse in marriage is about love and intimacy. One is exclusive of the other. I didn't know how to be intimate, so sex ended up with me using my wife as an outlet for my lust.

Jeanne knew something was wrong and felt the lack of intimacy, but I wasn't about to expose my thoughts or actions. I kept them hidden. I figured that I would deal with it somehow, sometime—just not now.

God had other ideas. I learned that if I won't deal with what God is talking about, He will tell my wife. If I won't listen to her, He will tell my friends. If I won't listen to them, He will tell the church and then the whole world. Trust me, it is better to deal with sin in private than having the whole world disgusted with you.

Since I was not responding, God told my wife. Jeanne started to share with me the dreams she was having about lust. They were *my* dreams. I thought, "Oh my God. She can read my mind." I attempted to stop thinking in front of her, reasoning that I would make her draw a blank.

She started seeing visions and even hearing music from movies I had watched. I was afraid to move. The prophetic is scary when you sleep with the prophet. My conscience kept convicting me. I felt dirty. I avoided sexual relations with Jeanne because the lust that came in made me feel even guiltier. I hated communion at church because I felt like such a sinner. It was hell, so would I masturbate for comfort; and the cycle would start all over again.

Get the picture? Then one day, God came up with a solution: "Expose the sin! Tell Jeanne! Bring it to the light."

I started to argue, "This will kill her. It'll cause a big war. This will wreck our marriage. She'll hate me. I'll look bad."

The last one was the real reason. That was why I couldn't repent. I believed that if I did something wrong, I was bad. If I was bad, God would hate me. So I couldn't be bad. I had to hide my sin, even from myself, but especially from God.

God was persistent. Finally one night, I confessed. It wasn't pretty. Most of my fears were realized, but Jeanne was amazing; she forgave me. What I didn't realize was the effect exposure would have on my spirit. I now hated masturbation and all its cling-ons. I was free! In one glorious moment of death, I was raised up to liberty.

Repentance is power. My spirit had never been free to function in the realm of my sexuality because I always considered that part of my life fleshly and sinful. With the spirit in charge instead of my drives, I was able to love my wife as God had intended, with passion, pure passion. God sanctified me at that point, over 30 years ago, and I have never gone back to that sin.

Shift into the supernatural realm! It's a lie that you can't be free.

GOD IS FAITHFUL

We can and do overcome satan *"by the blood of the Lamb, and by the word of* [our] *testimony; and* [we] *loved not* [our] *lives unto the death"* (Rev. 12:11). I was mortified of how Jeanne would feel if I aired my sin before her. But she forgave me and our intimacy was finally free to grow. We've been now happily married 40 years.

What I regret is that I didn't realize sooner that restoration is part of repentance. In fact, one of the root words for "repent" is the same root in Hebrew for restore which is *shuwb*. It means to return back to that original place.

I had hurt Jeanne; it would take years till I could stop loving myself more than I loved her and start the process of restoration. Had I kept short accounts with God instead of stuffing my stuff, I could have gotten to freedom much sooner.

Understand that we have layers in our character. Just because you've dealt with a sin on one level does not mean it will never reappear. It will likely crop up again as you get more intimate with God and in closer fellowship with others. Neither does the reappearance of that sin indicate that the earlier dealings weren't successful.

God showed me once that my sin was like a cancer. The cancer was not just a mass that could be extracted. It was fibrous and had tentacles going into every cell of my body. God said, "You can't cut it out. You need to kill it so that it will separate without destroying the surrounding cells." Sin must be put to death on the cross for victory to be complete.

Our sins, as was stated earlier, are removed as soon as we put them under the blood. Our sin nature, however, must be put on the cross daily (see Luke 9:23). If it were a one-time event, we would not have been told to make it a daily practice. For my sin of lust *"I made a covenant with mine eyes; [to not]...think upon a maid..."* (Job 31:1). I fasted all lust and came into total liberty and love.

God worked with me every step of the way. He taught me where my "off switch" was. Just as my television has an off switch, so my thoughts have an off switch. I just have to have the desire to turn off the switch when a bad picture appears. Remember, God is looking at our hearts, not our actions.

As mentioned earlier, when the Lord passed through the land of Egypt on the night of the last plague before the exodus, He wasn't looking to see who was in each house. He said *"...When I see the blood, I will pass over you..."* (Exod. 12:13). In fact, many people outside the covenant of Israel, must have put the blood on their own doors because, as you will recall from our earlier discussion, *"a mixed multitude"* left Egypt with the Israelites (see Exod. 12:38).

This mixed multitude included people who placed themselves under the blood, but had not covenanted (committed) themselves, to the Lord. We are the same. We have many areas of our hearts that are under the blood, but still need to be converted before we can walk in true fellowship with God and His people.

Our goal should be to expose all these areas. We want to *"repent… and be converted…"* (Acts 3:19), so that we can take on the image of Jesus and bring Him to others. Jesus told Peter, after taking communion with him, *"…when thou art converted, strengthen thy brethren"* (Luke 22:32).

Peter didn't believe Jesus. He was overly confident and thought he was ready to die for Him. Jesus prophetically told him that, *"…you will deny three times that you know Me"* (Luke 22:34 NKJV).

Peter couldn't see the areas of his heart that were not committed to Jesus. After he repented and was filled with the Holy Spirit, Peter operated in power. Even the Sanhedrin *"…observed the confidence of Peter and John…and began to recognize them as having been with Jesus"* (Acts 4:13 NASB).

Peter and John had started to take on the appearance and nature of Jesus. They spoke with authority. After his sin was exposed, Peter had to turn himself around (change his thinking); then he was not only powerful, but also profitable in the Kingdom.

> *Arise, shine! For your light has come! And the glory of the Lord is risen upon you. For behold, the darkness shall cover the earth…but the Lord will arise over you, and His glory will be seen upon you. The Gentiles shall come to your light…"* (Isa. 60:1-3 NKJV).

Shift the way you think, for the Kingdom is coming. Repentance is a gift from God; embrace it, for it is a powerful tool.

SHIFT INTO PRAYER

Lord, I pray that You would help us to repent and come out of our natural thinking and strongholds. I pray that our thoughts would become Your thoughts and our ways, Your ways. I pray that we would bring to the light those things that oppose You and Your Word; and that we would walk in a new level of supernatural thought life. In Jesus' name.

ENDNOTES

1. Merriam-Webster Online Dictionary. Merriam-Webster Online 2009, s.v. "penance," http://www.merriam-webster.com/dictionary/penance (accessed May 21, 2009).

2. Foxman, Paul. *The Worried Child* (Alameda, CA: Hunter House Publishers, 2004), 62–68.

3. Xavier, Francis. 1506–1552, www.quotationpage.com.

Chapter 4

INSIDE THE CORPORATE WORLD

Multilevel Unity

I (Ken) came into this world as a self-centered, self-serving individual with the world revolving around me. Feed me; hold me; comfort me; burp me; change me. If my parents didn't do it to my satisfaction or at my pace, then I started to holler at everybody around me.

I was demanding and ungrateful; still, my mother and father were excited that God had given them a lovely little baby like me. Even though I was totally dependent on them in my physical body, my soul and spirit were totally independent. God used my family to train me to become more corporate-minded: that is, I learned that it wasn't all about me.

So began my journey into the world of unity. Our family traditions were British in nature, which meant we had a stiff upper lip in the face of difficulties, with a slight bent toward superiority and arrogance. Both sets of my grandparents immigrated to Canada. One set came from the British Isles and the others were pioneers from the United States.

Being raised in the province of Alberta in western Canada fueled more of my natural rugged individualism. In this part of the country, independence is not only admired, but necessary for survival.

The farm is a familiar setting for me. I grew up on a farm, the second oldest of six children. My father was fun-loving but stern and had little time off from work to worry about me. That was OK, because I liked being independent and on my own.

As mentioned earlier, I used to hitchhike to town with all my hockey gear as a nine-year-old. That's how I got to my games. Think about any nine-year-old you know. How comfortable would you be with him setting off on his own to catch rides with total strangers so he could play sports? I thought it was normal. I got rides with Greyhound buses, gravel trucks, police officers, and the usual people who would feel sorry for a little guy packing a hockey bag (that was almost as big as me) and stick at minus -20°C.

I guess God had mercy on me and people took pity on me because I was never abducted or late for a game. This fueled my independence day by day.

At about this same age, I graduated from working in the garden (actually three gardens), doing chores, and mowing the lawn. Instead, I began working in the fields ten hours a day. I was actually excited with my new duties, as all my friends were driving tractors before I was allowed to do so. Though I had felt deprived by the delay, I was hardly strong enough to handle the equipment. The clutch on our tractor was so stiff I had to use both legs and all my strength to push down the clutch and shift gears—all while hanging onto the steering wheel.

The fields were big and the equipment was small; it would take me the better part of a week to cultivate one-quarter section of land. I was alone all day—no friends, no radio, just my imagination and me. My mind wandered off my work all the time. Once I found a buffalo jawbone in the field. I played with that bone so intently while I was cultivating that I wandered off my line by over 100 yards and knocked down three fence posts before I got the tractor turned around. There was no way to cover those tracks.

All these experiences solidified the independence that was in my DNA. Many of us come from families that actually promote corporateness. Even so, wounds, hurts, and disappointments lower our ability to trust those around us. Some come from totally dysfunctional families and have no sense of what a good family is supposed to look like.

Whatever our individual backgrounds may be, we are the material with which God forms His corporate body: the Church.

THE TEAM

God is not worried about our dysfunctionality; nor is He mad at us. He is thrilled at the prospect of our coming into our destiny in Him. God said, *"I know the plans that I have for you...plans for welfare and not for calamity to give you a future and a hope"* (Jer. 29:11 NASB).

We are like a high school football team. We join the team thinking we know how to run, catch, kick, and throw the ball. The problem is, we don't know or trust each other and we don't know or trust the coach. And besides that, there is this other guy (satan), who has been around for a while and is telling lies about everybody involved in the team.

Oh, we want to play football, all right. But in this atmosphere, what kind of a team are we going to have? How will we manage to come together as a unit after all the fights and arguments we've had at practice? We all want to play; we all want to do well, but we are a sorry excuse for a team.

Still, God is excited at the prospect of our "kicking some butt" during this season. He knows we have a ways to go. He's well aware that we'll need a paradigm shift in our thinking if we are to become a team (let alone a championship team for Him).

That is why God created families: to change our thinking. Moses, in the book of Genesis prophesied that *"...a man [shall] leave his father and his mother, and shall cleave unto his wife: and they shall be one flesh"* (Gen. 2:24).

Adam didn't even have a father or a mother. Yet, God's intention for marriage was apparent: to take two independent individuals and make them one. This is God's primary method for developing unity.

God planned to take marriages and, through their modeling of covering and submission, build families. These families would develop into clans, which would make up ethnic groups, which would form nations. At the same time, He would integrate these family cells into cell groups, which would form churches, which would usher in the Kingdom of God so they could have authority and dominion in the earth.

Satan had a strategy to prevent family units and their resulting authority from being established in the earth. He wanted to be the *"the god of this world"* (2 Cor. 4:4). All he had to do was cast doubt upon God's words (His truths) and His character (His motives).

Satan realized that even though Adam was the head of this first little family, he had actually never exercised that authority. Eve had never learned to submit or come under Adam's covering. Also, Eve had not actually heard God's instructions to Adam. She had only secondhand knowledge of the command God gave Adam concerning eating from the tree of the knowledge of good and evil (see Gen. 2:16-17).

With this scenario in place, satan went after Eve, challenging what she knew concerning eating from the trees in the Garden. When her reply was not exactly as God had spoken, satan knew he could twist the words, confuse, and deceive her. Adam, *"...who was with her..."* (Gen. 3:6 NIV) didn't correct the lie or prevent her actions. He let Eve take the lead.

The Hebrew primary root from which the word *with* is derived is *amam*. It means "to associate," but also by implication to "overshadow"—"become dim," or "hide."[1] That is literally what Adam did. He was overshadowed by Eve and said and did nothing. He let her do the talking; he just acquiesced. He was neglectful; she was deceived.

As a result, both experienced things they had never felt before: shame, fear, and guilt. Their reaction was to hide from God and to blame others. These feelings and reactions became part of man's DNA and have been passed down to every generation.

If illegitimate authority separated Adam and Eve, it follows that proper authority or order in relationships will bring unity. The boss who is reluctant to make decisions throws the whole company into confusion when he yields final say to subordinates. Many fathers fail to take their proper place as the covering for their wives and children. Fathers do not have to make all the decisions for the family, but they have to take all the heat resulting from decisions without blaming anybody else for what transpires.

TRUST GOD'S EFFECTIVE ORDER

According to God, Eve did not sin; Adam did. He was the one to whom God gave authority; he was the one held responsible for sin entering the world (see Rom. 5:16-19). Adam's authority wasn't granted on the basis of merit, but of election: God chooses whom He will.

The relations and roles in marriage don't operate on the basis of merit and worth either. They function on the basis of modeling of the Godhead; the model, therefore, is one of mutual respect, submission, and covering.

Marriage is the role model of unity displayed to the cosmos—both to the angelic and to the demonic. *"Therefore the woman ought to have a symbol of authority on her head, because of the angels"* (1 Cor. 11:10 NASB).

I (Ken) used to think, "Why do the angels care if my wife is in submission or not?" Now I see that marriage is the picture that God is using to manifest His wisdom to His creation. Jeanne's submission is not a sign of her inferiority to me; rather, it is a display of her trust in the goodness of God.

We need to shift our thinking if we are to gain the supernatural benefits of marriage. Instead of looking at His order through the lens of human perspective, we need to see it through His eyes. When we do, His ideas of leadership and submission make practical sense.

For example: My wife is in no way inferior to me. I owe her everything for bringing me out of my isolation and independence. She taught me, by example, how to love. She is the main reason that this book has made its way into your hands in its current form.

My role is to be the head and covering of the family; but I do not have the personality or the character to properly do this job. She is the heart of the home and the main reason it functions in love and order. To do this, she submits to my final authority. We both need grace to do our jobs.

The outworking of this role definition requires faith on the part of both husband and wife—and *it works.* I was teaching an adult Sunday school class many years ago; a woman named Maria who had just recently become a Christian was attending. She came to church alone because her husband was of a more conservative bent and did not agree with his wife's newfound born-again experience. He was actually angry with her as she grew more excited with Jesus. He finally demanded that she not go to church. He was feeling jealous and insecure with the sudden change in his wife.

Maria was a strong, independent woman and refused to obey what she considered to be an unreasonable demand. She asked me what strategy she should use on her husband so she could still come to church and not have to obey him. I quoted a Scripture to her:

> *...wives, be in subjection to your own husbands; that, if any obey not the word, they also may without the word be won by the conversation* [lifestyle] *of the wives;* (1 Peter 3:1).

I told Maria to trust God, claim this Scripture, and go home. I said, "Tell your husband that I said you should stay home and not come back to church until he said it was OK."

She was unsure about yielding in this way, but was willing to try. We prayed for her and she went home.

The next week, Maria was back and Ron, her husband, was with her. He wanted to see the guy who told his wife to submit to the husband whom God had given wisdom to be the head of their home. The outcome was that Ron became a Christian, their children became Christians, and many of their family followed. That was 25 years ago and they are still pillars in their church. God's principles work!

I (Jeanne) also am strong-willed, but as I studied God's Word I realized that I needed to submit to my husband. I still speak my mind, but if Ken decides to go ahead when I disagree, I am willing to submit to it and trust God that He will correct Ken if necessary.

I (Ken) sometimes joke that I make all the important decisions in our house such as how the national government should function and how the physics of the universe affect the planet and the cost of time travel. Jeanne is delegated all the minor decisions: where we live, what we spend, where we go on holidays, what we eat, and so on. Seriously, it's not about who makes which decisions; it's about this: Can I love enough to cover her, and can she trust enough to come under that covering?

Jeanne is far more prophetic and hears from God more easily than I do. I needed to learn how to submit to that functional, prophetic authority just as she needed to learn to come under my governmental authority. I learned this the hard way through many of my "good idea" investments that she told me were not "God idea" investments. I really know what is meant by the saying, *a good education is expensive*; mine sure was.

The marriage is the physical demonstration of how *"the husband is the head of the wife, even as Christ is the head of the church..."* (Eph.

5:23). The modern Church is struggling because so many Christian marriages do not operate on this biblical model. Thankfully, God is raising up leaders in the Body to minister healing to the hearts of those wounded in their attempts to love a wounded spouse.

Before we continue, I'd like to speak a word of hope and healing to all whose hearts have been broken in a difficult marriage:

> God sees all your tears. He will redeem all the years that seem to have been eaten up in sorrow. I speak now that you will have good reward for your love. By faith, start to receive your healing.

FAMILY COURT

The family was designed as the building block of society. God said of Adam, *"It is not good that the man should be alone;"* (Gen. 2:18). So he set up families as the vehicle used to subdue—that is, *exercise dominion* over—the earth.

Children of functional two-parent families have a lower incidence of criminal activity,[2] go further in school, and live in higher-income households[3] than do children where one or both parents are not present. God can intervene for a praying, loving single parent, but it was not God's original plan (see Matt. 19:8).

Part of the Church's function is to act as the surrogate family. *"Pure religion and undefiled…is this, To visit the fatherless and widows in their affliction…"* (James 1:27).

God says he will be *"a father to the fatherless, and a judge of the widows…"* (Ps. 68:5). He also says He *"sets the solitary in families…"* (Ps. 68:6 NKJV). This is a subject emphasized in the Bible. The fatherless and the widow are mentioned 42 times in the Old Testament alone.

The world system has helpful organizations such as Big Brothers and Big Sisters that meet important needs, but God had the idea first.

We, as the Church, need to listen to the Spirit so the world doesn't have to do our job.

Unity in the home is the testing ground for operating authority in the Church. The Bible asks, *"...If a man does not know how to manage his own household, how will he take care of the church of God?"* (1 Tim. 3:5 NASB). Authority begins at home. If fruit is produced in the home, it can be planted in the Church. If the husband does not lead his family in prayer at home, he should not lead prayer at church. Neither should an overweight person teach on dieting at the church. We are not trying to disburse knowledge or perform functions in a role of leadership; we want to impart life.

The importance of unity cannot be overstated. We had a cell group years ago that flowed in tremendous love and unity. We were from various churches, all living in a town about 20 minutes from Edmonton. The favor of God was on this group and He gave us a word to "be a light in our community." We went out in faith and called a pastor to help us start a church. With just five families, we were able to pay a full-time pastor and all the church's expenses. The church grew quickly over the next six years until it had over 500 members.

That is the power of unity!

ANOINTED SANDPAPER

Unity at the church level takes on a whole new set of parameters. When contemplating marriage, you take your time and make a careful choice before you commit to loving someone for the rest of your life.

In the Church, though, the intimacy is not as intense as in marriage; you don't get to choose whom you love. Jesus commanded the disciples to *"...love one another, as I have loved you"* (John 15:12). He then explained what He meant by love: *"Greater love hath no man than this, that a man lay down his life for his friends"* (John 15:13).

Laying down your life for someone else is impossible unless you shift your thinking and allow God to give you the grace to do it. Dying for someone you love is difficult enough; but we are told to die for people we might not even like. God showed His love towards us for, "...*while we were yet sinners, Christ died for us*" (Rom 5:8). We are to do the same. Even allowing people into your "space" can be challenging. That's where an understanding of boundaries is key.

You can tell how close people want to be with you in the Spirit just by checking how far into their physical space they allow you. We all have what psychologists call our personal space or boundaries—the invisible wall designed to keep others at an "acceptable" distance.

Two people who love each take down this "force field" and desire to have the other as close as possible. But approach too close to a stranger and the person will either back away or tell you to back off. Why? They have a fear of intimacy. It is too uncomfortable for them to let you get that close when they don't love or trust you. Healthy boundaries are good, but they are an indication of how much we love the ones we exclude from the inner circle.

I (Ken) was not a touchy, feely sort of a guy. When I became a Christian I might shake your hand and acknowledge that you exist, but my attitude was, "Stay out of my world and I will stay out of yours." Jeanne and the kids were allowed in, but I didn't want or "need" anybody else. I was independent, as you know. The first crack in my wall of self-protection came at a Charismatic Lutheran camp.

I discovered a problem that I didn't even know was a problem. I couldn't feel any sympathy or empathy for anyone in trouble. If someone was hurting, I assumed they had done something to create the situation that was buffeting them. I knew in my spirit that this idea was wrong, but there I was, stuck in my own stronghold.

This lack of love meant I had no power in my prayers. Miracles require faith; faith is powered (*energeo* in the Greek) by love (see

Gal. 5:6). No love, no faith; no faith, no miracles. So I decided to go forward in the prayer time and deal with the hardness of my heart.

I'm not sure what I expected would happen, but I wasn't prepared for what I got. As the man of God prayed for me, it was as if a stone in my chest started to fracture. I actually felt this mass or lump dissolve from off my heart. I started to cry (that's not me) and get emotional (that's not me). A lightness in my spirit came over me as though a burden had lifted. After that experience, I could empathize with people, and my prayers started to produce results.

Foolishly, I thought my hardness of heart was all that needed healing within me. I discovered later that there were many other wounds buried in my soul and spirit. God does not want us to be dependent on others, but He wants us to be interdependent, so that we all "rub" each other.

Think about those people who feel the most like sandpaper to you. They are the ones who get on your nerves, right? Well, they are also God's special gifts of grace.

God has designed these people to rub off our "sharp" edges. He goes to great lengths and expense to bring them into our lives. We need to embrace these people that Jeanne lovingly calls "grace builders."

Our family moved, for a short time, to another city so I could work on a large oil refinery project. The first Sunday there, we visited a church that was close to our house. I walked in, and a friendly looking gentleman, Les, grabbed my hand to give me a warm welcome. I attempted my usual shake and run routine (after all, we wouldn't be in the city very long, so I felt no need to make friends).

However, when I attempted to pull my hand away, Les hung on. He just smiled and proceeded to get to know me a little better. For five minutes he talked and asked questions, all the while clasping my hand in his iron grip. For the next two years, that man "invaded" my isolation fortress and forced me to become his friend.

Thinking back, I am so grateful that he did. I am writing this 17 years later and I am crying at the remembrance. God is so good! Les wasn't particularly prophetic, but he knew how to love and how to spot someone who needed love. That is the power and authority of fellowship. Les broke down a prison door behind which I had hidden for 30 years. He did it just by getting close and being corporate with me.

God is so pro-unity that He says:

> *...how pleasant it is for brethren to dwell together in unity! It is like...the dew of Hermon...upon the mountains of Zion: for there the Lord commanded the blessing, even life for evermore* (Psalms 133:1-3).

He commands the blessing (the empowerment) whenever He finds unity. If we want power and authority, we need to shift—change our minds and stop being independent and isolated. Factions in the Body of Christ must do the same thing individuals do; realize that we need each other. We need to love each other so God can be free to bless us. That means Evangelicals, Catholics, Charismatics, mainline churches, Pentecostals, Assemblies of God, Baptists: We are one.

We need to be *"...forbearing one another in love; endeavoring to keep the unity of the Spirit in the bond of peace. There is one body, and one Spirit....One Lord, one faith, one baptism, one God and Father of all, who is above all, and through all, and in you all"* (Eph. 4:2-6).

Know that God loves all His children and does not take it kindly when someone bad-mouths them. We also must love them, speaking and believing only good about all of God's kids.

This is the perfect opportunity for me to pray on behalf of all of us:

> Father, I stand in proxy for the Body of Christ which names You *Lord* and ask You to forgive us for allowing tradition or fear or pride or bad experiences to keep us from truly extending the hand of fellowship

to Your children. We take our authority in Christ on the basis of our receiving forgiveness and command this spirit of suspicion and independence to be banished from our relationships. In Jesus' name.

The more we pray this kind of prayer, the more power it will produce. If we submit to God and resist the devil, the devil *will* flee (see James 4:7).

WAGING STRATEGIC WARFARE

Satan's kingdom is made up of independent rebellious beings. They have rejected God and His Kingdom. They are like the servants in the parable who said of the nobleman, *"We will not have this man to reign over us"* (Luke 19:14).

Hell is made up of those who do not want to be in Heaven under God's rule. God is more loving and merciful than you or I. We don't have to worry about people missing God. If they are redeemable, God will find a way. If they refuse to come under His rule, He will not force them. If you don't want to be in Heaven, hell is your only choice.

Ever since the tower of Babel, satan has tried to bring a false unity (one not based on love). He understands that unity brings power and creates counterfeits he believes will be effective.

Regarding the tower of Babel, God said, *"They are one people, and they all have the same language* [they are saying the same things].... *Nothing which they purpose to do will be impossible for them"* (Gen. 11:6 NASB). Their unity that achieved the tower of Babel and the unity in satan's kingdom are built on fear and ambition.

In such situations, anything that goes wrong results in blame and accusation. Such reactions are a strong indication of the lack of unity. An organization can be made up of independent individuals; but an organism must be one. If 20 percent of my body's cells are in rebellion, cancer is raging in me. True health, for an individual or a church, requires all members to function in unity.

The Church has been waging trench warfare for years, with each individual church or denomination defending its piece of ground (that which it thinks is important). Through fear, confusion, and isolation, the enemy has kept them from advancing.

As a Church, we have spent all our time and energy putting out fires and defending "our turf." We cannot even conceive of victory because we have lost so many battles. We are locked into our bunker mentality; we think only of hanging on instead of having a vision of how we can change.

God is calling us to come out of our bunkers and attack strategic, winnable targets. He wants a good cross-section of the army to leave the trenches and join a unified force that is equipped to cross into enemy territory and cause a breach in his lines. The power and grace of that moment of unity will send confusion into the enemy's camp.

Each city or region may require a different attack strategy, but one characteristic will be common to all successful forces: unity.

I (Jeanne) had a vision of a mass of people of every sex, race, and age holding a flag in the middle of a piece of ground. They were planting the flag, like marines taking a beachhead. God was saying that unity is required to establish a city of refuge. For a citywide victory, there must be a citywide Church. This will require a shifting from denominational thinking to Kingdom thinking.

Denominations need not end, but divisions must. Projects will not win the day; anointings will. Satan does not possess superior numbers or authority; all the authority belongs to Jesus and those to whom He imparts it. The only authority satan has is the authority people give him. If we repent, stop resisting each other, come together in unity, and take back our legitimate authority, satan must retire from the battlefield or bring in reinforcements.

In an attempt to resist this unified local army, satan will draw some of his troops away from other arenas of battle. Putting this scenario into a Star Wars terminology, this action will cause "a tremor in the force."

In the areas satan vacates, resistance to God's purposes will lessen. The churches in those regions can then break through satan's bonds, provided they, too, are in unity. This will cause a domino effect as satan becomes increasingly preoccupied with putting out fires throughout his realm.

We must shift; we must acknowledge that what we have been doing isn't working. God has a better way: fight the enemy, not your brothers. If we unite, we can cause satan's forces to accuse their own. Then, we will see Jesus' words come true: "...[a] *house divided against itself shall not stand*" (Matt. 12:25).

REDEEMING THE ENTIRE CREATION

Satan originally took *two* people captive. Yet, their fall caused the whole of creation (over which they had authority) to come under satan's domain. The Church has occupied itself with redeeming people, but God is interested in restoring His whole creation. The Bible says that "*God so loved the **world** [the cosmos] that He gave His... Son...*" (John 3:16, emphasis added). God loves the whole of His creation, not just the people in it.

The people in God's Kingdom, united under their Commander have the authority to take back the world. We are not talking church here; we are talking Kingdom. The Bible says that "*...the creation itself also will be set free from its slavery to corruption into the freedom of the glory of the children of God*" (Rom. 8:21 NASB). This is our destiny and calling.

After Jesus' resurrection, the early Church was instructed to "*... tarry [wait]...in...Jerusalem, until ye be endued with power from on high*" (Luke 24:49). Jesus was saying, in essence, "Just wait together, in one place and in unity until the Holy Spirit comes. Then *everything* will change."

We are not going to change the world the way we are. Unity comes from being united first with God; then with our families; and, finally, throughout our churches. Until we get that far, there is no point trying to go any further. Every journey begins with the first step; we must take that first step. Love the ones God puts within our reach before we try to love those far away. Jesus laid out the order, "*...Jerusalem ...Judea ...Samaria ...the uttermost part of the earth*" (Acts 1:8).

FOREIGN FIELDS

Reaching out to the hurting in our own communities and in foreign fields will bring us together simply because we are operating in selfless love. Jeanne and I took a team to Guatemala. There were no pastors on this team, just 12 Christians united for a common cause: to set people free.

We needed to come together as a team in unity first. We met every week for three months of prayer and fellowship. We "sanded" each other, irritated each other, and forgave each other. We worked out our issues until we could love each other and then we were free to love others.

Once the team was in unity, the church body got involved. We took more than 600 pounds of provisions for the churches in Guatemala. We came under the anointing of our local pastor and he sent us to minister under the covering of a missionary down in Guatemala. Our anointings were added to the missionary's and we were able to minister in the prison, the streets, an orphanage, some churches, and in a pastors' conference. We saw salvations, healings, deliverances, and people set free.

The trip changed all of us. Since then, two other groups have gone to Guatemala and have met with great success. We have sent close to 60 individuals out of our church to that field alone. Others have gone to France, Serbia, Nicaragua, El Salvador, Cuba, Malaysia, Ireland, Singapore, Holland, Korea, the United States, and other parts of Canada.

We have been able to do this, as a church, because many of our members have been healed of their independence and have replaced it with a single vision to bring the Kingdom back to the earth. *Division* (in Latin, *di*, meaning "two" and *visio*, meaning "vision") means "two or separate visions."[4]

We must see as God sees and agree to walk together (see Amos 3:3) with Him in His vision and with each other.

OPEN HEAVENS

We need to shift in our view of the Church that has been described in the Bible as both the *Body of Christ* and the *house of God*. Both views had similar attributes; both were to become a door or a gateway to Heaven with "...*angels of God ascending and descending...*" (Gen. 28:12; John 1:51). That is how the Church is to operate: under an open Heaven. When the heavens are open, the veil that blinds people (see 2 Cor. 4:4) is removed and they can receive the truth.

One part of that truth is that God is no respecter of persons and will respond to any group of people that comes together in unity around a righteous goal. At the start of World War II, the U.S. merchant marine was vastly under-equipped to meet the demands of war. Merchant shipbuilding was crowded out by the navy's military requirements. As a result, there were not enough cargo ships to meet the growing need.

During World War I, it had taken 10 to 12 months to produce a single oceangoing ship. A shift in methodology and production had to occur if the quota of needed ships was to be met.

The man with the new vision was Henry J. Kaiser, who had just completed the Hoover, Bonneville, and Grand Coulee dams ahead of schedule. He had never built a ship before, but understood modularization and mass production. Critics laughed at his theories, but he astounded them by continually reducing the delivery times of the new Liberty ships until his shipyards were producing one every ten days!

By shifting production to thousands of factories nationwide and coordinating all their efforts, Kaiser changed the way ships were built. The production of the Liberty ships, which were a third larger than earlier cargo ships, was averaging 70 days by the fall of 1942. By 1944, the average time had been reduced to 42 days. One efficient (united) West Coast shipyard was averaging 16 days per ship and the *S.S. Robert E. Peary* was produced in a record time of just one week from the time the keel was laid until she was launched.[5]

That is the outcome of unity of purpose.

Unity is a principle that works. We need to shift the way we think about walking in unity so we can access the supernatural blessings of God. The early Church was *"...with one accord in one place"* (Acts 2:1) when the power of the Holy Spirit fell. When we are in unity, a commanded blessing opens Heaven and we become the true manifestation of the Kingdom of God.

The Kingdom of God includes all ages and maturity levels. It includes, but is not limited to, the Church. Jesus said, *"...the kingdom* [not the Church]*...is at hand"* (Matt. 4:17). He also said:

> *...I will build My church; and the gates of hell shall not prevail against it....I will give unto thee the keys of the kingdom...thou shalt bind...and...thou shalt loose...* (Matthew 16:18-19).

Jesus has given us the keys to a Kingdom that hell cannot resist or stop. Those Kingdom things that are locked up now will be loosed by the unified Church; and those demonic things that operate freely now will be locked up by the same unified Church.

That is authority! That is our glory! But until the last prayer of Jesus is answered, we will have no power. The last thing Jesus asked the Father concerning His disciples before He went to the cross was

...that they may be one, just as We are one;...that they may be perfected in unity, so that the world may know that You sent Me...[and] that they may see My glory...(John 17:22-24 NASB).

When that glory comes and we are changed into one Body, then the power and the authority of the Kingdom will be released on the earth and the *"...kingdoms of this world* [will] *become the kingdoms of our Lord, and of His Christ..."* (Rev. 11:15).

Unify us to hasten that day, O Lord!

SHIFT INTO PRAYER

Lord, forgive us where we walk in independence from one another and from You. Cause us to come into corporate unity first in the home, then in the Church. Cause us to believe that You supernaturally provide for the vision that You give Your people. In Jesus' name.

ENDNOTES

1. *Biblesoft's New Exhaustive Strong's Numbers and Concordance with Expanded Greek-Hebrew Dictionary.* CD-ROM. Biblesoft, Inc. and International Bible Translators, Inc. s.v. "amam," (OT 6004).

2. Fagan, Patrick F. , PhD, "The Real Root Causes of Violent Crime: The Breakdown of Marriage, Family, and Community," *The Heritage Foundation* (March 17, 1995), www.heritage.org/Research/Crime/BG1026.cfm (accessed May 22, 2009).

3. "Children's Health Encyclopedia: Single-Parent Families," *Answers.com*, www.answers.com/topic/single-parent-families (accessed May 22, 2009).

4. *Webster's New Twentieth Century Dictionary*, s.v. "division."

5. "Liberty Ships," *Global Security.org*, http://www.globalsecurity.org/military/systems/ship/liberty-ships-production.htm (accessed May 22, 2009).

Chapter 5

REIGN FROM HEAVEN

Grace

IT was payday, just before Christmas. All the guys piled into the lunch shack at noon. I pulled out the pay checks and started to hand them out. The usual grumbling and checking of the pay stubs filtered up from the table.

"Is that all we get for working the extra overtime?"

"Look at the deductions. Man, they take 40 percent of the gross."

"$#%&!*@ government, into my pocket again!"

All these comments were addressed to checks that netted these ironworkers between $850 and $1,000 for the week. I then proceeded to hand out another packet of envelopes. The mood changed.

"Hey, look at this—a bonus!"

"Wow, 250 bucks. Hey, thanks."

"Three hundred bucks. That'll help with the expenses."

"Gee, I've been here less than a month and still get $100? Thank you!"

As I was driving home that night, God started to talk to me. "Why would a man thank you for a $100 or $250 check, yet complain and snipe about an $850 check?"

As mentioned earlier, when God asks a question, it isn't because He wants to know something. He is asking to see if we know the answer.

I started to ponder and realized the difference had nothing to do with the size of the check, but rather, with the reason for the check. The large checks were wages that had been earned and were owed. The reactions indicated the men felt they were not being rewarded according to the effort they had exerted.

The bonus—unearned, technically undeserved, and unexpected—was received with joy. There were no complaints about the varying amounts, and all were thankful for the gift.

This picture parallels the distinctions between law and grace. If we labor under the law, always trying to do what is right, we will be disappointed with our wages. If we work in faith, we will always be delighted in the gift we receive.

Hirelings work for the wages and "...*because he is a hireling... does not care about the sheep*" (John 10:13 NKJV). Hirelings are concerned about their wages. The wages for the religious are tied to their attempts to keep the law, to do it right, and to be righteous. However, "...*there is none righteous, no, not one...*" (Rom. 3:10). We are all charged under sin and "...*the wages of sin is death* [separation from God]; *but the gift* [grace] *of God is eternal life...*" (Rom. 6:23).

We are trying to do work that we don't have the capacity to accomplish. We want to get paid for the effort we put out. But if we are getting paid for the job and not the time, then until the job is complete there will be no wages paid. That is the difference between a hireling and a son: The son gets his inheritance on the basis of relationship, not productivity.

We can never produce the fruit of righteousness by attempting to do everything right. Why? Because there is only one law made up of hundreds of commandments originating with the Ten Commandments. It is like a chain with many links, *"for whoever keeps the whole law and yet stumbles in one point...has become guilty of all"* (James 2:10 NASB). Break any one link and you have broken the chain. Trying to put together a chain that we continually break is frustrating; it is toil. That is why legalism produces cold, angry people. It doesn't seem fair to try so hard and then have that labor go unrewarded, or, even worse, rejected.

Enter *grace*. The very word has a beauty and ease about it. The Hebrew root is *chanan*; it literally means "to bend or stoop in kindness to an inferior."[1] As I read that, I picture a father bending over to help his child.

The Greek word *charis* denotes "graciousness,"[2] as in favor and a kind disposition toward a person or thing. It is a free act, on God's part, no more hindered by sin than it is conditional upon works. Just like the bonus checks we don't earn, grace cannot be earned or received because it is "deserved."

Grace is *"the goodness of God* [that] *leads you to repentance..."* (Rom. 2:4 NKJV). That is how we are converted. *"For by grace you have been saved through faith...not of works, lest anyone should boast"* (Eph. 2:8-9 NKJV).

The message of grace is displayed when a father speaks comfort to a child, "Don't worry if you broke it (or spilled it, or got mad and threw it away). I'll make it better. Come into my arms."

Grace is not about our choosing God; He must choose us (see John 1:13). Even our ability to turn to God comes from Him; unless the Holy Spirit convinces us of our sin, we cannot even repent (see John 16:8-9).

"Let us labor therefore to enter into [God's] *rest..."* (Heb. 4:11). To rest in Him, we need to change the way we think. As Paul said: "... *Be transformed by the renewing of your mind, that you may prove what is that...perfect will of God"* (Rom. 12:2 NKJV).

Our hearts need to be *"established with grace"* (Heb. 13:9) so that the *"...word of Christ* [dwells] *in* [us] *richly..."* (Col. 3:16).

This was a hard concept for me to grasp. I had always believed in working hard to supply everything my family and I needed. I had to learn instead to do my part, but trust in His grace rather than in my sheer "earning power."

UNFATHOMABLE EXTRAVAGANCE

I (Ken) was praying about whether Jeanne and I should attend a conference in Florida. It would be an expensive trip and would also entail my missing work. In my mind, I could not justify that kind of expense for a three-day conference.

God started to speak as I decided to forgo the conference. He said, "If I supplied the money for the trip, would you go?"

I replied, "Yes."

God shot back, "I already gave you the money. It is in your bank account. Use it to pay for the trip."

I now had the choice to obey or disobey. This was no longer a debate about justifying an expense. Instead, the issue involved my perceptions about money.

One thing is crystal clear: If we desire God to supernaturally bless our finances, we will have to shift the way we think about money. If our money really is His, then He has the final say on how it is spent.

Jeanne and I took the money and went on the trip. We were blessed, too. God had a divine appointment arranged with some prophets; we also combined the conference with a small vacation. We figured, "Hey—if God had already paid the airfare, we might as well take advantage of His generosity."

God continued to surprise us with His goodness. As we prepared to fly home, the airline announced that our flight was overbooked. They asked for volunteers to be bumped onto a flight leaving four hours later. Jeanne and I got off the plane; each of us received a free flight for our inconvenience. The extraordinary part was that we were flown *first class* to Detroit and Minneapolis, where we caught up to our original flight!

We arrived home at the same time and on the same plane that we originally booked, but with a pair of free tickets in our hands. We used those tickets for another conference in North Carolina and received further blessing from the Lord.

That is the grace of God, but I had to relinquish my fears for finances before He could release the blessing.

Remember: The battleground is in our minds. The war is waged in our thoughts. Most of us were taught as children, through the example and urging of our parents, to earn what we need. Religion has reinforced that idea by insisting that good people—the ones who do it right—earn entrance into Heaven. Religious definitions of what is right vary, but the principle remains the same: you will get what you deserve (what you work for). That is most often how we think.

The Bible says we all deserve separation from God (entrance to hell), yet God offers us eternal life (see Rom. 6:23). Our thoughts about God and the consequences of our sins have been hardwired in us since infancy. Those thoughts separate us from God's will for us. Jesus said:

> *Except ye be converted [change your mind], and become as little children, ye shall not enter into the kingdom of heaven"* (Matthew 18:3).

When I was younger, I (Ken) used to believe that I had to become a missionary for the rest of my life and die a martyr's death. I believed that was my fate. But Christians aren't doomed to fate; we have a destiny. I assumed that God required a sacrifice from me to satisfy Him. I had bound myself under fatalism. Where did I get such a twisted way of thinking? My thoughts came from my perceptions, which were determined by my upbringing.

In no way do I want to dishonor my parents. They weren't perfect, but they were great parents. They did the best they could with what they knew and made the best of our circumstances, which were demanding. We lived on a farm and there was never an end to the work that needed doing every day! I wanted to play and have fun, but the work always came first.

I remember the first day of summer holidays after grade three. I had to work in the garden the very day school let out for the year. All of the other kids were going off to play. When the garden work was finished, the lawn needed mowing. After that, the farm chores needed doing. The next day, we would be stacking hay. On and on it went.

I developed the mind-set that my life was doomed to be devoid of pleasure and full of work. I could only please my Dad (God) if I did my duty. I developed that attitude as a way of thinking. Thank God, He gave me a wife who loved life and understood the value of play; He used her to balance me.

Thoughts are actually neuro-pathways in the brain. When these thoughts are reinforced repeatedly, they become the default pathways through which the brain sends electronic signals. These paths become so well-worn and rutted that it is hard for the signals (thoughts) to go in a different direction.

NOT HIRELINGS, BELOVED CHILDREN

Grace, the idea that God actually is disposed toward us, is hard for most of us to accept because we have been taught to think otherwise. These thoughts (neuro-pathways) are powerful. Sports psychology studies done since the early 1970s have examined visualization and its effects on performance. They tested the hypothesis that performance could be improved by visualizing (thinking about) a specific action.

The studies used two groups: one group practiced each day; one group practiced *and* visualized. What were the results? In all studies, the performance of the visualizing groups improved significantly more than that of the control group. Those who visualized the specific activity developed a neuro-pathway to the relevant muscles that sent just the right amount of electricity to accomplish the task.[3]

Such is the power of thought. As visualization works for the physical, so it affects our mental processes. We need to think God thoughts consistently to train our minds to habitually think like Him.

God needed to change my "African missionary martyr complex" if I was to be profitable to my family and ultimately to the Kingdom of God. He had to have me think in terms of grace rather than works. Otherwise, I would be judging myself and everyone else on the basis of how hard we work. God helped me to "...[bring] *into captivity* [redirect the neuro-pathways of] *every thought to the obedience of Christ"* (2 Cor. 10:5).

God had to shift my view of myself from that of a hireling to that of a son; from one who had to work for all he gets to one who had an inheritance waiting for him.

That was hard for me because my view of God developed from a perception of my relationship with my father. I thought my dad only cared about the work getting done and not about me. (This was not the truth, but my perception of the truth.) From this, I developed a "counterfeit" priority list: work first, relationships second. Of course, since there was no end to the work, toiling became Priority 1, 2, 3, through 99. Relationships ran a distant 100.

You can imagine how this affected my relationships with my wife, children, and everyone else. They just weren't on my list of priorities! Oh, I could work for God but I couldn't love Him or His people. I became a Pharisee and a hypocrite who would "...*tithe of mint and anise and cummin,* [but] *omitted the weightier matters of the law, judgment, mercy, and faith..."* (Matt. 23:23). I could have added love, kindness, gentleness, and so on to this list.

I was cold, hard, and driven. Plus, I lacked love. Why was I like that? I found it impossible to think any other way. *"As* [a man] *thinks in his heart, so is he"* (Prov. 23:7 NKJV). I needed deliverance, not from a demon (although there was one associated with my thoughts), but from my stronghold of works in place of grace.

These thoughts were so pervasive that once I started down that path, I couldn't untangle myself from it. So what was the answer? At the time, my only thought was, "Just don't go there." Do not allow those thoughts to form. Refuse them. Since then, we have discovered how to heal these memories (a subject not within the scope of this book).

To get to that place, I had to repent of all my judgments against my parents (these were at the root) and ultimately against God. I had to repent of believing the lie that my dad and God were hard and that I was only good for serving and work (and had no real value in myself).

I had to refute my own words and vows about my life (for instance, about being a martyr) and take them to the cross. I had to let Jesus reap what I had been sowing there. After that, I could finally ask God to tear down this stronghold in my mind and to put to death every lie (every thought pattern and structure, every neuro-pathway) that had programmed my beliefs. Finally, I asked God to give me a new heart to believe the truth about God, my father, and myself.

What freedom...what power there is in being able to walk in grace. My flesh still believes the lie that I have to work for what I get, but that thought no longer has the ability to control me. If I were to give it life (agree with the thought and meditate on it) then it would take me back into captivity. This is why we are told to "... *deny* [ourselves], *and take up* [our] *cross daily, and follow* [Jesus]" (Luke 9:23). The blood of Jesus cleanses our sins; but the cross is designed to daily deal with our fleshly nature.

It goes back to the "off switch" I mentioned earlier. Turning off a thought is no different from turning off the TV when a sexual image appears. We can't stop the image from coming through the airwaves, but we can switch the channel or discontinue the transmission of the image into our minds. If we have not repented and broken the power of "old" thoughts (the errant desires of our hearts), then the TV screen in our minds will pop on unassisted and the thought will reappear. If we maintain command of the remote control, it becomes easy to shut off images and thoughts as soon as they crop up.

Now I am free to receive God's grace because I believe I am His son and He loves me. I am free both to try and even fail while enjoying the process. I no longer believe I am more loved when I succeed or less loved when I blow it. I can have fun with my heavenly Dad because *"a righteous man falls seven times and rises again..."* (Prov. 24:16 NASB).

We are shocked when the righteous fall; God is not. We think falling makes us unrighteous; God does not. We need to change the way we think; God does not. Our righteousness comes from Christ, not our walk (see 1 Cor. 1:30).

THE ELECT

A baby's tendency to fall while learning to walk is an indication that he is still a baby and is appropriately immature. This is not a bad thing; this is proper order. We must be immature first; it is a vital step toward maturity.

Likewise, our ability to walk is an indication of our maturity, not our righteousness. If we understand that it is Christ's grace that makes us righteous, then we can extend grace to others when they don't do things "right." The grace we extend to others is not our stamp of approval upon their actions (or works); it is our approval of them as people.

This is how God deals with us. He calls us by *"the election of grace"* (Rom. 11:5), not by our *"having done any good or evil, that the purpose of God according to election might stand, not of works, but of Him that calleth..."* (Rom. 9:11).

Our standing, then, is based in God's love for us. He is kindly disposed toward us. He can see the future, and He sees us as we are going to be in Christ, not the way we are now. He sees our growth in His Spirit. It is our destiny, our calling, that excites Him. A baby who fills his diapers has a healthy bowel. That is good. Cleaning the diaper is not a problem for those who love the baby.

I remember checking my kids' bowel movements to make sure they were healthy bowel movements. If everything was OK, I was happy, not upset. As the kids matured, we taught them how to control these bowel movements and to do them in appropriate places. That was a sign of their maturity.

THE LAW

Consider this passage from Romans to understand God's view on our actions:

> *The law entered, that the offense might abound. But where sin abounded, grace did much more abound: that as sin hath reigned unto death, even so might grace reign through righteousness unto eternal life by Jesus Christ ...* (Romans 5:20-21).

God is not worried by the sin in us. He has grace through Jesus to overcome it.

We are actually locked into the laws of physics. The second law of thermodynamics states,[4] in part, that everything in the universe is running down. This is called *entropy*. When entropy is connected with biological organisms, it is called *atrophy*. The Bible calls this *"the law of sin and death"* (Rom. 8:2).

The opposite of this death is life. Science has determined that one of the markers of life is the ability of an organism to take simple unorganized molecules and arrange them in complex structures. A baby drinks milk, forms molecules inside its cells, and grows. That is an indicator that the baby is alive. The Bible calls this *"the law of the Spirit of life in Christ Jesus* [which] *hath made me free from the law of sin and death"* (Rom. 8:2).

My self-effort did not set me free. It is not the baby's ability to drink that makes him grow; it is the presence of life that allows our efforts to change us. We do not create our own life; it is a gift to us.

It is grace.

THE GIFT

I (Ken) remember taking a job to erect a curtain wall. A curtain wall is the glass and aluminum exterior of an office tower. I had no experience at all in this type of construction; I had to go back to my apprenticeship books to even remember the terms so I wouldn't look stupid.

About three weeks after I started the job, the vice-president of the company came from Quebec to Alberta to visit the site. He introduced himself to me and immediately began to ask me if I liked to travel.

I thought he wanted me to work up in northern Canada in the small cities that were rapidly growing up there. I was wrong; he wanted me to run a couple of jobs in London, England. I was flabbergasted. A few weeks earlier, I didn't have a clue what I was doing, and now he wanted to put me in charge of a large job in a foreign country. The interesting thing was that, a month or so before this conversation, I had experienced two vivid dreams about being in England.

That very day, I (Jeanne) had been talking to God and asking Him if I could fly on an airplane (I had never flown).

He replied, "If you could go anywhere in the world, where would you like to go?"

I said wanted to go to London, England. In that moment, a strong sense of peace and well-being descended on my spirit. God spoke to me clearly: "Yes, you will go."

When Ken got home, he asked me if I wanted to go on a trip. In those days, we never had enough money to go on trips. I excitedly asked if we were going to England, as God had told me earlier that day in prayer. Within two weeks, we were walking outside Buckingham Palace.

God spoke into my (Ken's) spirit later that He was displaying His grace and power to us because we were His children. I didn't earn that trip; I wasn't qualified to do the work, but God gave us favor in the eyes of the company. They became the agents of His grace.

We had a wonderful time in England, exploring and sightseeing, all at the expense of the company. God supplied the trip; they paid for it. We never ended up working in England, but God wanted to show us his grace and power. It was part of changing my way of thinking about my relationship to God as His child. It was becoming abundantly clear that God delights to bless His children with their hearts' desires.

NOT UNDER THE LAW

If we are trusting in the grace of Christ, then we need to let go of our own strength and ability to do it right. If you are depending on being *"...justified by the law; ye are fallen from grace"* (Gal. 5:4).

In fact, Paul said, *"I do not frustrate the grace of God: for if righteousness come by the law, then Christ is dead in vain* [for no purpose]*"* (Gal. 2:21). Grace and law (self-justification) are mutually exclusive. It is either one or the other.

Jesus was *"...full of grace and truth"* (John 1:14). We are full of our flesh and *"...by works of the law shall no flesh be justified"* (Gal. 2:16).

God knows the truth about us, which is why He offers grace. Our works cannot justify us; we are only *"...justified by His grace..."* (Titus 3:7). Look at it this way. We are made to sit in heavenly places in Christ (see Eph. 2:6). This is our position, purchased by grace.

When we are accused of wrongdoing, the accusation itself is an appeal to the law, and says that we didn't fulfill the requirements of the law. If we try to defend ourselves (appealing to the law to say that we did it right), we forfeit our position of grace—which is not our righteousness, but Christ's, in the first place.

To defeat us, all satan has to do is to sucker us into a fight and draw us down to his level. If we leave our position of grace, then the effects of the law (sin and death) come upon us. We must learn to keep our mouths shut and not defend ourselves. Jesus, as always, is our example *"...that* [we] *should follow His steps...who, when He was reviled, reviled not again..."* (1 Pet. 2:21,23). When He was accused, *"Jesus yet answered nothing..."* (Mark 15:5) *"...but committed Himself to Him that judgeth righteously"* (1 Pet. 2:23).

Thus, our response is not about winning an argument or looking good. That is what our flesh wants. Rather, it is about bringing spiritual power and authority into the equation. We must accept our responsibility even if we have only 1 percent of the blame. Jesus, who was sinless and never had to take blame, accepted our blame, for our sakes.

Jesus was about to win the greatest victory ever accomplished when Peter tried to "rescue" Him. Jesus had no fewer than 72,000 angels at His personal beck and call (see Matt. 26:53); He did not need Peter's help.

Despite His legions of angels, Jesus accomplished His victory, not by fighting but by keeping silent. He *"disarmed the rulers and authorities...having triumphed over them..."* (Col. 2:15 NASB).

SILENCE

Jesus said, *"...The works that I do shall* [you] *do also; and greater works than these..."* (John 14:12). Our efforts may not save the world, but the battles we fight are significant.

I (Jeanne) once had a conflict with the teacher of one of our children. Our daughter liked to draw and often expressed her feelings through her drawings. The teacher was so concerned about our daughter's mental health that she spent much of her time psycho-analyzing the drawings rather than teaching the child.

This teacher often shared her own childhood problems with our daughter at lunchtime. On those days, our daughter would come home withdrawn and depressed. She was passing in other subjects, yet failing in all of this teacher's courses.

I phoned the teacher to address the situation; the teacher got offended and walked away from the phone without hanging up. I prayed. The Lord told me to wait. I waited on the "dead" line for over half an hour until the teacher came back. She was surprised that I had waited her out. I suspected that she wanted to accuse me of hanging up on her.

She would not yield to my demands to focus on teaching and not analyzing. She felt her priority was to continue her "crusade" to fix our daughter. So, I arranged a meeting with the school board.

God gave us a strategy: "Keep your mouth shut. Don't engage in battle; don't try to justify and don't attack." We arrived at the meeting, but the teacher was late. The board asked us if we wanted to start without her, but we declined. We sat around for a long time waiting until she showed up. She was nervous, confused, and very agitated. Her comments seemed so off base, that the board members gave each other questioning looks.

Suddenly, the teacher bolted for the washroom with the explanation that she needed to take a pill to calm down. While she was gone, the chairman told us that we didn't need to stay any longer. The problem was solved. They realized our child was not the one who had an issue. The teacher quit within a week because of "nerves."

We never had to open our mouths to explain our side of the conflict. God fought for us because we held our peace and God's grace carried us through the battle. Instead of complaining, we rested in God's ability to resolve the situation.

When we refuse to continually complain about our difficulties, we give God permission to work in our lives. The Bible says, *"Do all things without murmurings and disputings: that ye may be blameless... [and] shine as lights in the world"* (Phil. 2:14-15). We are relying on God's grace

When we are resting in Him rather than being contentious and fighting for ourselves, we are truly relying on God's grace. We are not called to contend with God or others, but to rest and receive from Him.

Solomon said: *"Cast out the scorner* [mocker], *and contention shall go out; yea strife and reproach shall cease"* (Prov. 22:10). The mocker isn't always the "other person." Sometimes the mocker is in us and is expressed through our opinions and thoughts. We are supposed to *"...speak as the oracles of God..."* (1 Pet. 4:11). If we can't, then we should keep silent.

IMPERFECT AND CALLED

Our opinions serve only to cloud God's will. Our willpower cannot accomplish the will of God. His will is performed *"...not by might, nor by power, but by* [His] *Spirit, saith the Lord..."* (Zech. 4:6). The Spirit adds that His work is also accomplished with shouts of, "Grace!" (see Zech. 4:7).

We need to shift our thinking and embrace the idea that God can be glorified through us even when we and our situations are less than perfect.

God loves to use broken vessels to accomplish His work. Paul discovered this when God told him, *"My grace is sufficient for you, for power is perfected in weakness"* (2 Cor. 12:9 NASB). Paul responded, *"Most gladly, therefore, I will...boast about my weakness, so that the power of Christ may dwell in me"* (2 Cor. 12:9 NASB).

If we believe in God's grace (His kind disposition toward us), then we can actually be *"...content with weaknesses, with insults, with*

...s, with persecutions, with difficulties, for Christ's sake; for when I am weak, then I am strong" (2 Cor. 12:10 NASB).

A situation arose in a church where Jeanne and I were part of the leadership team. God was directing us as a church to move into more radical worship. We had just brought in a new pastor who was helping to facilitate that move, but there was a great deal of opposition. Even the leadership was divided: three elder couples against; two couples for the new worship. Four deacons were also against the new direction; three deacons were for it. A church split was brewing.

God spoke a strategy into our hearts. We who wanted change were not to push for it; we were not to politic for it; we were to keep our mouths shut and only pray for it. Weekly, we gathered for prayer, asking God to make a way in this situation. We were to simply love the resisters and try to develop better relationships, leaving the church direction in the Lord's hands.

It was very difficult and many conflicts arose due to people's strong opinions. Within four months, all three of the elder couples resigned, as did the four opposing board members. I could hardly believe it. They had held the power in voting numbers and seemingly controlled the situation.

In reality, God had everything in His hands and prevented a war from erupting. There is power and authority in being gracious to others and submitting to God's grace. But, to access this grace, we must shift our thoughts off ourselves and our desires, and onto God.

SHIFT INTO PRAYER

Dear precious Father, help us to receive the gift of Your love. Lord, help us to believe that You love us so much simply because we are Your children. You are pleased with us. Therefore, cause us to come out of a mind-set of duty into a place of joy—out of works and into Your full grace. We declare that we love You and we receive Your love and work of grace for us. In Jesus' name.

ENDNOTES

1. *Biblesoft's New Exhaustive Strong's Numbers and Concordance with Expanded Greek-Hebrew Dictionary.* CD-ROM. Biblesoft, Inc. and International Bible Translators, Inc. s.v. "chanan" (OT 2603), www.eliyah.com/lexicon.html.

2. Ibid., s.v. "charis," (NT 5485).

3. Plessinger, Annie. "The Effects of Mental Imagery on Athletic Performance," *Vanderbilt University Psychology Department,* http://www.vanderbilt.edu/AnS/psychology/health_psychology/mentalimagery.html (accessed May 23, 2009).

4. http://en.wikipedia.org/wiki/Second_law_of_thermodynamics.

Chapter 6

SING AT YOUR TROUBLES

Releasing Power With Praise, Worship, and Thanksgiving

"BOY, does this taste good! Thank you for this meal, it's great." These are my usual comments when I am famished and I sit down to eat. It doesn't matter whether it's beans or meatloaf; it all tastes like fillet when I am starving. However, when I am not hungry (likely because I snacked), my comments might run more along this vein: "It's OK," or, "It is a little sweet, but it tastes good."

The Bible says, *"The full soul loatheth an honeycomb; but to the hungry soul every bitter thing is sweet"* (Prov. 27:7). Jesus said, *"... those who hunger and thirst for righteousness...shall be filled"* (Matt. 5:6 NKJV).

If we want to be filled, we must get hungry. If we get filled with other things: self-righteousness, pride, ambition, people, or things, then we won't want to digest anything else or change our condition. We'll be stuffed and any attempt to get us to "eat" will result in resistance and complaints.

God is challenging all of us to narrow our focus. We are not superheroes; we can only squeeze so much into our lives before we become overwhelmed. If we want more of God, then there has to be less of us. The problem is, we don't want to give up anything. We defend the status quo and resist change.

The Bible refers to people with this attitude as being stiff-necked. They are inflexible. It's a serious condition; God showed me how it isolates us. I know He's right, because Jeanne and I have experienced it.

After we'd had a certain argument, I wanted to make peace but Jeanne wasn't quite ready. We were lying in bed and I reached over to turn her head and give her a kiss, as a peace offering. She would not let me turn her head; she was still mad and stiff-necked. God spoke to me, "That's how you act when I want to love you. You won't let Me turn you toward Me."

I realized I needed to continue to love Jeanne while she was mad, so that she could relax with me. It worked. When we are resistant in the face of pressure to change, we will start to murmur and complain. The Hebrew root for "murmur" is *luwn*, meaning "to stay, to not go on, to become obstinate."[1]

The problem with being stiff-necked is that it forces you to swim against life's currents. Life is about change; it's not frozen in a still photo—it's a movie that's always running. Life requires us to be willing to shift over and over again.

Of course, God loves us as we are. But He loves us too much to leave us where we are. He wants us to hunger for more. He calls us out of one mind-set and into another. This requires us to change our minds, because the Kingdom mind-set and its resulting power are totally opposite to the world's ways.

That is why we are told to *be not conformed to this world: but be... transformed by the renewing of your mind...* (Rom. 12:2). Our thought patterns or mind-sets are structures set up by us to process the information and situations we encounter in this world. As we have discussed, these structures become inflexible and incapable of change simply because they are structures.

Mind-sets can be compared to the walls of the house in which you live. It takes a great deal of effort to change the framework of your house. Because it is so labor-intensive, it's not something you would do every day to suit your changing moods.

Likewise with your thoughts. They cannot be changed easily. Yet, if we are going to flow with God, we will have to abandon these fixed structures. We'll need to exchange them for something more fluid—mind-sets that flow freely with the Spirit.

The Holy Spirit is never depicted in the Bible as a lake, placid and calm; He is like a river always moving. He is like the wind or a fire, always shifting and transforming energy.

The New Covenant allows for this kind of fluidity. The Bible says it is a better covenant, based on better promises (see Heb. 8:6). The passage goes on to say that *"if that first covenant had been fault-less, then should no place have been sought for the second"* (Heb. 8:7). The Old Covenant did not accomplish the fullness of God's plan. It was designed for a finite season to address the mind-sets and capacities of the people at that time.

To them, God was far off and unapproachable. God does not want us to stay stuck in that limiting thought pattern. To move to the next level, God requires us to commit to new paradigms, inside and out.

"No one puts new wine [new ideas] *into old wineskins* [thought struc-tures]; *or else the new wine bursts the wineskins…"* (Mark 2:22 NKJV). In other words, the new ideas would blow your mind! Kingdom thoughts don't make sense to the natural man. *"…They are foolishness unto him…because they are spiritually discerned"* (1 Cor. 2:14).

For example, God wants us learn to love the unthankful. Why? So we can be like Him who *"…is kind unto the unthankful and to the evil"* (Luke 6:35). I was unable to fit that particular thought into my way of thinking (my wineskin). So God brought someone into my life to help me change the way I thought; we'll call him Randy.

Randy and I worked together. Even though I was older and more experienced, he was my foreman. The economy was slowing down during this time and construction was dying. I had been offered a new job close to our residence. It was a job that would effectively "hide me" until times got better and construction picked up.

I had a direct word from God to bring Randy with me to the job. He and I decided to ride together to do our sign-on paper work. When we completed our paperwork, I placed my form in the basket and Randy tossed his on top of mine.

The secretary processed Randy's application first. Because of this, he was effectively given seniority over me, even though I was the only person the manager had requested. No big deal right?

Wrong. A year later it became a very big deal. Cutbacks occurred and Randy got laid off. Because this was a union job and Randy had seniority, he decided to "bump me." According to union rules, his seniority allowed him to take my job. Well, so much for friendship and being grateful for my getting him the job in the first place.

I was not ready to rejoice and be thankful in this situation. I was mad and felt betrayed. Of course, God was not caught off guard by this "sudden" turn of events. In fact, that very day, God supplied me with four different offers for work. Even the manager who hired me phoned up and offered to get me a new job with a different company. God was teaching me to trust Him and thank Him in *all* situations.

ENJOY THE RIDE

Often the very thing we see as a problem is the thing God wants to develop into a feature. To get on board with His perspective, we have to shift our viewpoint regarding our problems and allow God to work His power.

There was an open cupboard above the stove in our house. It was an eyesore, as the fan vent was visible. Jeanne and I decided to make an improvement. I built a door to hide the vent. We then designed

and created a beautiful grape-pattern glass mosaic to finis'
The area that was ugly became a pleasing focal point in the room.

God loves to do that in our lives. He wants us to view our problems as possibilities. The layoff prompted Jeanne and me to start our own company. We did more than $30,000 worth of work in the first three months of the company's existence.

I got recalled to the mine after about four months and was able to honestly forgive Randy. God however, was not done with me in this area. Three years later, both Randy and I left the mine.

Again, I felt God tell me to hire him. This time he was working under me as one of my ironworker foremen. It was only a few years later that he "knifed me in the back" again. I asked God whether I had made a mistake bringing him along.

God told me He was using Randy to reshape my thinking. I started to thank God for fast-tracking my development. I had prayed earlier and seen a picture of Jeanne and me taking a short cut. God said in the dream that the quickest way to get to our destination in Him was through persecution. We learned that we must change our attitudes concerning difficult situations and relationships. We must embrace those people who rub us the wrong way. They are God's gifts to us. They challenge us at our very core; therefore, we need to strive continually to see them as God does. This is not easy to do; but if we do it, our mind-sets (and therefore, our outcomes) will be transformed.

This is the price of the shift from the natural to supernatural. It never happens while gliding through life on autopilot. It requires focus and an openness to what God is doing. After all, His bringing these people into our lives is never an accident; God does it purposefully. We need to thank Him instead of murmuring and complaining about it.

Graham Cooke at a 2001 conference in Kelowna, British Columbia, shared a powerful insight into this process. He once related a dream he had concerning it: In the dream he saw three sculptors working on a marble statue. They were chipping away the marble that didn't fit into the final form the statue was to take. As he went around to the front of the statue, he realized that it was a statue of him.

When he saw the faces of the sculptors, he recognized them as people who were persecuting him. God was using their actions to remove the attitudes God wanted Graham to reject. Graham got the point; he was able to shift from fighting with these people to blessing them.

The children of Israel continually murmured against God in the desert. They were still complaining when they arrived at the very doorstep of the Promised Land. The basis for most of the complaining was fear. They were afraid of the Egyptian army, they were afraid they would die of thirst, they were afraid they would starve, and now they were afraid of the giants in the land. Their fear was an indication of their lack of faith in God's ability or willingness to look after them.

The Israelites could not adapt to change and just wanted to go back to Egypt. They seemed to forget the suffering they'd endured in Egypt. Under Pharaoh, they were slaves. They were afflicted and sorrowful. Their children were killed. As long as they stayed in Egypt, things would get worse.

Yet, once they were out of Egypt, the Israelites backed away from the freedom they once craved. In reality, they were backing away from the shift that would be necessary to enjoy that freedom.

They had physically left Egypt, but their minds were still enslaved. So they murmured. They literally announced their resistance to going forward. They could not fathom making it on their own; they felt unable to fight their own enemies. They were stuck in a slave mentality, and any attempt to change their minds was met with resistance.

God was angry with their refusal to believe Him. He expects us to *"...believe that He is, and that He is a rewarder of them that diligently seek Him*" (Heb. 11:6). When we don't believe, we are saying to God, "I don't *think* you are really God or really in control."

Imagine the potential for God to change us through the situations we get into! These situations are designed to create in us a hunger for something better. When we put that hunger to constructive use (beyond self-pity), anything is possible; God is more than able to transform our circumstances.

MURMUR OR MAGNIFY GOD?

While I recovered from cancer surgery, I (Jeanne) shared a hospital room with another woman. Her surgery was similar to mine. My roommate was not a Christian, so she often complained and had very little hope. I was trying to be positive in a difficult situation

I knew my life depended on a godly attitude. I had to choose to speak right and meditate correctly; I listened to praise music and gave thanks in my distress. However, my roommate continued to be unable to see good in any situation. I pleaded with Ken, "We have insurance coverage for a private room. I needed to get into a positive atmosphere to be able to believe for my healing." Finally, we were able to get a private room where friends could come in and sing and pray over me to speed my healing.

Recovery came more quickly with praise and gratitude rather than negativity. I remained focused on God and continued to express my worship to Him. In my private room, I had the freedom to pray and sing whenever I wanted. I brightened up; my cheerful attitude brought life instead of death to my wing of the hospital.

One day, as Ken sat with me in the room, the cleaning lady came in and closed the door. She came up to the bed and spoke to me. She said, "I know you are Christians from the way you act. I want what you have. Can you pray for my family, and for me to receive the Holy Spirit? I want to have the joy you have."

We prayed for her family and then for her to receive the baptism of the Holy Spirit. She received immediately and was filled with joy.

After she left, Ken remarked that, since I was able to minister in the hospital, it was probably time for me to go home. That sounded good to me.

Meanwhile, my former roommate experienced complications. It seemed to me that her focus on the negative had only aggravated her medical situation. I was able to leave the hospital, but she would have to remain awhile longer.

Whatever the challenges we face, our protection is the life and joy we have in Jesus. It's not something we hide behind; it's the wonderful life we are privileged to live.

TRUE MEASURES

All of us have a measure that we use to determine whether things are getting better or worse. Often we miscalculate, putting too much weight on insignificant information.

Take the case of the Israelites who escaped Egypt. After being freed from 400 years of slavery, Israel's mind-set was stuck on something inconsequential: food choices.

Even after God provided manna to sustain them, they lusted for what they perceived as being better, including *"...fish, which* [they ate freely] *in Egypt...the cucumbers...melons...leeks...onions, and the garlick"* (Num. 11:5). Instead of being grateful for the manna, they complained that *"...there is nothing at all, beside this manna..."* (Num. 11:6).

This food fetish continued even until Jesus' time. He said *"... you seek Me...because you ate of the loaves and were filled"* (John 6:26 NKJV).

The Jews seemed incapable of changing their minds. Jesus came to them with new thoughts, but instead of being able to challenge them, He only succeeded in offending them. They took offense because Jesus showed them that both He and the Father saw things differently than they did.

Consider the parable of the laborers who worked in the vineyard. The first group was hired for a standard daily wage. The owner hired more workers later in the day and chose to pay them the full day's wage. The group hired earlier took exception to the owner's generosity:

> *When those hired first came, they thought that they would receive more; but each of them also received a denarius. When they received it, they grumbled at the landowner* (Matthew 20:10-11 NASB).

Jesus' own disciples took offense when Mary poured expensive ointment on Jesus' head:

> *The disciples were indignant when they saw this, and said, "Why this waste? For this perfume might have been sold for a high price and the money given to the poor"* (Matthew 26:8-9 NASB).

Jewish leaders were frequently incensed with Jesus' approach to ministry. Here they took exception to His and His disciples' association with sinners:

> *The Pharisees and their scribes began grumbling... saying, "Why do you eat and drink with the tax collectors and sinners?"* (Luke 5:30 NASB).

Jesus would introduce any new concepts; but the people resisted. The result was judgment from God. If they had understood that God loved them (instead of perceiving God to be demanding, as the law was), they would have been able receive the benefit of His love and would have shifted their thinking to be aligned with His.

Jeanne and I learned long ago to declare that our God is good and does only good for us. Jesus said, *"Out of your own mouth I will judge you..."* (Luke 19:22 NKJV). If we say God is good; then He is good to us. If we say He is harsh and hard; then He will be hard to us. We say negative things about God because we have hard places in our hearts (see Luke 6:45).

We must be careful to assess our progress in life according to God's "measuring stick." We must also remember that His supernatural benefits are always available. However, they can only be fully accessed when we shift our thinking to trust Him—even when we cannot see the solution.

HEALING HEARTACHE

As Christians who have been "converted," we tend to speak with a "divided tongue"—we bless God one minute and curse people the next.

James 3:10 says it this way: *"Out of the same mouth preceedeth blessing and cursing...."* James goes on to ask: *"Doth a fountain send...sweet water and bitter? Can the fig tree...bear olive berries? either a vine, figs? so can no fountain both yield salt water and fresh"* (James 3:11-12).

James is saying that the fruit (what people see or hear coming from us) cannot be different from the root (the source) within us. If we are both blessing and cursing, there must be two opposing roots.

We have good areas in our hearts and evil areas. I realize Jesus' blood covered all my sin, but certain areas of my sin nature (parts of my character) have not been fully submitted to Jesus. This is why I don't always act like a Christian.

We need to shift our thinking to recognize that, although our souls are saved, areas of our souls have not yet been sanctified.

The prophet Bob Jones once told me that I had negative speech. I couldn't see it and thought he was crazy. I was the most positive person I knew. I hardly ever worried and had a good outlook (to the point of foolishness) all the time.

What God showed me was that my negativity was not with situations, but with people. I knew they would disappoint me, so I defiled them to do just that. Defilements are like vibes transmit which causes people to react to those signals. A dog will respond to fear and be aggressive where it would normally be passive.

My expectations were rooted in a wounded part of me that had never healed or been converted to the life in Christ. That part still sat in darkness, coddling and nursing its wounds. That part of my heart could not rejoice or be thankful for people; thus, I was at least partially powerless to love them.

A young driver cut me off one night as I was driving home. I was furious and sped up to get right behind him. My loving intention was to give him a good dose of my high beams. I couldn't catch up because he kept going faster so I stepped on the gas. In no time we were both flying down the highway at breakneck speed.

My anger was burning when I heard a small voice whisper, "You like this feeling, don't you?"

I knew the voice of God and immediately backed off. I realized I liked the anger, which was one of the few emotions in which I functioned. The problem was that the anger proceeded from the flesh and not the spirit; therefore, it could be manipulated by satan. I did not hate that area of my flesh and thus had no power to defeat it. I needed to take my anger to the cross, repent of it, and leave it there.

My experience became the catalyst God used to heal the heart attitude of my friend, Ron. Jeanne and I were ministering to him, trying to uncover the wounds that caused him to feel rejected and unloved by his wife. He was carrying a "love package": a way in which he required people to act in order to demonstrate their love toward him. Needless to say, Ron's wife could not fulfill his strict requirements.

He felt wounded and hurt and lived in self-pity. His constant need of ministry for this hurt showed me that he liked self-pity . He held this emotion close in his heart, coddling and rehearsing it—in a way, loving it. But Scripture says that "...*by the fear of the Lord men depart from evil"* (Prov. 16:6). Ron had to learn to hate those feelings before he could be free.

Ron's murmuring and complaining indicated that this wounded area of his heart did not trust the Lord. Once he realized what he was doing, he repented of his attitude and came against a spirit of self-pity. A great sense of freedom swept over him as the Holy Spirit began to burn away his woundedness.

The Spirit came with such an intense, cleansing fire that he was soon drenched in sweat and his shirt was soaked. We had to give him a fresh T-shirt, which we later joked was won for the best manifestation of the week. Ron's new freedom, resulting from a shift in his attitude, increased his prophetic gift dramatically.

It is not just a death to complaining that the Father wants, but also a resurrection, indicated by praise and power in every situation. We use complaining, anger, and self-pity as methods of protecting ourselves so we won't get hurt. God wants to be our protection. He wants us to operate in freedom and love—willing to get hurt and positioned to be immediately healed.

This is what I call the power of an indestructible life. We need to embrace the battles, not run from them. This indestructible life is a reality. The Lord is speaking this word into the cosmos:

> *The heavens declare the glory of God.... Day unto day utters speech.... There is no...language where their voice is not heard* (Psalms 19:1-3 NKJV).

SUPERHEROES

Hollywood has heard the sounds described in the nineteenth psalm. Most of the people in Hollywood are probably not Christians. As a result, their perceptions are distorted. Yet, they still see and hear *something*.

Many artistic people possess an unredeemed prophetic gift and can discern the sound God is speaking into the airwaves. How many movies are made about superheroes (or villains) who seemingly cannot be destroyed? They get wounded or blown apart, but have powers to rejuvenate and repair themselves. Because of this ability, they scoff at fear and can fight unbelievable odds and awesome powers.

God is trying to imprint this image onto Christian hearts: We can be healed; we can be resurrected. We can love, be hurt, and be healed. We can bear the situations that confront us and overcome. Jesus is our model. If He can do it, we can:

> *...For the joy that was set before Him [He] endured the cross, despising the shame* [seeing the shame as not worthy of consideration], *and is set down at the right hand...of God* (Hebrews 12:2).

It should be with joy and excitement that we go into a situation that is going to hurt us and shame us and maybe kill our flesh. Why? Because we have an indestructible life; when we come out of this particular "death," we will have power that will force our enemy (mainly our flesh) to withdraw from the field of battle.

We can't hide behind structures (thought patterns) of false protection; they themselves are death. Isaiah talks about Israel making a covenant with death, saying: "*...we have made lies our refuge, and under falsehood have we hid ourselves*" (Isa. 28:15).

Our old structures and agreements will not work in the Kingdom. We must shift our thinking to avoid making covenants of self-protection and death (the natural). Instead, we must embrace the New Covenant we have with God (the supernatural). This is true for individuals, churches, nations, and races.

NEW-WINE TIPSY

New wine (a new way of thinking) has life in it. It bubbles and changes flavors as it matures. New wine cannot be stored alongside vats of matured wine because it will actually cause the old wine to start working again and change its flavor. This happens because the carbon dioxide bubbling from the new restarts the yeast in the old wine, thus changing its flavor.

The maturing new wine may have to be poured from barrel to barrel to clarify it and get rid of the dregs and lees. This process is illuminated in the Bible: "[We have] *settled on* [our] *dregs and* [have] *not been emptied from vessel to vessel…. Therefore* [our] *taste remained in* [us]…" (Jer. 48:11 NKJV). Jeremiah goes onto say that God will "… *send to …those who tip …and they will tip him over…"*(Jer 48:12 NASB). God is going to upset our "apple carts."

In this passage, God is saying: "No problems; no progress." Every time my (Ken's) plans have been upset, I have ultimately profited from it—I resisted, but I profited. Having to move off the family farm ended up a being good thing. Losing my job at the mine was a good thing. Losing money on investments was a good thing. I didn't want to make any of these moves, but I was forced to and God prospered us. I am now preparing my heart to accept whatever God brings and not complain.

We need to let the new wine make us "tipsy," or we will never change. We need to be affected in our minds and in our hearts. This is a change by the Spirit. If we choose the Spirit, then God can make us sensitive to areas of woundedness and wrong thinking. Through forgiveness and repentance we put these areas to death on the cross and are made free.

If we cannot see or refuse this change by the Spirit, the God who loves us will bring the fire into our lives. He will lift His grace off of us and will allow people and/or situations to expose our own hearts. As the pressure increases, whatever is on the inside of us will come out. This is a much more painful method.

We typically refuse to see our own sinful nature until pressure causes us to react and expose it. If we think we are strong, God will expose our weakness; if we think we are wise, God will show us our foolishness; if we think we are righteous, God will show us our depravity; if we think we are brave, God will expose our fear.

Character is developed in adversity and humility. We should ask God to show us our hearts before He has to expose our actions. The amount of love and trust we have for the Father will dictate the method by which we are ultimately changed.

God has told us that "...*all things work together for good to them that love God...who are called according to His purpose*" (Rom. 8:28). "All things" may not seem to suit our purposes at the moment; but our highest purpose is tied to His. We can trust God, for "*if God is for us, who can be against us?*" (Rom. 8:31 NKJV).

POWER PRAISE

We can be thankful no matter what comes our way. We need to understand how God intends us to respond to Him; we need to understand His strategy to bring us power.

Our English word *thankfulness* is translated from the Hebrew word *towdaw,* meaning "to extend the hand," and often translated *praise*. The root is tied to the Hebrew word *ya'dah,* meaning "to use the hand," and is often translated *to worship*. All of these words derive from the Hebrew word *yad,* meaning "to open the hand," and often translated *power*.[2]

Worship, praise, and *thanksgiving* all have the same root indicating *power* or the release of power. Jesus confirmed that connection when he quoted Psalms 8:2 and substituted the word *praise* for *strength*.

> *Out of the mouth of babes...hast Thou ordained strength...*
> (Psalms 8:2).

> *...Out of the mouth of babes...Thou hast perfected praise...*
> (Matthew 21:16)

Jesus himself was of the tribe of Judah, whose name also means "praise." Jacob's prophecy for his son Judah includes the statement, *"Your hand shall be on the neck of your enemies..."* (Gen. 49:8 NKJV).

God used names as prophetic pictures so that we could see spiritual truths. For Jesus, the words *praise* and *strength* were synonymous. *Judah* or *praise* was to exercise strength over the enemy.

Power and strength comes from a releasing of words and sounds of *shabach,* a shout or praise into our realm of authority.[3] This is an authoritative shout that brings order and stills turbulence. David said that God *"...stilleth (shabach) the noise of the seas"* (Ps 65:7). Jesus demonstrated this release of words and sounds when He calmed the sea. Joshua released an ear-splitting shout (the Hebrew word here is *ruwa*) that brought down the walls of Jericho (see Josh. 6:20).

This concept of using praise and thanksgiving as a weapon to release power is used often in Scripture. Jehoshaphat, king of Israel *"...appointed singers...that should praise...as they went out before the army.... And when they began to sing and to praise, the Lord set ambushments.... [And their enemies]...helped to destroy another"* (2 Chron. 20:21-23).

Praise sets the stage for victory at a time of crisis. Jeanne and I made a habit of going out to an extra-special restaurant and celebrating God's provision every time I got laid off or a job ended. I was in construction, so this usually happened several times a year.

Fear says don't spend money and celebrate at a time like that. Faith says trust God and celebrate His provision. Our meal was an act of worship and submission, declaring that God would now supply for us beyond our understanding. Psalms declares: *"Whoso offereth praise glorifieth Me; and to him that ordereth his conversation aright will I shew the salvation of God"* (Ps. 50:23).

Salvation is deliverance from disaster. We were determined to turn bad situations into good ones. Peter and the apostles were more than once hauled in before the Sanhedrin (religious council) and threatened or beaten, or both. They responded with praise and boldness and "[rejoiced] *that they were counted worthy to suffer shame for His* [Christ's] *name"* (Acts 5:41).

They thanked God for being beaten! Some of us feel persecuted when we are not properly greeted at the church door. To move into the supernatural, we will need to shift our thinking about persecution.

While on a mission trip, Paul and Silas were beaten and jailed. *"At midnight* [they] *prayed, and sang praises unto God.... And suddenly there was a great earthquake...foundations...were shaken...all the doors were opened, and every one's bands were loosed"* (Acts 16:25, 26). The doors opened, the shackles came off, but nobody tried to escape.

The prisoners knew what had happened because they heard Paul and Silas praising. They could make the connection and knew that God was in the place. I think reverential fear fell over that prison. That is the power of praise.

God gave us a testimony of praise when we moved to the city of Lloydminster on the border of Alberta and Saskatchewan. God had given me (Ken) a specific word to move. Strangely enough, the word came from out of a movie. I had been working out of town and getting home only on the weekends for about a year. Things were not going well with our two youngest boys. They were in their early teens and needed Dad's firm hand. Jeanne and I were looking to God for a strategy, since it looked like I wasn't going to be able to stay home for a while yet.

One evening after I had talked to Jeanne on the phone, I sat down to watch TV. I saw a show about a family that got marooned on the Alaska coast during the wintertime. The father and son made a valiant attempt to get help, but left the girls stranded by themselves on the shore with just a tent. The family's separation almost cost the girls their lives. It was many months before the father could return with help; he found the girls close to death.

I was deeply moved by the movie. In prayer afterward, I felt God said, "Don't leave anyone behind." The job I was supervising was only supposed to last another five months, but I heard God say it would last much longer.

We packed up the four kids who were still at home and moved the family to Lloydminster. The economy was so hot in that part of the province that we couldn't rent an apartment or a house so we had to buy a house and lease out our old one. This was a great move for the family; our boys got involved with the youth at church and our neighbor was a pastor.

The only problem we encountered occurred when the job finished, two years later, and houses weren't selling. For most of the construction workers, the job was over. Nobody was renting and people were dumping their homes; it was definitely a buyers' market. We had our house listed for three months and received no offers. We prayed and reminded God that He had gotten us into this situation: He was the one who told us all to come.

God replied with, "Trust Me." We took the house off the market and decided to rent it. A couple in the church agreed to rent the house and then decided to buy it. We had sold the house within a week, by ourselves. Jeanne got a big banner and put it in the window. The sign read "SOLD BY THE LORD." That sign sat in the midst of at least a dozen "For Sale" signs that lined our street. The economy does not dictate to God what He can to do, if we are thankful and acknowledge Him.

God makes a way where there is no way, but we have to cooperate. One of the ways to cooperate is with our attitudes. If you asked me and I were to give you a glass of water, how would you respond? Most likely, you would thank me for the water while the full glass was still in your hand. Even though the water had not yet slaked your thirst, you would thank me. Why? Because you have it in your possession and you know all you have to do is drink it.

THANK YOU

We should respond in like manner whenever God grants our prayers. Once we have prayed and we know by faith that He has granted our requests, we should thank Him. He has done His part; He has given us our requests. If we want them to manifest in our physical realm, we need open our mouths and praise Him, saying, *"Lift up your heads, O ye gates; and be ye lift up, ye everlasting doors; and the King of glory shall come in"* (Ps. 24:7).

We rejoice to *"...call...Thy gates Praise"* (Isa. 60:18). Our praise allows God to manifest in our realm of authority and to open gates that were previously closed.

I remember hearing a man telling the story of his adult daughter who was in a mental institution. She had been in there for almost two years and was totally unresponsive to any stimuli. He had been crying out to God, but heard no answers. One day, as he was driving out to visit his daughter, his faith reached the bottom.

He came to a red light and waited for it to turn green. There were no other cars at the intersection; he waited and waited and waited. The light didn't change. The man was so despondent about his daughter that he sat as if in a trance. Then it dawned on him that God was controlling the light. For whatever reason, there were no other cars on the road. This light was all about him. Weakly he asked, "What do You want from me?"

The answer came softly, "Thank Me for your daughter's condition." Nothing else was spoken, just that soft command. The man started to cry and then gave it all to God in tears and prayer. He followed the command: *"Be anxious for nothing, but in everything by prayer and supplication, with thanksgiving, let your requests be made known to God..."* (Phil. 4:6 NKJV).

As the man released his praise to God, the light turned green. He had lost track of time, but it seemed as if that light had stayed red and that street remained empty for almost ten minutes. He drove up to the hospital and went up to his daughter's room to discover her sitting on her bed, bright and chipper. She was completely in her right mind. In less than a week, she was home, whole and free of medication. There is power in thanksgiving and praise!

THE CENTER OF WORSHIP

God used the Old Testament to create pictures of what He wants to do and how He wants us to respond to Him.

In Moses' tabernacle, the priests had a thanksgiving offering that they presented every day (see Lev. 7). David also set up a tent to house the ark and bring praise. God said that in the last days (in our time) He would *"...rebuild the tabernacle of David...so that the rest of mankind may seek the Lord..."* (Acts 15:16-17 NKJV).

The tent of David was a 24-hour, seven-days-a-week praise and worship service (see 1 Chron. 16). The physical presence of the Lord could be visibly seen there. David declared that he wanted to *"...see thy power and glory, ...as I have seen thee in the sanctuary"* (Ps. 63:2 also see Ps 50:2 and 68:24). David even had a recorder (see 2 Sam 20:24) to record the Psalms as David was inspired by the worship and the Spirit in the tent. This went on for 33 years, the length of David's reign in Jerusalem. (This time frame was the exact length of Jesus' life and was a type, or foreshadowing, of Jesus' spending his life in worship.)

As soon as David set the ark of God in the tabernacle, victories came on every side for David and Israel. David's kingdom grew until it occupied all the land from Egypt to the Euphrates River (see 1 Chron. 18:3). The fear of David and his God caused all his enemies to sue for peace and to pay tribute. It only took 10 to 15 years for David to take Israel from a disorganized group of tribes to the most powerful and richest kingdom of its day. Putting God in the center of the nation and in the center of Israel's affections accomplished these victories.

This worship in the tabernacle was not static. David made over 4,000 different instruments for the worshipers (see 1 Chron. 23:5).

Every hour a new batch of praisers and musicians took over. They sang unrehearsed songs as the Holy Spirit gave direction (see 1 Chron. 25). The victories and the power may not have seemed connected to the praise, but as soon as the praise stopped, the victories stopped. Solomon, who enjoyed the benefit of David's victories, moved the ark out of the tabernacle and placed it behind the veil in the temple. At that point the expansion of the kingdom ceased. True praise changes things. Praise is to be our lifestyle as it was for David. Many Old Testament prophets mirrored that lifestyle. Daniel continued to thank God three times a day even after a law was enacted in Babylon that made it illegal to pray to anyone but King Darius (see Dan. 6:7-10).

Jonah had a revelation of praise while in the belly of the whale. He said: *"They that observe lying vanities forsake their own mercy. But I will sacrifice…with the voice of thanksgiving…. Salvation is of the Lord"* (Jon. 2:8-9). Jonah refused to acknowledge that his circumstances (in the fish) could prevent God from accomplishing his purpose in him.

The same was true in the New Testament. Paul could take bread, give thanks, and eat in peace (see Acts 27:35), trusting that he and 275 others on board an imperiled ship were all were safe, despite the storm. Why? Because an angel had told him everyone would be safe. He had his promise; he didn't need to see the storm stop in order to give thanks.

When I (Jeanne) was seven months' pregnant, my daughter and I went to a doctor's appointment. When we came out from the visit, the car wouldn't start. I was desperate; I had no money for a tow truck. We lived 30 miles away in the country, far beyond any bus routes. Not only that, but it was the middle of winter!

I prayed, and praised God that He was going to start the car for us and when I tried again, it started. I thought, "Maybe it's just a fluke that the starter didn't work." When I got home, I tried the car again, but it wouldn't start. Ken looked at the car and found that the starter was fried. God had been gracious in a response to praise.

HE IS LORD

Acknowledging God's sovereignty allows Him to work. Our job is to remain thankful to Him. *"In everything give thanks: for this is the will of God in Christ Jesus concerning you"* (1 Thess. 5:18).

The Lloydminster house God sold for us was a good example of this truth. It is best to leave things in God's hands and not worry. God had told us that He would sell it, and He did. I had to leave Lloydminster before Jeanne to start another job back in the Edmonton area. We had already bought another house in the Edmonton area, but hadn't taken possession yet. Meanwhile, I got a call from Jeanne saying that the man who had bought our house in Lloydminster was being transferred.

I talked to him and discovered that the company he worked for was going to close the branch office in Lloydminster and run it from Edmonton (150 miles away). I asked him if he had prayed before he put the offer on the house, which he said he had. God had told both of us to enter into the deal. That was enough confirmation for me. This little hitch was just a lie; the truth was the house was sold and this man was going to live in it. The "subject to" clause had already been taken off. Legally, the deal was done, but I felt God wanted to teach the man greater faith.

I told him I would let him out of the deal, but we needed to give God a week to fix the problem. "Just wait a week and thank God that everything will work out," I said.

Jeanne and I committed ourselves to thanking God for the sale of the house. Five days later, the man phoned back. All his company's customers had protested so loudly about the plan to shift operations to Edmonton that the company reconsidered and gave him back his position in Lloydminster—with a raise! Praise works.

The Bible says to *"…do all in the name of…Jesus, giving thanks to God…"* (Col. 3:17). God is for us. We can sing His praises continually. God inhabits His people's praises (see Ps. 22:3). In Israel, when the people broke out in praise at the dedication of the temple, the glory of the Lord filled the place (see 2 Chron. 5:13-14).

Praise is a powerful weapon. Psalm 149:6-9 says:

> *Let the high praises of God be in their mouth...to execute vengeance upon the heathen... to bind their kings with chains, and their nobles with fetters of iron; to execute... the judgment written: this honor have all His saints....*

Today, we still operate as priests; but our offering is a *"...sacrifice of praise to God...that is, the fruit of our lips giving thanks to His name"* (Heb. 13:15). We praise Him with understanding and through the Spirit. *"For if I pray in an unknown tongue, my spirit prayeth..."* (1 Cor. 14:14). Praying in tongues seems foolish, but it is in the Word of God. In fact, one of the Hebrew words for praise is *halal,* from which we derive the word *hallelujah*. The Hebrew root *halal* means "to be clear (dealing with sound and color) to shine or boast, to be clamorously foolish, to rave about."[4]

I (Jeanne) love to *halal,* or boast on the Lord. Years ago, I sprained my ankle badly and could hardly walk. The pastor told me to go to the hospital, as the swelling was severe.

God was teaching us about "clamorously foolish" praise and the power it produced. I heard God tell me to praise Him and stand on His Word for my healing. So I limped up to my feet and started to jump up and down shouting, which is *shabach,* another form of praise[5] given to God for His goodness. When Ken got home, the swelling was gone and I was healed!

This principle doesn't only apply to physical healing. God gives us *"...the garment of praise for the spirit of heaviness* [depression]*..."* (Isa. 61:3). The Hebrew word for this kind of praise is *tehillah,* also from the root *halal*. It means "to laud or extol with words."[6] We are to speak praise words to depression and cover ourselves in words of praise as with a garment.

God is not an egomaniac who needs to be stroked. He is the creator; the Holy Spirit is the instructor; Jesus is the example; and the Bible is the instruction manual. Praise is designed for us. Praise pleases God because it is our expression of love to Him. We need to praise Him because it supplies us with enough power to walk in this life.

There is an interesting passage in Habakkuk that sums up what we studied here. It talks prophetically about the Jesus, but by implication includes us, since we are in Him:

> God came…. His glory covered the heavens, and the earth was full of His praise. And His brightness was as the light; He had horns coming out of His hand: and there was the hiding of His power… (Habakkuk 3:3-4).

The word *horn* is the Hebrew root *geren,* meaning "to push."[7] The word *hand* is the Hebrew word *yad,* meaning "open hand."[8] The word *power* is *yadah,* which means "praise" in the Hebrew.[9]

The passage from Habakkuk tells us that strength comes from Jesus' open hand of praise. That strength manifested in light and sound. That is how God created the universe. That is how we create what we need in our own realms.

The worship, praise, and thanksgiving that God gives us will manifest to the world as we give it back to Him. Israel *"…sang this song, Spring up, O well: sing ye unto it;"* (Num. 21:17). We need do the same. We need to shift our thinking until we can sing at our troubles and call forth the water of life into our dry situations!

SHIFT INTO PRAYER

> Lord forgive us for not seeing You through the storms of our lives. Help us to see You clearly, regardless of the circumstances. Forgive us and help us to shift our thinking when we don't trust You enough to thank

You for Your love and protection in every situation. Change the way we think so that we can release a praise that will chase away every fear from our hearts.

ENDNOTES

1. Zodhaites, Spiros. *The Complete Word Study Dictionary: Old Testament* (Chattanooga: AMG Publishers, 1994), s.v., 3885.

2. Ibid., s.v., 8426, 3034, 3027.

3. Ibid., s.v., 7623.

4. Ibid., s.v., 1984.

5. Ibid., s.v., 7623.

6. Ibid., s.v., 8416.

7. Ibid., s.v., 7176.

8. Ibid., s.v., 3027.

9. Ibid., s.v., 8426.

Chapter 7

GET YOUR LIFE IN LINE

God Empowers Our Obedience

OBEDIENCE is an action; submission is an attitude. The Bible says that whatever is inside of us will eventually come out. Outwardly, we may act differently from the way we feel inside; but eventually, our hidden attitudes will manifest themselves in the open.

I think of the story of the little boy who was constantly told to sit rather than stand in the pew at church. When the frustrated father finally applied enough discipline to elicit the proper decorum from his son, all seemed well. However, with a pout, the little boy declared defiantly, "I may be sitting on the outside but I am still standing on the inside."

Many Christians exhibit the same attitude: They give God religious duty instead of joyful obedience. The problem is that, instead of entering into the grace of the New Covenant, they have exchanged the tree of the knowledge of evil for its seemingly better side: the knowledge of good.

The tree of the knowledge of good produces at best nothing more than a sense of duty. There is no life in it, only death. God does not reward duty, because dutiful actions do not have their source in

Him. Therefore, if all we do is modify our behavior for the sake of duty, we forgo the life Jesus died to give us.

Even the conscience is not salved by duty, because we know in our spirits that God is not pleased by our acts of obligation. As a result, we try ever harder to please God doing the only thing that is left for us: sacrifice.

Sacrifice is never accepted when birthed from a selfish motive (see Ps. 40:6). Furthermore, if we strive to please God through a sacrifice that wins us nothing, we become discouraged, as Cain did. We need to rethink our natural thoughts toward obedience and begin to see it in a different light—His light.

THE CAIN MISCALCULATION

Cain brought his sacrifice to God and it was rejected (see Gen. 4:3-7). Cain became envious of his brother Abel. He obviously believed that he had tried at least as hard as his brother, Abel, to bring a pleasing sacrifice to God.

Abel offered God a lamb, which grew by itself. Cain toiled to raise the crops he would offer to God. Cain failed to see the important difference between the two offerings: Abel obeyed and offered what God called for; Cain simply made a sacrifice.

Cain murdered Abel because of envy. The root of that envy came from a religious spirit that was furious when its religious duty was rejected.

I can relate to this spirit firsthand: I have fasted in the past, hoping to twist God's arm to answer my prayer. I tried to manipulate God with my "great" sacrifice. I have learned the hard way that you don't manipulate God by fasting; you just get hungry.

Jesus said to the Pharisees, *"Ye seek to kill Me, because My word hath no place in you....Ye seek to kill Me, a man that hath told you the truth..."* (John. 8:37, 40).

When it came to religious service, the Pharisees were the most righteous people on the face of the earth. Unfortunately, their reliance on doing things right blinded them from seeing the Son of Righteousness who was manifesting God's power right before their eyes.

Their self-righteousness demanded that God should appear only within whatever bounds they determined. The Scriptures say that they "...*rejected the counsel of God against themselves, being not baptized of* [John]" (Luke. 7:30). This is why Jesus said that prostitutes and tax collectors would get into Heaven before the Pharisees. In Kingdom terms, "*Many that are first shall be last; and the last shall be first* (Matt. 19:30).

The prostitutes knew they were sinners; the Pharisees thought they were righteous. They failed to judge themselves accurately. We must be the first to judge ourselves and ask whether we truly are obedient or just doing what we think is right. There is literally a world of difference between the two.

We counseled with a man who wanted to buy a new truck. He claimed that God had told him to buy it; he said he wanted to buy the truck so he could take his pastor hunting. This man had big debts; his decision was causing a great deal of contention between him and his wife. Good ideas are not necessarily God ideas, and most often are not even good ideas.

The truth was he wanted that truck for himself. He couched his desire in religious jargon to appease his conscience and silence his wife. In another case, someone told us that God led him to buy a raffle ticket on a dream home. The problem was that another family in the church believed the same thing—but there was only one house. Neither family won the prize, but both of their grocery budgets got tighter that month.

It is vital that we separate those things that are pressing us in the soul realm from the things God is saying in the spirit realm. Absent this distinction, we'll tend to believe that whatever concerns us also concerns God. Unless we admit our errors, we will never learn to hear His voice.

Jesus never based His actions on His own perception of right and wrong. Instead, He made decisions based on what the Father showed Him. When He was challenged as to why He healed on the Sabbath, He said: *"My Father worketh hitherto, and I work....The Son can do nothing of Himself, but...what things soever He doeth, these things also doeth the Son likewise"* (John 5:17,19).

In other words, "I do nothing on My own initiative." Jesus modeled how to know and obey the Father. This knowing is vital, because without a revelation of what God is doing, any response we give is necessarily from the flesh.

You've already read about my dreams involving work in England and how I was offered a job there shortly after having these dreams. At the time, I wanted the job and I wanted to be important. While God was talking to me about family, I was focused on my career; I even took a job in another city in preparation for the assignment in England.

My striving caused problems between Jeanne and me and, in the end, did not produce the job overseas. God did send us to England at the company's expense for an eight-day trip, but He never intended for us to live there.

My own ideas caused me to "hear" from God things that never really happened. We must be honest with ourselves; If things don't come to pass as we "saw" them, they were not from God (see Deut. 18:22).

God is calling us to higher ground. He is urging us to shift out of our natural patterns and self-centered desires to walk circumspectly in the precise things *He* desires for us. Our own desires are not sufficient impetus upon which to act; we need a genuine word from the Father.

CHRISTLIKE COMPASSION

We often want to help people who are in trouble because they are in trouble and plainly need help. We let our human compassion dictate what we should do.

Jesus never acted out of His own compassion! If God chose mercy, Jesus was merciful. If God meted out judgment or chose to allow consequences to manifest, Jesus did not interfere (see Matt. 12:20).

Even in the healing from John 5 described earlier, Jesus had to literally step over *"...a great multitude of impotent folk, of blind, halt, withered..."* (John 5:3). He didn't heal any of them except the one lame man.

Why didn't Jesus heal those in obvious need? Because, in the Spirit, He only saw God healing the one man. Why? The Bible doesn't tell us why and Jesus didn't question God; He only obeyed, saying: *"I can of mine own self do nothing: as I hear, I judge..."* (John 5:30).

Years ago, out of human compassion, we responded to a need in our congregation. A couple was bemoaning the fact that they didn't have money for a financial difficulty. We gave them some money, only to discover later that they were in a far better place financially than we were. I realized I had let emotions make my decision rather than hearing from God. That gift was a sacrifice for us; unfortunately sacrifice moved by human compassion rather than Holy Spirit guidance is not true obedience. Often, we get smart to this truth too late—after we make decisions that are not of genuine benefit.

Human compassion is also fickle. If we help people for their sakes (or ours) and not God's, we are prone to becoming offended if they don't respond to our assistance with gratitude. Our reactions to such situations provide a test of our original motives. If you are disappointed with someone's reaction to your good works, you probably didn't do it for God, for God never disappoints.

Human compassion or human love often turns to hate when the impetus for the original action is no longer present. The Bible illustrates this point in the story of Amnon and Tamar (see 2 Sam. 13).

Ammon thought he had a true love for Tamar; in reality he only had lust. That human emotion turned fickle once it was satisfied:

> Amnon said...I love Tamar, my brother Absalom's sister....Being stronger than she, [Amnon] forced her, and lay with her. Then Amnon hated her exceedingly...greater than the love wherewith he had loved her... (2 Samuel 13:4,14-15).

So it is with us. Actions not initiated from God have no life in them; in the end, they hurt the ones we intended to help. Bob Mumford, who was a prominent prophetic teacher in the 1970s, in teachings often said, "God fixes a fix to fix us; but if we (or others) fix the fix before we are fixed, then God has to fix another fix to fix us."

Human compassion just gets in the way of God's purposes and prolongs the process. We can only obey when we truly hear what God is doing.

Jesus and Mary's interaction during the wedding at Canaan of Galilee is instructive on this point. The first thing that becomes apparent is the need brought to Jesus' attention by His mother, who "...said to Him, 'They have no wine'" (John 2:3 NKJV). Mary was concerned, because running out of wine would have caused great embarrassment in the Jewish culture.

The next thing we see is Jesus' response to Mary: "My hour has not yet come" (John 2:4 NKJV). In other words, "This is not My problem."

Mary picked up something in the Spirit. Up to that time, Jesus had not performed any miracles. She sensed that God wanted to do something, so she prepared the servants to participate. She "...said unto the servants, 'Whatever He says to you, do it [obey]'" (John 2:5 NKJV).

When Jesus was ready, He gave instructions and the servant poured out the wine He miraculously produced. The result was that Jesus *"...manifested His glory; and His disciples believed in Him"* (John 2:11 NKJV).

Our obedience, like the servants', glorifies Jesus.

ACTIONS AND OBEDIENCE

As we said earlier: *obedience is an action; submission is an attitude.* God is always looks beyond the action to judge the heart. Sometimes we act "in obedience," but we respond in our own time. This kind of slow obedience indicates an unsubmissive heart and is actually a passive form of disobedience.

God told me (Ken) to get ready for a move to a different city. He wasn't specific on the timing. Since I was working a steady job and not planning on changing our family situation, I didn't respond.

Instead, I increased my activities outside of work by buying several cars to repair and sell. I also started building a stone fence with a large ornamental iron gate. Life for me was not changing; it was just becoming more cluttered. God, however, had an agenda and a time frame that I needed to heed.

Two years later, when the need to move came "suddenly," I wasn't ready. I worked for almost two months steady to get our acreage ready to vacate and rent. Had I obeyed God promptly, the project would have been finished already and the move would have been easy. I had to repent of my disobedience and the extra strain it had put on the family.

The children of Israel also disobeyed by walking in slow obedience. They had come to the edge of the Promised Land. God ordered them to scout it out, go in, and conquer. Only 2 of the 12 spies returned with a good report. Ten allowed fear to come in, saying:

> *We be not able to go up against the people for they are stronger than we. The land...eateth up the inhabitants....*

And there we saw the giants...and we were in our own sight as grasshoppers... (Numbers 13:31-33).

The people's response was predictable:

...the children of Israel murmured...and...said...Would God that we...had died in this wilderness!...Hath the Lord brought us...to fall by the sword, that our wives and our children should be a prey?... (Numbers 14:2-3).

Fear nullified the people's faith and left them unwilling to obey. God responded by determining to destroy them. Moses interceded fervently and God replied:

...as ye have spoken in Mine ears, so will I do to you: your carcasses shall fall in this wilderness.... ye [shall] bear your iniquities...forty years... (Numbers 14:28-29, 34).

As God promised, a plague went out and consumed the ten spies who brought the evil report (see Num. 14:37).

After sleeping on their decision, the children of Israel changed their minds and *"...rose up early in the morning...saying, Lo, we be here, and will go up unto the place which the LORD hath promised..."* (Num. 14:40).

Unfortunately, it was too late; the window of opportunity in which to obey God had passed. God had given new instructions, but the people decided (against God's warning) to go up and fight the Amalekites and Canaanites anyway. They assumed that, since they had changed their minds, God would change His also.

They went to battle, not in faith but presumption, and were soundly defeated (see Num. 14:44-45). They had no authority or power because they were in disobedience; God was not committed to helping them continue in their ways.

Shift your thinking; Slow obedience is not obedience at all—it is disobedience!

MOTIVES AND ACTIONS

We cannot judge the heart. Only God can do that. When asked about obedience, Jesus relayed a story that demonstrated the subtleties of motive and actions.

He told of two sons asked by their father to work in the fields. One son refused; he then repented and went out to work. The other immediately agreed to do the work, but never did it (see Matt. 21:28-32). Ironically, the son who at first resisted obedience was the one who obeyed in the end.

Obedience is defined not by intent but by action. I (Jeanne) was prompted to go to the hospital and share the Lord with Ken's uncle. I was a young woman and too frightened to share the Gospel. Instead, I just prayed for the man.

On three consecutive Sundays, that prompting returned, but because of my fear, I couldn't do it. The next week, Ken's uncle had a heart attack and died. I was devastated and repented, asking God to forgive me.

Would I have been able to lead him to the Lord? I don't know. I do know that, although I did not discuss the Lord with Ken's uncle, his Christian roommate did. They had many good conversations about God in that room. Nevertheless, I earned myself a hard lesson. Thankfully, God is gracious; I now lead people to the Lord on a regular basis.

God challenged the thinking of the children of Israel regarding His preference of obedience over sacrifice. In Jeremiah, He made clear that the sacrifices of Israel were not His highest desire:

> *This thing commanded I them saying, Obey My voice, and I will be your God, and ye shall be My people: and walk ye in all the ways that I have commanded you, that it may be well unto you. But they hearkened not...and went backward, and not forward* (Jeremiah 7:23-24).

Obedience was the key. Sacrifices and offerings were added later to teach the people how to approach a holy God; they were not designed as substitutes for obedience.

We as husbands (Ken speaking) sometimes offer sacrifices of flowers or gifts instead of regularly showing our wives the love they need. Sacrifice is a poor substitute; it does not represent passion, but duty. God and wives hate dutiful actions; they want obedience to love.

Jeanne's friend and her husband were having a hard time with intimacy in their marriage. Neither they nor we had any clue as to how to solve their situation. But, as always, God had a strategy prepared. All it took was for someone to listen to Him.

The wife had bought some golden, tinsel-like material to make dance props for the church. As she sat down to sew, she felt no inspiration and laid the material aside.

A month later, God started to talk to her about her role in putting some zing back into her marriage. She was fighting against intimacy with her husband, but knew she needed to change. God told her to take some material she had purchased for the church and make a hula skirt. She obeyed and made herself a golden hula skirt.

This was totally beyond her reserved nature. Later that evening, she decorated the room with candles and prepared for her husband. Needless to say the hula skirt had the desired effect.

Yielding to the Lord allowed this woman to love and bless her husband. Obedience will *always* bring an empowerment from God. In the days that followed, she felt inspired to use the rest of the golden material and some white cloth to create a canopy which she then draped over four posts. She had no idea what she was building; she was just being obedient to what she saw in the Spirit.

When she took the canopy to church the next Sunday, she was told she had built a *chuppah* (pronounced *hoopa*), which is used in Jewish wedding ceremonies. There was a powerful anointing for anybody who passed under the chuppah that Sunday. Obedience in using the gold material to bless the intimacy in one marriage allowed God to give inspiration to bless the whole church with more marital intimacy.

Obedience does not require understanding, only a joyful response. Samuel said that *"...to obey is better than sacrifice, and to hearken than the fat of rams"* (1 Sam. 15:22). God desires no substitutes for obedience.

COMMANDED TO LOVE

Jesus said to His disciples, *"A new commandment I give unto you, That ye love one another; as I have loved you"* (John 13:34). That command supersedes all others.

Paul further explained the superiority of love over sacrifice: *"And though I bestow all my goods to feed the poor, and...give my body to be burned, but have not love, it profits me nothing"* (1 Cor. 13:3 NKJV).

As Cain found out, God has the right not to accept our sacrifices. Cain gave of his produce when God wanted a blood sacrifice. Disobedience caused his sacrifice to be rejected. Cain showed his unsubmissive nature when he reacted in anger. His sacrifice had been all about him, not about pleasing God.

The writer of Hebrews picks up the same theme: *"In...sacrifices for sin Thou hast had no pleasure. Then said I [Jesus], Lo, I come...to do Thy will, O God"* (Heb. 10:6-7).

Jesus knew the difference between obedience and sacrifice. Our goal is to be like Jesus. He never did anything for selfish reasons; He always did what pleased the Father.

Sacrifice uncommissioned by God is, at its core, selfish. It is an attempt to buy off God. We know He has a right to expect our obedience, which is why we don't ignore Him completely. Our conscience is pricked to do *something,* so we choose to do something less (in our estimation) than what is commanded.

Hosea discovered that all of God's commands are chances for us to gain victory over our flesh. Hence his words: *"For I desired mercy, and not sacrifice; and the knowledge of God more than burnt offerings"* (Hos. 6:6).

Any resistance to obey is an attempt to maintain our independence. What we fail to recognize is that God wants to give us, as it were, signing authority over this earth. In resisting God's authority over us, we miss out on the opportunity to wield that same authority.

An employee endowed with signing authority can write checks against the account of the one who delegated this authority. As long as the employee conducts business according to the will of the one he represents, his name on those checks will be honored at any bank. However, as soon as the employee attempts to do his own business with his patron's funds, he is guilty of fraud and banned from wielding his former authority.

God wants us in that place of authority so that we can *"…ask anything in* [His] *name* [knowing He] *will do it"* (John 14:14). We can chase away the most powerful evil in the universe if we will *"submit…to God. Resist the devil, and he will flee from* [us]*"* (James 4:7). He won't flee because of us; he will flee because of the authority we have in Jesus when we are submitted to God.

CONSCIENCE AND CONSEQUENCES

We cannot with impunity pursue our own courses of action and not expect consequences. God knows that we are often not ready to obey in certain areas. He has made provision for that.

God always wants to move us from judgment to a place where He can show us mercy. Even in the tabernacle of Moses, the mercy seat was above the law, which was placed inside the ark (see Exod. 25:21). It is from the mercy seat that God chose to speak to Moses (see Num. 7:89). However justice demands that *"…the wrath of God cometh… upon the children of disobedience"* (Col. 3:6). *"But God …is rich in mercy, for His great love…"* (Eph. 2:4). This is the dilemma: Justice demands judgment and love cries for mercy. God solved the problem by blinding those who would not obey so that He could leave them in unbelief and show mercy.

This principle is laid out by Jesus as He quotes Isaiah. Speaking to the disciples, He said, *"It is given unto you to know the mysteries of the kingdom of heaven, but to them it is not given …therefore I speak to them in parables"* (Matt. 13:11,13). He goes onto describe what is happening to the people who can't believe. *"…For the hearts of this people have grown dull. Their ears are hard of hearing and their eyes have closed lest they should see …and hear …[and] understand with their hearts and turn, so that I should heal them"* (Matt. 13:15 NKJV).

The parables are not so they could understand the principles but rather so they couldn't. God's love was protecting them. Paul said of Israel that *"…the elect have obtained* (righteousness by faith) *and the rest were blinded"* (Rom. 11:7 NKJV). He goes on to say *"…blindness … is happened to Israel, until the fullness of the Gentiles … come in. …For God hath concluded them all in unbelief, that He might have mercy on all"* (Rom. 11:25,32).

I remember desperately wanting to be involved in a particular condominium project. I didn't wait to get an answer from God because I knew what He would say. Jeanne had already gotten a "No" from the Lord, but I harangued her, saying that her fear was speaking.

I chose to go into the project blind, without the guidance of the Spirit. God didn't speak to me because my heart was not ready to obey. My flesh felt great about the deal, so I jumped blindly in. (Where guidance is concerned, the stronger the excitement in the flesh, the less likely there is any Spirit involved.) The project worked out, but the principals of the management company siphoned off all the money.

When I repented of my independence and willfulness, God was forgiving; unfortunately, nature was not and I lost my investment.

The mercy of God restored what was lost, but not through that investment.

Jesus warned that disobedience (knowing God's will and resisting it anyway) will bring *"many stripes."* But sinning (not knowing His will and doing your own will) will bring *"few stripes"* (Luke 12:47-48). My blindness still cost me a lot.

The danger in disobedience above the punishment is that, in time, we will lose the ability to hear the Spirit plead with us. Continual disobedience will attract spirits who are also disobedient.

Paul warned that *"some shall depart from the faith, giving heed to seducing spirits...speaking lies...having their conscience seared..."* (1 Tim. 4:1-2). A cauterized conscience (which is the forerunner to a hardened heart) deadens our capacity hear the conviction of the Spirit.

If there is no conviction of sin, we will never by our own will desire to repent. You can only be called to repentance; you cannot fabricate it yourself, as Esau discovered. The writer of Hebrews admonishes us to "[look] *diligently lest any...fail of the grace of God... as Esau.... For ye know...he found no place of repentance, though he sought it carefully with tears"* (Heb. 12:15-17).

Esau could not, by his own volition or emotion, bring himself to repent of his casual approach to God's will. Esau's rejection of the birthright (which he valued as nothing) caused him to also lose the blessing (the empowerment of authority).

Please take to heart the consequences Esau reaped. The hardening of your conscience, left unaddressed as Esau's was, will eventually destroy all God wants to do in you, too.

Paul also admonishes us saying:

> [Hold onto] *faith, and a good conscience; which some having put away...have* [become shipwrecked]*...delivered unto satan, that they may learn not to blaspheme* (1 Timothy 1:19-20).

Our conscience is the main voice God uses to speak to the spirit. When the conscience is seared, communication with God is disrupted. The problem can be compared to having a poor telephone connection. You can hear the party on the other end, but cannot make out what they are saying. A seared conscience separates us from the very voice that can save us.

ANTICIPATE CONSEQUENCES

The arrogance of disobeying and saying "No!" to God has consequences that can be anticipated and avoided.

When Israel wandered in the wilderness, they were led by the cloud during the day and the pillar of fire at night. When the cloud lifted, the children of Israel had to move with it. If they stayed behind, they would have lost the benefits of God's presence: shade by day, warmth and light by night; spiritual drink from *"that spiritual Rock that followed them"* (1 Cor. 10:4), as well as physical water; the manna that sustained them; the protection afforded them; and the leadership that guided them.

God is not trying to punish us or bring judgment. He is always trying to bring mercy. This concept is best illustrated by comparing it to the use of an umbrella in a storm. Protection is found under God's "umbrella." We can relinquish that protection two ways: We can step out from under the umbrella, or refuse to stay under its protection when it moves.

God is training us to prophetically anticipate consequences rather than endure judgment. God wants us to grow up. Just because we are His children does not mean that we should remain immature. Mature people can anticipate consequences. Children or novices do not see problems coming; they expect adults to deal with the problems for them, even when they create the problems themselves.

One of our sons got the idea to take off and go to the United States. Without informing anyone of his plans, he took our car and left with a buddy of his. The two then dumped the car in a town north of the U.S. border and sneaked across the line.

They were apprehended about 20 miles down the turnpike and detained by the border patrol. Jeanne and I had to travel close to 2,000 miles to collect the car, collect our son, and travel back home. On our way down to pick up our son and the car, we saw a large billboard that boldly declared, "FORGIVE."

Our attitude up until then had been to punish our son for his foolishness. But God wanted us to come into a more mature, giving spirit. We prayed and God worked on our hearts as we drove. By the time we picked up our son, we had shifted our thoughts and met him with love and forgiveness. Our son displayed immaturity, but we forgave him. However, there were consequences to be faced for his actions. It was some time before our son was given privileges with the car again.

Immaturity is, in essence, the inability to hear and obey. It causes us to disobey and prevents us from stepping into places of authority. People display immaturity in many ways.

For instance, we have dealt with people who have gone on costly mission trips, only to struggle with finances for food when they arrived back home. They said God told them to go, but God supplies where He calls. We must always look at the fruit of our actions to determine their source.

Recently, a young man in our county went to a bush party where over a hundred young people (mostly under age) had a large bonfire and drank beer.The party turned bad and another youth was beaten to death. Although the young man tried to break up the fatal fight, he ended up being charged as well. Yes, he was trying to help. The problem was that he should not have been there in the first place.

When I was younger and immature, I did what I wanted. As I have gotten older, I am learning to do only what God wants (see John 21:18). There are consequences for every action; it is a law of God's universe.

The problem we have obeying laws is that we have learned that we can break some of man's laws and get away with it. The greater the time period between the incident and its consequences, the less likely the two are to be connected.

Not so with God's laws. We cannot break them, only confirm them. Israel experienced a drought in the time of David that God said was ...*for Saul, and for his bloody house, because he slew the Gibeonites* (2 Sam. 21:1). Almost 40 years had transpired before this judgment came to fruit. Unrepented disobedience brings judgment.

SPIRITUAL WEAPONS

Obedience immediately releases God to deal with the people and situations in our lives:

> *(For the weapons of our warfare are not carnal, but mighty through God to the pulling down of strong holds;) casting down imaginations, and every high thing that exalteth itself against the knowledge of God, and bringing into captivity every thought to the obedience of Christ; and having in a readiness to revenge all disobedience, when your obedience is fulfilled* (2 Corinthians 10:4-6).

The ability to release God into a difficult situation created by others hinges on our ability to obey God ourselves. Our death to our own desires begets new life (see 2 Cor. 4:12) A work of grace through faith allows us to prefer Christ's life to our own, if we are willing to die to self. If we submit, then God enters in and can work on all other disobedience that affects our lives.

Jesus was our perfect example. He could not be killed. He said, *"No one takes* [My life] *from me.... I have power to lay it down, and I have power to take it again. This...I have received from My Father"* (John 10:18 NKJV).

This is the power of the indestructible life. Because His life could not be taken from Him, Jesus had no fear in laying His life on the line. He was totally submitted to God and God was totally responsible for what happened. That is the safest place to be!

Jesus says we are in the same position. He promised that "...*whosoever shall lose his life for My sake and the gospel's...shall save it*" (Mark. 8:35). He also said, "*Whosoever believeth in* [Me] *should not perish, but have eternal life*" (John 3:15).

Jesus died for us. Therefore, the test is never *Will you die for Him?* but *Will you live for Him and not yourself?* Because Jesus was fully obedient, God could orchestrate all the events that were necessary to bring our redemption.

Remember, God doesn't ask us to do things; He gives commands. We either obey or disobey. His intention is expressed in the following words: "*If ye will obey My voice...then ye shall be a peculiar treasure unto Me above all people...and ye shall be unto Me a kingdom of priests, and a holy nation....*" (Exod. 19:5-6).

God is setting up a Kingdom. He is just checking out who should rule it for Him. This is the testing ground where each of us decides whether we want to participate.

PASSION FOR GOD'S WILL

A prophet had a vision in which he said he went up to the throne room with Jesus. He saw many people whom he recognized in the Spirit. There were other people close to the throne whom he did not recognize. Near the throne were two empty seats. He asked, "Who were these seats reserved for?" Jesus told the prophet that the empty seats near the throne of God were for anyone who wanted them.

Do you want them? Be careful how you answer. Jesus said it was better not to vow than to vow and not complete your vow. But God wants you to dare. He loves those that value what He values. He loved Jacob, who desired the birthright and the blessing so much that he was willing to lie, steal, and cheat to get them. We may abhor Jacob's actions but God didn't. His response, in a sense, declared,

"I like this boy." Jacob had to repent for his actions, but he was commended for his attitude.

I (Jeanne) once prayed for a minister's wife who was going up north. As we were talking on the phone, my right leg began hurting terribly. As it had never hurt before, I felt that God wanted to heal my friend. She admitted that her leg was in bad shape and surgery had been recommended. I prayed and claimed her healing.

I never heard from the woman after she left, but a year later, while talking to another pastor, the issue came up. I asked how the woman's leg was doing. "Oh didn't you hear? She didn't have the surgery. She was completely healed after you prayed for her."

We must do what God has commanded us to do and leave the results up to Him. We pray, not worrying about a response, or thanks, or reward. God wants us to trust His Word. If we don't get the results we expect, we just go back to God and find out why.

Authority in any realm comes from faithful, persistent obedience. In fact, Jesus said, *"Ye are My friends, if ye do whatsoever I command you"* (John 15:14). Notice He didn't say "…whatsoever I *ask* you."

Jesus went on to say, *"…I…ordained you, that ye should go and bring forth fruit, and that your fruit should remain"* (John 15:16). He is talking about our living eternal, fruitful lives. If we yoke ourselves with Him in whatever He is doing, this fruit bearing will be easy and our souls will be at rest (see Matt. 11:29-30). But we must do it with Him, not just agree with Him. We must shift our thinking to embrace the fact that if submission is our attitude, then true obedience is seen through our actions.

HEARING AND LEARNING TO OBEY

James explained that we are not to be *"…forgetful* [hearers], *but…* [doers] *of the work,* [and therefore] *blessed in* [our deeds]" (James 1:25).

We can follow Jesus' example, knowing that *"by the obedience of one* [Jesus] *shall many be made righteous"* (Rom. 5:19). He had to learn, as strange as that may seem, to walk in this authority. Though His spirit was God, His body and soul (where His will dwelt) were human and had to learn to obey the voice of the Spirit. The writer of Hebrews wrote that *"though He was a Son, yet He learned obedience by the things which He suffered"* (Heb. 5:8 NKJV).

Jesus, in His earthly form, was just like us, of the same make up: Paul said He was *"the firstborn among many brethren"* (Rom. 8:29). Jesus chose to use the title Son of man when referring to himself. He *"...took upon him the form of a servant, and was made in the likeness of men"* (Phil 2:7).

Jesus prayed *"**Our** Father,"* (Matt. 6:9, emphasis added), just as we now do. He had a body; we have a body. He had a soul; we have a soul. His Spirit was the Spirit of God; once we're saved, we also have God's Spirit. Conversely, Paul explained: *"If any man have not the Spirit of Christ, he is none of His"* (Rom. 8:9).

Therefore, if we would submit our bodies and souls in every aspect to the Spirit of Christ, these bodies and souls of ours would be in exactly the same situation as Jesus' was.

Do you realize how hard it was for Jesus' body and soul to live with Him? Every thought, every action was under the control of His Spirit. Even at the end, a vain attempt was made by the human soul of Jesus to bargain with the Spirit. Jesus allowed His soul to express its reservations about going to the cross, saying, *"Father, if Thou be willing, remove this cup from Me: nevertheless not My will, but Thine be done"* (Luke 22:42).

Jesus' will resided in His soul and was opposed to the plan of going to the cross. The pressure was enormous—both fleshly from within and satanically from without. But God sent an angel to Jesus, as He would to any man or woman, to strengthen Him for the test.

The ferocity of the pressure Jesus experienced is evidenced in this account from the Gospels: *"And being in an agony He prayed more earnestly: and His sweat was as it were great drops of blood..."* (Luke 22:44).

In staying fixed on what His Spirit knew was God's plan, Jesus the Man experienced such turmoil that He actually ruptured the blood vessels in His brow. Remember, the will had to decide to obey the Spirit: The man part obeying the God part. It was a real battle, because it could have been lost. But Jesus had learned the obedience that is the response of a dependent child to a loving Father.

Abraham prophesied the victory centuries before the cross when he said to Isaac, *"...God will provide Himself a lamb for a burnt offering..."* (Gen. 22:8). Obedience gave Abraham great authority; it gave Jesus absolute authority.

Our authority grows as our obedience is perfected. Jeanne and I have spent thousands of hours ministering to hundreds of people. We have made many mistakes and gone down many blind alleys. That is part of the learning curve. Our training has taken several decades. We sacrificed our time and energy because the Father called us to set captives free.

It has been a great joy for us to see others changed in God. The Holy Spirit hid us from sight because we weren't ready to handle the pressure of public ministry. Even Jesus obeyed the rules concerning a priest and did not start His public ministry until He was 30 years old. He was the perfect example of an obedient Son.

> *...He humbled Himself, and became obedient unto death, even the death of the cross. Wherefore God also hath highly exalted Him, and given Him a name which is above every name: that at the name of Jesus every knee should bow, of things in heaven, and things in earth, and things under the earth; and that every tongue should confess that Jesus Christ is Lord, to the glory of God the Father* (Philippians 2:8-11).

It was so vital to Jesus to obey that He said, *"My meat is to do the will of Him that sent Me…"* (John 4:34). Jesus' love of the Father compelled His actions; Jesus calls us to the same response, saying, *"If ye keep My commandments, ye shall abide in My love; even as I have kept My Father's commandments, and abide in His love"* (John 15:10).

It is not law but love that motivated Jesus. Once we make the shift out of our natural thinking then our obedience is no longer duty. Instead, obedience becomes joy *"for the love of Christ constraineth us…"* (2 Cor. 5:14).

LOVE, NOT DUTY

If love doesn't empower your walk, then your faith—which dictates your actions—will be compromised. Why? Because *"faith… worketh by love"* (Gal. 5:6). With your faith compromised, there will always be a place or situation in which satan can tempt you to turn your back on God.

In that place, God will appear, demanding His own glory. If we are in love with Him, we will interpret His every action as an extension of His love for us, even if it appears to the natural eye to be completely the opposite. We can see Him this way because we know He loves us and would never hurt us.

This is the essence of our call. *"…We have received grace and apostleship* [or whatever our callings], *for obedience to the faith…"* (Rom. 1:5). We have grace to obey but we must learn, as Jesus learned, how to walk in it.

Every saint is called to this truth.. *"By faith Abraham, when he was called to go…obeyed…not knowing whither he went"* (Heb. 11:8). Our obedience is learned through our experience in obeying.

Our obedience grows as we gain trust in following His Word. I (Ken) once felt compelled to stay home from an important meeting. We were expected to attend, but God said, "I want you at home this evening."

As a result, I was out in the front yard when a neighbor came over, crying. Her father was dying and she needed some comfort. I was able to lead her to the God of all comfort; I was also able to lead her to the Lord for her salvation. That night impacted her whole family. I was just obeying God's command to stay home, though I didn't know why. He orchestrated the results of my obedience.

On another occasion, I was driving to work early in the morning while it was still dark. I felt compelled to slow the car down. I came over a rise and there, in the middle of the road was a whole herd of white-tailed deer. I managed to make my way through the herd without incident. Had I been traveling at highway speed, any attempt to maneuver through or around them would have resulted in disaster.

Once, during the middle of the night, we were returning from a ministry trip in a remote northern city. Except for the driver, the whole team was asleep. I (Jeanne) had been dozing and quietly praying when God prompted me to sit up and declare aloud protection from all wild animals.

I felt kind of stupid for shouting it out, but the driver was aptly alerted and immediately slowed down. Just moments later, we encountered a herd of wild horses wandering across the road. It was to be the first of six encounters with herds of animals, including deer, moose, and elk crossing the road in front of us. We didn't know it, but we needed protection from the Lord that night.

When we love Him, we trust Him. Therefore, we are more open to obedience, which, in turn, results in the Holy Spirit being poured out on us. He is *"the Holy Ghost, whom God hath given to them that obey Him"* (Acts 5:32).

It is our response of love in obeying and that will allow us to abide in Him. Right to the end of the Bible the same theme is emphasized. John wrote: *"Blessed* [empowered] *are they that do His commandments…"* (Rev. 22:14).

God is going to do great things in these last days, but He has limited himself to work through us just as we work through Him. He has ordained us to enter into what He is doing; but we will need to have hearts that are obedient to respond. We must respond accurately if His work is going to be accomplished.

There was a man who sat for eight years in a church we attended. How he had managed to avoid giving his heart to the Lord all that time is a mystery to me, but he did. God started to stir up the Body one week, to intercede for him: some prayed; others fasted.

During the Sunday service, an expectation for his salvation rose up in several people at the same time. People were interceding for him in the pews and in the hall. The minister felt compelled to stop the service in the middle of his message and ask if anyone wanted to meet God right then.

When this gentleman finally responded, the church went nuts. Many people had been willing to obey God's call of love. The result was a release of power that convicted this man of his need for God.

David said of godly willingness: *"The Lord shall send...strength out of Zion: rule Thou in the midst of Thine enemies. Thy people shall be willing in the day of Thy power..."* (Ps. 110:2-3).

The Kingdom isn't about us, but He will prepare us. We must lean on His grace to be able to accomplish what He asks. We only have grace for today, but we will be supplied with more to obey in the future. God is building a habitation for Himself and He will do it in us, if we obey Him.

Zechariah 6:15 says: *"They that are far off shall come and build in the temple...if ye will diligently obey the voice of the Lord your God"* (Zech. 6:15).

BEING USEFUL

God conquered the land of Canaan, but He waited until the disobedient generation died. Their disobedience was the result of a self-centered focus about how war was going to affect them. Therefore, instead of being part of the promise manifested, an entire generation fell by the wayside.

Let us not be the "useless" generation that died in the wilderness. Let us be a generation God can use. To be that generation, we need to have a Kingdom mentality. Jesus said, *"I came down from heaven, not to do Mine own will, but the will of Him that sent Me"* (John 6:38).

Likewise, He calls us to *"...endure hardness, as...good* [soldiers] *of Jesus Christ. No man that warreth entangleth himself with the affairs of this life; that he may please Him who has chosen him to be a soldier"* (2 Tim. 2:3-4).

God calls us to a higher plane. If we will concern ourselves with what concerns Him, He will attend to the details that concern us.

Jeanne and I have experienced that kind of provision. God has always supplied for Jeanne and me, especially when we were led to give generously, even beyond what we thought we could handle. For example, we have spent much time counseling, but God has redeemed the time for us with small jobs that produced huge profits.

He has blessed our obedience in many ways, not all of them financial. Not long ago, I was building a fence with my neighbor and his son when my oldest boy called from his home in Winnipeg. Because I was working with my neighbor, I wasn't able to walk away and talk to my son privately. Instead, I turned on the speakerphone, hung the phone on the front of my shirt, and continued to work.

God had revealed to me just that morning a Scripture that required me to repent to my son concerning some mistakes I had made raising him some 18 years before. The neighbors listened to the conversation as we worked. When it was all over, they had some questions.

We sat down later and had some coffee as we talked. The neighbors' son, who was in his early thirties, told his dad that he (the father) needed to repent because he had done some of the same things I'd just confessed. A discussion then ensued on how repentance and forgiveness operate in the Kingdom. The net result was that the father, who was Catholic but didn't know Jesus personally, committed his life to Jesus.

Simple obedience to the prompting of the Spirit and a humble, open attitude will open doors to people's hearts. We might not always see the connection between what God tells us to do and the work He is trying to accomplish; yet, we can trust that the connection is real.

God always wants to commune with us and show us His purposes, so that we can join with Him in ruling His creation. Without our response, God's hands are tied even in bringing salvation to this world.

Do you want to be used to stop wars, end disease and cruelty, extinguish perversion and pain? Somebody is going to do it, but it won't be us unless we lay down our lives in obedience to Christ and make ourselves available on behalf of those who are captive.

Jesus heard from the Father. He didn't rebel no matter what He was called to do. Isaiah describes the attitude of Jesus: *"The Lord God hath opened Mine ear, and I was not rebellious, neither turned away back"* (Isa. 50:5).

If we are to be like Jesus, we can't rebel, either. God wants to establish us. Jesus said, *"Whosoever heareth these sayings of Mine, and doeth them, I will liken him unto a wise man, which built his house upon a rock"* (Matt. 7:24).

Even though storms will come, they won't bring us down. *"I am the Lord thy God which teacheth thee to profit, which leadeth thee....O that thou hadst* [listened] *to My commandments! Then had thy peace been as a river..."* (Isa. 48:17-18).

As we obey, we will be imbued with power and authority and even blessed, because *"...Blessed are they that hear the word of God, and keep it"* (Luke 11:28).

If we allow it to, the Word will touch every area of our lives. Years ago, we had a prayer group in which a discussion on tithing came up. Everyone agreed that tithing was in the Word and every couple, save one, responded to the Word and started to tithe. Everyone prospered except that one couple, who continued to struggle financially.

We need to change our minds to line up with the Word if we are to be blessed (see James 1:25). In some instances, Jesus questioned even the salvation of those who were disobedient, saying, *"And why call…Me, Lord, Lord, and do not the things, which I say?"* (Luke 6:46). *"Not every one that saith unto Me, Lord, Lord, shall enter into the kingdom of heaven; but he that doeth the will of My Father…"* (Matt. 7:21).

There is a door of obedience that opens unto a world of authority and power. On which side of the door will we choose to stand? Yes. The door is open to all. Jesus is that door. He invites us to push it open, change our thoughts and actions, and come into the Kingdom through Him (see John 10:9).

The question is, will we enter?

SHIFT INTO PRAYER

Lord, give us a willing heart to obey You. Open our ears to hear what You are saying. Open our eyes to Your Word so we can obey and do the things You are showing us to do in and through our lives. Cause us to be led by Your Spirit to choose life in You—the life that glorifies You most. Help us to shift our actions, always learning to become more like You. In Jesus' name.

Chapter 8

GIVE IT AWAY; PASS IT AROUND

Sacrifice: The Expensive Free Gift

JESUS said, *"If any man will come after Me, let him deny himself, and take up his cross daily, and follow Me. For whosoever will save his life shall lose it: but whosoever will lose his life for My sake...shall save it"* (Luke 9:23-24).

Denying ourselves means rejecting all our good ideas, ambitions, agendas, techniques, excuses, accusations, diversions, or pet projects that interfere with the plan God has for us.

Years ago, I (Ken) had a dream in which I was in the middle of a shallow ocean and my ship had sunk. I could still see its masts and hull about 15 feet below me. As I surveyed my predicament, I spotted several low islands surrounding me, arranged roughly in a circle.

Each island had a name, one was *Business*, another was *Education*, one was called *Success*, and so on. As I rotated in the water, the last island I saw was named *God's Will*. No other information was given; there was no hint what God's will might be.

Then God spoke, "I will bless you in whichever island you choose, but once you arrive there, you will not be able to reach any of the others."

The dream ended and I woke up knowing I had to make a choice. My ship was sunk and I couldn't stay where I was. I had to quickly make a life choice. I had to make a conscious decision to choose God's will at the expense of ever being able to choose another course. Making the choice was a form of death to me; I would need several lifetimes to even come close to finishing all the things I had started or wanted to start.

Knowing the other islands would have to be sacrificed, I chose to swim, rather slowly, toward the island called *God's Will*. If we are truly determined to follow Christ, we must reckon with the same spiritual juncture Peter traversed. When asked if he was going to leave Jesus, he replied, *"Lord, to whom shall we go? You have the words of eternal life"* (John 6:68 NKJV).

So even though we are talking about sacrifice as a means of stepping into power and authority, the only one who really sacrificed (gave up more for less) was Jesus. He left the realms of glory and intimacy with the Father to secure a place for us. We, by contrast, only give up the illusion of more for the reality of more.

CHOOSE TREASURES IN HEAVEN

Concerning this concept, renowned Christian missionary and martyr Jim Elliot said, "He is no fool who gives what he cannot keep to gain what he cannot lose."[1] Jesus' words agree, saying: *"Lay up for yourselves treasures in heaven, where neither moth nor rust doth corrupt, and where thieves do not break through nor steal"* (Matt. 6:20).

God comforts us with the guarantee that, when we follow Him, we lose nothing of value. All that said, there is one part of us that loses big time; that is our flesh. The flesh (the carnal mind) *"...is not subject to the law of God, neither indeed can be"* (Rom. 8:7).

I learned a long time ago that my flesh has a mind of its own. It is interested only in self-satisfaction and will not obey unless forced to do so. The mechanical part of the carnal mind is like a television receiver. It picks up whatever signals float about. It also continually replays the "old movies" stored in our memories. Needless to say, some of those images are contrary to a Christian lifestyle.

The only way to short-circuit the carnal mind is to change channels as soon as carnal images show up. This is the "off switch" I mentioned earlier; you could also call it the "don't-go-there" switch. Sin and temptation evaporate when we refuse to dwell on images conjured by the mind.

Problems start when we postpone throwing the switch and decide instead to process what we are seeing. Our flesh wants to linger and look. How long we choose to linger is telling; the speed at which I switch off mental images (or even actual television pictures) is usually a good indicator of where I am in my thought life.

You cannot lose this battle if you choose to win it. We are in total control of our choices. Overcoming this temptation takes the same skills required to overcome overeating or fits of anger—it takes discipline. This is why Christians are called *disciples,* or *disciplined ones.*

We are not volunteers in this war; we are disciples. Therefore, by the power of God we can rule over our bodies just as one day we will again rule over this creation.

Sacrifice is part of discipline. To sacrifice is to refuse our fleshly desires and crucify them on the cross. This is always painful. If we quit the process every time it hurts, then the pain (not God or us) will dictate our measure of success. The purpose of going to the cross is not to hang there and suffer forever. Rather, it is to put to death what is carnal.

Since the flesh doesn't want to die, it will kick and scream all the way to the cross. The best remedy? Put the flesh out of its misery quickly. Then, when it is dead, we are *"...freed from sin....*[and] *death hath no more dominion over* [us]*"* (Rom. 6:7,9).

Let me assure you that I no longer have a martyr complex; nor am I a masochist. Yet, I know something in me must die if I am going to win this war.

Let me also assure you that God is always faithful to keep His part of the bargain in making us more like Jesus. The rest is up to us to decide: will we keep our part willingly through the Spirit or reluctantly through the fire of circumstances?

In other words, will we choose to let the flesh suffer, or the spirit? I chose to sacrifice the flesh.

SEEDS SOWN

The rest of this chapter is written from the same perspective of "life and death" choices.

We know that to reap a harvest, a seed has to be sown. Spiritually speaking, that seed is the Word of God. Paul said that "...*what you sow is not made alive unless it dies....*[*The body*] *is sown in corruption, it is raised in incorruption. It is sown in dishonor, it is raised in glory....It is sown a natural body; it is raised a spiritual body*" (1 Cor. 15:36,42-44 NKJV).

Solomon declared, "*Cast your bread upon the waters, for you will find it after many days*" (Eccles. 11:1 NKJV). We must be willing to lose our seed when we sow it. Farmers sow seed in faith. They take grain that could have been sold, fed, or eaten by their livestock and they throw it out into a field and bury it. They have faith in the law of sowing and reaping and they understand how these laws work. Such farmers are mature.

Someone who is immature will not trust these laws because they don't understand the true value of things. You will never see a two-year old exchange the chocolate bar he is eating for a $1,000 bill. He can taste the value of the chocolate bar, but is unaware of the power of a $1,000 bill to purchase 1,000 more of them!

We are the same with spiritual things; we don't grasp their value. We compare them to the natural things we have or want, without realizing we are comparing apples to oranges. Unless we shift and operate on a higher plane than the natural, we will forgo spiritual blessings simply because we don't recognize their importance (their intrinsic value).

It's a matter of maturity. Paul, the apostle, exhibited his maturity by the things he valued. He said,

> *What things were gain to me, those I counted loss for*
> *Christ....I count all things but loss for the excellency of*
> *the knowledge of Christ Jesus my Lord: for whom I have*
> *suffered the loss of all things, and do count them but dung,*
> *that I may win Christ...that I may know Him, and the*
> *power of His resurrection, and the fellowship of His suffer-*
> *ings, being made conformable unto His death* (Philippians
> 3:7-8;10).

I still sacrifice, but I no longer consider it sacrifice, because God has always rewarded sacrifice with something greater than I could give.

Please understand that we are not talking about giving to get; the "blab it and grab it" or "name it and claim it" philosophy. I just know that whatever I give up, I get more value back. I left a job that was about an hour away from home to take a lesser-paying job that was within 20 minutes of our house. That move, based on the family-first principle, opened a financial door of opportunity that I am still walking through.

Our willingness to lay down everything that keeps us from God opens the door for Him to remove the things we see as hindrances.

We are the only ones who can stand in the way of our obtaining Christ. We often blame situations and circumstances for why we can't get somewhere in God. If we do, we are under a misconception. The truth is, that while our ambitions can be thwarted; our relationship in Christ cannot—not unless we allow diversions to restrict it.

In the quoted passage from Philippians, Paul explained that diversions could cost him relationship if he allowed them to. But

Paul saw the value of the riches of Christ, therefore he counted diversions as worthless by comparison.

Under divine direction, Jesus made the ultimate sacrifice. His flesh fought it to the end, but Jesus submitted. *"...He humbled Himself, and became obedient unto death, even the death of the cross"* (Phil. 2:8).

LAYING DOWN YOUR LIFE

Jesus had to put His flesh to death in order to allow His prophesied death on the cross. In the Greek, Mark's description of Jesus' death (see Mark 15:37) indicates that He had to "send his spirit away."[2]

Luke uses a more descriptive phrase (see Luke 23:46), saying Jesus "discharged his spirit to traverse or depart, piercing beyond or to the other side."[3] His flesh cooperated with His Spirit because it had learned suffering and sacrifice before (see Heb. 5:8). An athlete's body is able to go past what is comfortable because it has been disciplined to do so. The flesh doesn't enjoy suffering, but the spirit understands the crown to be gained.

When I (Ken) was in my teens, working on the farm, I learned what it was to push my body beyond its capacity. I remember helping the neighbors put up some silage on a quarter of land they had about 20 miles from the farmstead. We wanted to store the feed temporarily before we moved it back to the home place, so we packed it together right on the ground. A hired man named Dave packed the silage with a tractor while my friend Doug and I hauled it from the silage cutter.

The pile had grown to at least ten feet high when the tractor got too close to the edge of it and the tractor tipped over. It pinned Dave beneath it in such a way that he could not breath. I backed my truck up against the tractor and attempted to push it over, hoping to unpin Dave without killing him in the process.

It didn't work and I started to panic. Doug arrived at that point, too. Together, we tried to lift the seat off Dave's chest, but it wouldn't budge. Finally, with a swiftly sent up prayer, I grabbed the end of the seat and told Doug to pull on Dave.

With all the might I could muster, I pulled up on the seat and Doug slid Dave out from under the tractor. He recovered with no broken bones, but was bruised over his whole body.

It wasn't until we had the tractor righted that we saw what had happened. The two-inch steel channel that held the seat bent when I pulled on it—until it was at a 90 degree angle! It later took a torch and sledgehammers to straighten it out. It was clear that God had intervened, whether by sending an angel or by supplying superhuman strength to save Dave from suffocating.

We can, with God's help, go much further than we think we can. With Jesus as our example; we too will be able to do the works that He did. He promised as much, saying: *"...He that believeth on Me, the works that I do shall he do also; and greater works than these shall he do..."* (John 14:12).

God's definition of great works is slightly different from ours. It does not always involve our "doing." God prizes character development over accomplishments. His Word says: *"He that is slow to anger is better that the mighty; and he that ruleth his spirit than he that taketh a city"* (Prov. 16:32). To paraphrase: who we are is more important than what we do.

Character development accelerates when we come to the end of our own resources and let God take over. That is why Jesus never condemns us when we can't perform. He allows circumstances to aid us in our desire to look more like Him. He is waiting for the death of our self-life because *"...unless a grain of wheat falls into the ground and dies, it remains alone; but if it dies, it produces much grain"* (John 12:24 NKJV).

Ken and I were ministering to a couple that was having major marital problems. We were committed to helping them but, because of wrong thought patterns, Ken's advice to the husband was not well received by the wife. She wanted resolution, however, and continued to come to our house for personal ministry.

We had been under attack from people who had opinions, but not facts, about how we should deal with this situation. Ken had one very nasty call at 1:00 A.M.; it came from an outside party, challenging Ken's biblical advice.

The next day, the wife came for ministry. Another woman and I sat down to work with her. While I was ministering to her, the session deteriorated into an attack against Ken and his advice.

I started to get very angry. Ken had given scriptural counsel, but because of her own strongholds, the wife could not agree with the Word. I reacted poorly to her attacks and yelled at her to leave my house.

I could hardly believe my own reaction, as I normally respond in love and gentleness. The Holy Spirit convicted me of my anger; I remembered the Scripture that says, *"The wrath of man does not produce the righteousness of God"* (James 1:20 NKJV). I apologized to the wife for my outburst of anger. I truly loved her, but I also loved my husband and would not tolerate any negativity about him.

Normally, this woman could not handle anyone yelling at her, but the Holy Spirit kept her from running away. I also wanted to run away. Instead, both of us sacrificed the flesh and chose life. I wanted to see and her marriage made whole. She wanted to keep our friendship alive and see her marriage restored. Ten years later, both the marriage and the friendship are thriving.

Again, there must be a death for life to come. The apostles learned this early and could state with certainty that we *"...are always delivered unto death for Jesus' sake, that the life also of Jesus might be made manifest in our mortal flesh. So then death worketh in us, but life in you"* (2 Cor. 4:11-12).

To produce life in people, we must die to ourselves. Before we minister to them, pray for them, lay hands on them, or witness to them, we need only to die. Out of that death will come all acts of love needed to bring life.

ALL FOR OTHERS

In his apostolic position, Paul walked out this death in obedience to God saying:

> ...God hath set forth us the apostles last, as it were appointed to death: for we are made a spectacle unto the world, and to angels and to men. We are fools for Christ's sake...we are weak...we are despised...we both hunger, and thirst, and are naked, and are buffeted and have no certain dwelling place... (1 Corinthians 4:9-11).

Paul's authority, gained by laying down his life, allowed him to say "...ye [have] *not many fathers: for in Christ Jesus I have begotten you...*" (1 Cor. 4:15). Fathers produce children, but they must lay down their lives for them.

Mothers also sacrifice for their children. They change their eating habits while pregnant; they stop smoking and drinking; and they are extra careful not to bump themselves and the baby. After the baby is born, mothers get up during the night to feed and change their babies. These are sacrificial acts: it is the laying down of the parent's life and comfort so the baby can have life.

Sacrifice is always part of family and spiritual life—and it yields authority. We can gain this authority if we overcome our fears. One of the most common fears that hinder us is the fear of the unknown, which is essentially a fear of death in a certain area of one's life.

Here's the good news: once you have died and been resurrected (received sanctification) in a particular area, the fear of dying to self ends. In fact, we are to arm ourselves (get strong) by suffering (see 1 Pet. 4:1).

This is how an athlete brings his or her body into submission and becomes eligible for victory. I learned this while playing football. A large hill bordered our football practice field. By running up this hill, we used it to gain endurance. The drill was designed for us to make two cycles up the hill and then to race across the field to the goal line. Some of the guys would hide in the bushes and pick up the pack as they came by the second time. Their goal was to do the drill with as little pain as possible. The coaches' goal was to get us in shape.

I loved that drill even though my body rebelled against it. I liked to push my body and make it my servant. I especially enjoyed beating the guys who rested for the one lap. I defeated my fears of not making the team by sacrificing my body and making it my servant. I was one of the 30 players that beat out another 130 guys to make the team.

This is how Jesus won for us the victory over sin. *"…He appeared to put away sin by the sacrifice of Himself"* (Heb. 9:26). We are to enter into His ministry by rejoicing *"…in* [our] *sufferings for* [others], *and fill up that which is behind of the afflictions of Christ in* [our] *flesh for His body's sake, which is the church"* (Col. 1:24).

Paul is not saying that Christ's work on the cross is not complete. He is talking about the work of Christ in salvation being extended and our entering into it. Christ's suffering and sacrifice brought life to us originally. Our suffering and sacrifice can further enhance that life to the Body.

A similar concept is seen in the Garden. God planted it, but Adam was to guard and work it. In our case, God has allowed us to work in His harvest field. Being willing to enter into Christ's suffering is for the sake of the Church's edification. This is how we are to minister.

Jeanne and I dealt with a couple where the husband had gotten into sexual lust. During ministry, we encouraged the wife to vent her anger, which she had continually suppressed. The husband took offense at our techniques and later told others how abusive we were in ministry. He was neither repentant, nor willing to say why the ministry had been undertaken in the first place. We, under the obligation of confidentiality, could not disclose the issue. With this veil of silence, we would not defend our actions. We were forced to let our reputations take a hit.

The psalmist said to God "...*You have magnified Your word above... Your name*" (Ps. 138:2 NKJV). My word is my bond, which determines my integrity; my name is just my reputation. The final outcome of the ministry was that this couple healed their relationship and are prospering in their marriage.

Sometimes, we must make a shift in our priorities and sacrifice even our reputations if we are to keep our integrity and bring life to others.

This truth is further explained in the Scripture that describes Paul's "*bearing about in the body the dying of the Lord Jesus, that the life also of Jesus might be made manifest in our body*" (2 Cor. 4:10).

An Old Testament type of bearing death in the body is seen when Joseph's bones were carried across the desert during the exodus (see Josh. 24:32). This story demonstrates the dichotomy of the Christian walk: The people carried a mummy (the picture of death) while the nation was experiencing a birth after its slavery in Egypt.

It was, however, an expression of faith, and as a result, Joseph, though dead, was one of the only three that left Egypt that was allowed to inherit the land. Even death cannot separate us from the promises of God!

So then "*unto you it is given in the behalf of Christ, not only to believe on Him, but also to suffer for His sake*" (Phil. 1:29). This is an important part of our calling. Yet, because it is not gratifying to the flesh, we too often reject it. As a result, our children stand to inherit a powerless Church. Meanwhile, occultist groups (the new age, occultist practioners, and religious cults) are filling the void.

Any preaching on holiness that does not include a laying down of our lives has the ring of hypocrisy to our kids. To the world at large, the Church is often seen as being unloving. Why? Because people understand intuitively that real soldiers fight real wars and die to free those they love. We haven't been willing to die for each other even though Jesus said, *"Greater love hath no man than this, that a man lay down his life for his friends"* (John 15:13).

BEARING BURDENS

When I (Jeanne) was in the hospital recovering from abdominal surgery, two friends, Brenda and Myrna, came to visit me. Both women had to drive a long way and arrange care for their children.

On that day, I was in intense pain and started throwing up a green mess. Since I hadn't eaten for several days, vomiting indicated intestinal blockage. Immediately, the doctor sent me for X-rays. If there was a blockage, I would need immediate additional surgery.

Brenda and Myrna started to intercede for me. They prayed that God would clear up whatever was causing this complication. They were shooed out of the room as the nurses prepared me for tests. They stood in the hall praying in tongues as people curiously passed by them. They were slightly embarrassed, but died to their feelings in order to bring relief to me.

They waited and prayed until I returned from my tests, which was quite a while. We rejoiced to discover that their prayers had worked; the doctors could find no blockage. We thanked God that I didn't require another surgery.

These women were faithful to help bear my burden when I needed it most. The Scripture is full of this theme. Paul captures it with these words: *"...be thou partaker of the afflictions of the gospel according to the power of God"* (2 Tim. 1:8).

Burden-bearing does not come easily; it comes at a price. Remember, we are in a war. Therefore, we should not *"think it... strange concerning the fiery trial which is to try you...but rejoice, inasmuch as ye are partakers of Christ's sufferings; that, when His glory shall be revealed, ye may be glad.... If ye be reproached for the name of Christ, happy are ye; for the spirit of glory and of God resteth upon you:"* (1 Pet. 4:12-14).

This thought is so contrary to our view of power and authority that we cannot comprehend how suffering (and the associated appearance of weakness) makes us strong. Weakness is what the enemy sees; we are actually resting in God's strength. Then, like Christ, *"…we are accounted as sheep for the slaughter.* [But], *in all these things we are more than conquerors through Him that loved us"* (Rom. 8:36-37).

All these verses point to the same truth: Suffering produces power to overcome what we are suffering. Jesus didn't just go to the cross and die for us; He also rose again to bring us life. One day, the disciples were in grief and defeat; the next they were rejoicing at His victory.

It is the same way today. We must not look only at what we can see; we must also look to Him who is invisible and seated on the throne of power.

We once booked a plane ticket for a young man in our church in whom we saw great potential. The ticket was to enable him to go with us to a Morningstar Conference in Charlotte, North Carolina. He first got permission from his parents, then we paid for the ticket. Suddenly, everything changed. His father, who has a medically defined mental disorder, had an attack of fear.

The father became paranoid over his son leaving and accused us of trying to destroy his family. After a long session on the phone, I went over to their house to try and reason with him. I sat with this man for three hours as he went on a verbal attack, swearing at me and threatening me. In the end, we lost the price of the ticket and the young man missed a great conference.

God gave me a special grace to endure the assault that came our way. I believed that we would be rewarded for being called evil when all we were trying to do was to bless others. Sure enough, within a few weeks someone felt led to donate the exact amount that we had lost on the ticket price. (Later, this young man married and he and his wife came and gave us a gift. They said God had prospered them and told them to give us a check. It was for three times the amount we had originally lost). God was training us to endure suffering, realizing it is good for us. Our hope is that *"...after...ye have suffered a while,* [God will] *make you perfect, stablish, strengthen, settle you"* (1 Pet. 5:10).

To function this way we must have our mind-sets changed to *"... prove what is that good, and acceptable, and perfect, will of God"* (Rom. 12:2). If we know what God wants and we trust Him then we are able to *"...present* [our] *bodies a living sacrifice, holy, acceptable unto God..."* (Rom. 12:1).

Not every sacrifice is dramatic. A sacrifice can be something as simple as letting others talk when you are bursting at the seams with something to say. Regardless of the perceived magnitude, sacrifice always requires thinking about others and their good above our own.

Your sacrifice may come in the form of a prayer or blessing. It may mean helping and encouraging others. Whatever it is, sacrifice must always cost you something, otherwise it is not a sacrifice.

The law commanded the best of our first fruits be offered to the Lord. The same is true of what we give to Him as we bless others. For this reason, Jeanne buys jewelry to have on hand. That way, she always has something special to give when the Spirit moves her to bless someone.

THE COST

David walked out this principle when he bought the threshing floor from Ornan. David said to him:

> Grant me...this threshing floor...for the full price: that the plague may be stayed.... And Ornan said unto David, ... Lo, I give thee the oxen also for burnt offerings...and the

threshing instruments...and the wheat...I give it all....
David said... Nay; but I will...buy it for the full price:...I
will not...offer burnt offerings without cost....[And the
Lord] *answered* [David] *from heaven by fire upon the*
altar... (1 Chronicles 21:22-24; 26).

God responded to the sacrifice with a demonstration of His power. David knew that the offering had to cost him something to be accepted. He was not only willing, but also desirous to pay the cost.

God is pleased when we are willing, not constrained, to follow in His footsteps. God said, *"Be...not as the horse, or as the mule... whose mouth must be held in with bit and bridle..."* (Ps. 32:9). Indeed the mature are able bear the weight for others. Jesus *"...hath borne our griefs, and carried our sorrows..."* (Isa. 53:4).

God allowed Jeanne and me to take in her sister and kids when she and her husband were going through a rough stretch in their marriage. We were privileged to give them shelter for six weeks. Likewise, we interceded for our own children when satan was trying to draw them away from God. This is our calling to sacrifice. If we can take these opportunities to serve God, we will joyfully participate with the Spirit of God in loving His creation.

Sacrificial love insists that we should bear one another, but not for an earthly reward. If we seek glory or praise or even thankfulness from those to whom we minister, then we will forfeit praise from God. The Pharisees did this. They sought recognition from men. Jesus warned us, saying, *"Take heed that ye do not your alms* [good deeds] *before men, to be seen of them: otherwise ye have no reward of your Father which is in heaven"* (Matt. 6:1).

FALSE SACRIFICES

In other words, everything we do must be for God, not for self or for people. If God is not the motivator for an action, then our flesh is. The Bible tells me that *"...in my flesh...dwelleth no good thing..."* (Rom. 7:18) and *"...the flesh profiteth nothing..."* (John 6:63).

Therefore, even with seemingly the best motives, if I do it out of my flesh, it will not be of any use to the Kingdom. In fact, because the flesh wars against the Spirit, we will actually frustrate the grace of God that is available for the situation when we act presumptuously. We must have the mind of God even when we are trying to be compassionate.

Jeanne and I once rented a house to a couple who said they were Christians. They had a hard luck story and we felt compassion for them. We took a damage deposit, but let them move in two weeks early, before they paid any rent. That damage deposit was the only money we ever received from them. They were immature in dealing with their finances. We finally had to go to court and even arrange for the sheriff to evict them before we could get them out.

This couple even got some of the church leadership to come to settle the dispute. Fortunately, the elders had more wisdom and less misguided compassion than we did and properly saw the scam for what it was.

All too late, we checked with the church they had attended and learned they had a pattern of doing this. Their trick was to con some gullible Christian into renting them a place. Then they would sit in it for six months or a year until they were finally kicked out. Even the utility companies could not collect from this couple.

All the while, God wanted to reform them; we actually delayed that process. Compassion is a poor substitute for a God-ordained sacrifice. Our thoughts are not God's; we must shift our habit of listening to the wrong voices. We must hear the voice of the Spirit.

CHANGING FRUIT

The battle is in our minds; we have to allow God's thoughts and perspective or vision to become ours. God wants to access His creation, but He requires us to plant seeds so that He can legally produce the fruit.

Suffering and sacrifice are seeds that God can use. Jesus calls us to *"...endure hardship as a good soldier of Jesus Christ"* (2 Tim. 2:3 NKJV). As Paul said, *"I endure all things for the sake of the elect..."* (2 Tim. 2:10 NKJV).

God wants us to always see Him as a rewarder (see Heb. 11:6). Suffering always has a reward attached to it. *"For if we be dead with Him, we shall also live with Him: If we suffer, we shall also reign with Him..."* (2 Tim. 2:11-12). This is our ultimate goal: to *"...know Him, and the power of His resurrection and the fellowship of His sufferings, being made conformable unto His death"* (Phil. 3:10).

I (Ken) have been laughed at, ridiculed, and persecuted at work for my faith, but I don't see it as something to shun. Rather, it is something to embrace. All those people who persecute me need God. If I can act like Jesus, then He can speak through me. I enjoy being a witness for Him.

Once, when the phones went out at a job site on Lake Wabamun, the superintendent joked with me, saying I should walk on water across the lake so he could communicate with the crew on the other side.

Enjoy the joking. It shows seeking people that you are secure in God's love for you. I've been able to share Christ and lead someone to the Lord on every job I've worked. Few people really hate Christians; most have endured hurtful experiences and are afraid of God.

The greatest thing we can have on earth is fellowship with God. Adam walked in that fellowship in the Garden. The thing that separated Israel from the rest of the nations was that God was present in their midst. Any kind of fellowship is a privilege—even the fellowship of suffering. Remember, God is just; He sees all. Jesus said:

> *Blessed are they which are persecuted for righteousness' sake: for theirs is the kingdom of heaven. Blessed are ye, when men shall revile you, and persecute you, and say all*

manner of evil against you falsely, for My sake. Rejoice,
and be exceeding glad: for great is your reward in heaven:
for so persecuted they the prophets which were before you
(Matthew 5:10-12).

Jesus has just proposed what seems to be an oxymoron: *Rejoice because you are persecuted.* We've talked before about thanking God for our hardships. We must also remember, in the midst of the hardship, to be real with God and honest with ourselves. We need to pause and say, "Holy Spirit, I need Your help. I cannot rejoice in trouble without it." Whenever our mind-sets, experience, doctrine, or beliefs don't line up with what the Word is saying, we must be willing to change our point of view, knowing He *will* help us.

Faith is not meant to be blind. *"Faith is the substance of things hoped for, the evidence of things not seen"* (Heb. 11:1). We can ask God to reveal His wisdom and unravel the mysteries whenever we reach points of dichotomy or confusion. He knows that we need to see the final victory that our suffering helps to purchase if we are going to joyfully buy into the suffering process.

Suffering is not pleasant, but it often provides the impetus to move out of the realm where the suffering occurs and into a realm of glory. Neither is suffering strictly for situations in religious or spiritual contexts.

Ken and I have found that we always must bring our flesh under control or it will try and control us. I suffer from diabetes, partially because I let my weight get out of control. Since I brought my appetite under control and started exercising, I have lost 50 pounds. My eyeglass prescription has been reduced twice; so has my thyroid dosage.

I (Ken) had to learn how to repent. I've already explained how hard this was for me. Repenting meant that I had done something wrong; therefore I was bad and God couldn't love me.

Instead, repenting proved to be my door to freedom from guilt and shame. My thyroid medication has also reduced. We must believe that if *"...we suffer with Him...we may be also glorified together....The sufferings of this present time are not worthy to be compared with the glory which shall be revealed in us"* (Rom. 8:17-18).

IT WILL BE WORTH IT

Paul made this point another way, saying:

> *...though our outward man perish, yet the inward man is rewarded day by day. For our light affliction, which is but for a moment, worketh for us a far more exceeding and eternal weight of glory* (2 Corinthians 4:16-17).

A small seed of joyful suffering produces a great harvest of glory. This is why a national church under siege grows so dramatically. What is the old motto? "The seed of the church is in the blood of the martyrs."[4]

Jim Elliot and his three partners died attempting to reach out to Auca Indians in South America. Their deaths and the subsequent loving response of Jim's widow opened a whole tribe to the glories of the Gospel. When I first heard of their deaths, I thought, "What a waste." They never even got to speak before they were killed. It wasn't until later that I understood how sacrifice operates in the Kingdom of God.

Sacrifice is so foreign to what the Church has attempted to do lately. We have tried to be acceptable to the ways of this present age. We have been people-orientated rather than God-orientated. We have taken the sacrifice and the blood out of our walk and tried to be a big happy family. We try not to alienate anyone or make any enemies.

The result: The Church can't call sin, *sin*. We are losing members faster than we can replace them. Our children are bored; our divorce rate is as high as the world's rate; we are accepting abortions; we accept homosexual practices; and we can't even preach tithing.

Why? For fear we might offend someone or some group. We might be called fanatical or even religious. But our efforts to please the world are misguided. We weren't called to be just another part of society; we came to rescue society. Our citizenship is in Heaven; we are only pilgrims here.

The term *cult* was first applied to Christians because they were culturally different from the Roman Empire. The early Church believed that "[we] *are dead, and* [our lives are] *hid with Christ in God"* (Col. 3:3). These early believers were intimate with God and bold in their stance. They knew that when *"the sufferings of Christ abound in us, so our consolation also aboundeth by Christ. And whether we be afflicted, it is for your consolation and salvation..."* (2 Cor. 1:5-6).

They recognized that what happened to them didn't affect only them. They understood that the Kingdom of God is not limited by time and space; God resides outside of the physical realm. The seed we sow in suffering opens prison doors and sets captives free as far as our realm of authority reaches. It is like a pebble dropping into a pool; the ripples go right out to the edge and after a time come back again.

A LIFESTYLE

So what we do in worship and intercession or just dying to self can and does change the spiritual climate of a whole area. If the area responds to the new wave of life, it can splash over whole provinces and states, which, in turn, can change a nation.

I (Ken) was once asked if I would take a demotion because I had the skills that were required for a critical task performed below my foreman rank. I was opposed to the demotion because it would cost me income but, after prayer, I was prompted to accept it. I moved out of the foreman's shack into the lunchroom with the men.

The whole job was under a negative spirit that caused everybody to constantly complain about supervision and all other aspects of the construction. When I would come home after work, Jeanne often mentioned that I seemed a little off. She discerned that a negative spirit was over the jobsite, so we began to repent and pray against it.

I asked God what I could do to help. He suggested I start a chess tournament during our breaks. That simple act changed the belligerence into excitement. Men no longer grumbled and complained about the leadership of the job. They studied chess moves and strategies and began encouraging one another.

An entirely different spirit took over the site. God wants us to make a difference no matter what our realm, even if we have to be demoted to do it. My willingness to take a lower position allowed the jobsite and crew to be blessed. If we are willing to shift from the concerns that center on our individual well-being and concentrate instead on the greater good, God can give us authority and power over the enemy.

Jeremiah watched the potter flatten (demote) a clay vessel because he felt a hard lump in it. The pot was almost finished, but the potter wanted it to be perfect (see Jeremiah 18:4). Let's trust God to remove those things that would keep us from being vessels of which He is proud. We must learn not to complain, but to rejoice that He loves us enough not to leave us as we are.

RELEASING POWER

Jesus gave His disciples the "heads up" on what would take place in Christian's lives during the last days. He warned them of opposition, saying:

> ...they shall...persecute you, delivering you up to the synagogues, and into prisons, being brought before kings and rulers for My name's sake. And it shall turn to you for a testimony (Luke 21:12-13).

God was going to use trouble to give them a testimony. He was laying up treasure for them in Heaven. All the troubles God brings our way are to be used for the Kingdom's advantage.

Our son James developed schizophrenia 15 years ago. Our journey through this tragedy has drawn us closer to each other and to God. Our family's healing resulted in healing for thousands of other people, who profited from our experiences.

We compiled the principles God taught us into a course that teaches people how to remove generational curses from their families. Jeanne's experience with cancer brought us a new understanding of how to operate in faith for healing. Even the storms we experienced with our kids taught us how to navigate through certain difficulties.

God places doors of hope in valleys of trouble (see Hosea 2:15) to allow us to access knowledge and power that we would never have discovered otherwise. Though we would never pray to have these problems, when we come out the other side, we know the sacrifice has been worth it and has shifted our approach to difficulties.

Paul recognized the process and could confidently declare:

> ...we glory in tribulations also: knowing that tribulation worketh patience; and patience, experience; and experience, hope: and hope maketh not ashamed... (Romans 5:3-5).

The seed of suffering is the fast track to maturity in our lives and, therefore, in the release of power. There is a story in the Old Testament that demonstrates the principle of how sacrifice releases power.

The Scriptures tell us that the king of Moab was trapped and about to be defeated when "...he took his oldest son who was to reign in his place, and offered him as a burnt offering on the wall. And there came great wrath against Israel..." (2 Kings 3:27 NASB).

The sacrifice of his son released demonic forces against Israel and they had to back off from their assault. Principles or laws work on both sides of the fence. This is why satanic rituals still use blood sacrifices today. Satan will always counterfeit God's ways for the sake of acquiring power. But God released the ultimate power of blood when His son sacrificed Himself.

I (Ken) went on a Daniel's fast once for 21 days (no meat or sweets). At the end of the fast, I got a prophetic word that dramatically affected my decisions concerning work and ministry. The sacrifice of food released a spiritual dynamic that brought clarity and power into my life.

This principle works corporately, too. The church that we are in now started because five couples united and sacrificed by double-tithing, believing for a church in the area.

We have never truly understood the impact that sacrifice can have. All sacrifices are not dramatic, but all are effective. *"The sacrifices of God are a broken spirit...and a contrite heart..."* (Ps. 51:17).

God wants us to use His Spirit as our defense. We have to sacrifice our own soul power and force of our will to accomplish God's purposes. In the *Star Wars* trilogy, Luke was tempted to use the "dark side of the force" by allowing his anger to win him a battle. The same temptation is thrown at us. What we may not realize is this: When we use our own force, we are actually using demonic forces (see James 3:15).

As soon as we tap into those powers we are trapped. *"...To whom ye yield yourselves servants to obey, his servants ye are to whom ye obey; whether of sin unto death, or of obedience unto righteousness..."* (Rom. 6:16). We cannot use demonic structures to accomplish godly goals.

Our soul power is not godly.

WINNING AT ANY COST

Jesus said that if satan fights satan, his kingdom will fall (see Luke 11:18). The only reason satan will allow you to win using his weapons is because then you will become a greater evil than that which you defeat.

We have witnessed lately the fall of many religious leaders. Often, an overemphasis on some sin is an indication that something is wrong before it is fully exposed.

Such preoccupations usually come from unhealed wounds. These wounds leave us spiritually vulnerable. To go into a war wounded is to invite disaster. Satan is a predator. He loves to feed on wounded warriors; he needs our power—as much as he can get—to function. And he will use every means at his disposal to get it.

God, by contrast, always teaches us to come in the opposite spirit to that which guides the enemy's attack. We are to be *"…patient in tribulation…"* (Rom. 12:12) and *"…bless them, which persecute* [us]; *bless, and curse not"* (Rom. 12:14). We're commanded to *"recompense to no man evil for evil…"* (Rom. 12:17), *"…not rendering evil for evil, or railing for railing: but contrariwise blessing…"* (1 Pet. 3:9).

All these actions require us to understand that the Kingdom of God operates under different rules from the kingdom that satan has tried to maintain here on earth—and God's Kingdom will always prevail!

All the persecution that I have received on various job sites (all of which were designed to hurt me) provided instead an open door for me to witness. At the mine where I worked, I was able to share my faith with more than 200 men over the course of four years. I also had the privilege of leading a dozen souls to the Lord.

I (Ken) was removed from teaching an adult Sunday school class because it became too popular. I couldn't understand at the time how that could glorify God, but because I let that class go, God has allowed me to minister to the larger body of Christ.

We can trust that God is a God of justice. We know it is so because He said, *"Vengeance is Mine; I will repay"* (Rom. 12:19). Therefore, we don't have to worry about temporary losses. We can even welcome, as the disciples did, an opportunity to suffer loss because we know, as they did, that God has something better for us than a painless life.

By faith...

> *...others were tortured, not accepting deliverance; that they might obtain a better resurrection ...others had trial of cruel mocking and scourgings...bonds and imprisonment; they were stoned...sawn asunder...tempted...slain with the sword...wandered about...destitute, afflicted, tormented; and these all...through faith received not the promise: God having provided some better thing for us, that they without us should not be made perfect....Seeing we... are compassed about with so great a cloud of witnesses, let us lay aside every weight and...sin...and run...the race... set before us* (Hebrews 11:35-37; 39-40–12:1).

These saints were willing to suffer and seemingly not receive His justice in their lifetimes. They saw something more and refused justice for the opportunity to enter in with us (in the last days). They joined their faith with ours in bringing about the Kingdom of God to earth. This subject is too deep to be dealt with here, but it is a mystery that God is about to reveal to this generation.

THE GOD OF RESTORATION

We exhibit our beliefs by our actions. If we know that God has covenanted with us to supply all our needs as He did Abraham, then we can tithe as Abraham did. We will not be bound with the thought, "I can't afford this," for we know that He who told us to tithe also said He would supply all our needs (see Phil. 4:19).

In fact, in God's economy, nothing is ever lost: it simply changes form. This law is mirrored in the physical realm as stated in the first law of thermodynamics, which states: "Energy is neither created nor destroyed, it only changes form."[5]

If nothing is ever lost, then by faith we can claim back everything that has been stolen. Even family destinies that have been lost will be restored to the one who has faith to pick them up.

The law says that when a "...*thief is caught, he shall pay double*" (Exod. 22:7 NASB). Even if we are robbed, God will not allow us to lose the seed sown in hope. If we trust His Word and allow ourselves to be defrauded, that seed will appear through another source.

We need to believe and always come to the battle in the opposite spirit of the enemy. Paul asked, "...*Why do ye not rather take wrong? why do ye not rather suffer yourselves to be defrauded?*" (1 Cor. 6:7). Our answer to Paul's question would have to be that we are not willing to take wrong because we really don't believe God will look after us. We are not 100 percent confident of the benefits of walking according to Kingdom principles.

Jeanne and I were sitting at a table with friends waiting for a wedding reception to start. A couple came in and brashly stated that we were sitting where they wanted to sit. Jeanne immediately jumped up and offered them our seats. I was taken aback, but Jeanne led the way to a lower seat. I can imagine their chagrin when they heard us called up to give the speech to the bride and groom. We never have to fight for ourselves as long as we are submitted to God.

We often don't trust that if we obey Him, God will look after us. Because of that, He often can't. We are too independent and determined to look after our own affairs. People still believe the Bible says, "God helps those who help themselves." It does not.

Our efforts to defend ourselves are really efforts to keep our lives within our own control. The Bible says that "...*whosoever will save his life shall lose it: but whosoever will lose his life for My sake...shall save it*" (Luke 9:24). If we want power, we need to act in the opposite way of the world and of satan and even allow our lives (reputations, opinions, and desires) to die.

In dying comes victory.

...Now is come salvation, and strength, and the kingdom of our God, and the power of His Christ: for the accuser of our brethren is cast down.... And they overcame him by the blood of the Lamb, and by the word of their testimony; and they loved not their lives unto the death (Revelation 12:10-11).

All of these aspects, including dying to (as in not loving) our lives, must be present to overcome the devil. If we are willing to let Jesus reign freely in us, we can do it.

The point of our sacrificing our lives is not just to die, but to change the way we think so we can really live. The Jews didn't leave Egypt just to get out. God wanted to take them into the Promised Land.

So it is with us—"*...not...that we would be unclothed, but clothed upon, that mortality might be swallowed up of life*" (2 Cor. 5:4).

We are sowing seed in death expecting to reap life, not just in this time, but also into eternity. We are committing all we have into God's hands, trusting that He can bring a harvest out of our sacrifice.

It is a biblical truth that "*all that will live godly in Christ Jesus shall suffer persecution*" (2 Tim. 3:12). We must come to terms with this truth, and we do so by consciously shifting the way we think.

It's time to embrace suffering, for it is the gateway to power and authority.

SHIFT INTO PRAYER

Lord, help us to be that grain of wheat that falls into the ground, dies, and bears much fruit. Help us to die to the flesh and reap in the Spirit. Cause us to yield not 20-fold, or 40-fold, or 60-fold , but 100-fold fruit in our lives for the sake of others. In Jesus' name.

ENDNOTES

1. Elliot,Elisabeth, ed. *The Journals of Jim Elliot* (Grand Rapids, MI: Fleming H. Revell, 1978), 174.

2. Zodhaites,Spiros. *The Complete Word Study Dictionary: New Testament* (Chattanooga: AMG Publishers, 1992), s.v., 863, 575.

3. Ibid., s.v., 1606, 4198, 3984.

4. Tertullian, *The Apology*, 197 A.D. (Quotation is a paraphrase of: "The blood of Christians is seed.")

5. iptv.org/exploremore/energy/energy_in_depth/sections/potential.cfm.

Chapter 9

THE TWO PILLARS

Mercy and Justice Properly Represent God

I laugh when I see the portraits of Jesus painted by the old masters during the Reformation. He is portrayed as a milquetoast, lovingly and softly touching His world.

The Church must be portraying the same image to the world today, for we, as the Church, are neither loved nor hated. We are inconsequential as far as the media world perceives us. Politicians often suggest that we go back to our cloisters and stop interfering with the rough-and-tumble "real" world.

It's time for a reality check. The Church does not exist to blend into the background. History is *His story* and the Church is *His* Body, equipped to do His bidding at all times. Therefore, a shift must occur for both the Church and the world. Both must reckon with the assignment of the Church to a leading role in the world story.

God is both merciful and just. He wouldn't be God if He weren't. The world mistakes His goodness for permissiveness. Therefore, the world responds to God much as Pharaoh did when Moses demanded Israel's release from slavery. Pharaoh replied haughtily saying, *"Who is the Lord, that I should obey...? I know not the Lord, neither will I let Israel go....get you unto your* [labors]*"* (Exod. 5:2,4.) In other words, "What are you talking about? Shut up and get back to work."

Pharaoh believed himself invulnerable to Moses' God. He would soon experience a reality check. The Pharisees were just like Pharaoh. They had the power in their realm and expected God to work within their thought patterns. Then Jesus showed up, not "meek and mild," but in the full manifestation of divine authority and spoke the truth about the Pharisees' attitudes. He blasted them, saying:

> *They tie up heavy burdens and lay them on men's shoulders.... But they do all their deeds to be noticed.... They love the place of honor...and the chief seats...and respectful greetings....But woe to you ...hypocrites, because you shut off...heaven from people; for you do not enter in... you devour widows' houses...for a pretense you make long prayers....[You] make one [convert who becomes] ...twice as much a son of hell as yourselves. Woe to you, blind guides...inside [you] are full of robbery and self-indulgence...[and] dead men's bones and all uncleanness.... You...outwardly appear righteous...but inwardly you are full of hypocrisy and lawlessness....you are sons of those who murdered the prophets. You serpents, you brood of vipers, how will you escape...hell?...upon you may fall the guilt of all the righteous blood shed on earth...* (Matthew 23:4-7;13-16; 25,27-28; 31,33,35 NASB)

Whoa! I wouldn't want to be on the receiving end of that tirade. Right in the middle of His judgment against the Pharisees, Jesus described the characteristic of true disciples of the law. Jesus calls these characteristics *"...the weightier provisions of the law: justice and mercy and faithfulness..."* (Matt. 23:23 NASB).

Justice is defined as the virtue that consists of giving everyone his due. The Latin roots are *jus,* meaning "law or right."[1] The Hebrew root that was translated *mercy* means "to bow in kindness, grace and compassion."[2]

Jesus wants us to faithfully apply mercy and justice in every situation. We are not to be fickle in our application, but loving and honest as God is when He deals with us.

God's justice is balanced. *"The Lord is longsuffering, and of great mercy, forgiving iniquity and transgression, and by no means clearing the guilty..."* (Num. 14:18). The world wonders how God can both forgive and yet not clear the guilty. Yet that is the sign of a good Father—He forgives a child yet disciplines and brings consequences (see Heb. 12:7).

Discipline or judgment is actually an act of mercy and love. *"For those whom the Lord loves, He disciplines....He disciplines us for our good, so that we may share His holiness"* (Heb. 12:6,10 NASB).

Our problems understanding God's actions reflects on our upbringing. Many of us were disciplined harshly and without love. The perception then becomes that all discipline is hard and cold. Our lenses become distorted and we misunderstand godly discipline. God is not like our earthly fathers. He loves and everything He does is out of love (see John 3:16). Therefore, we need to repent (change our thinking) and be healed (see Heb. 12:13).

Soon after we bought our house, a young man broke into it. He wrecked the basement door and stole some food, money, clothes, and some comic books belonging to our kids. He was a friend of our son and we didn't suspect him of the break-in. He eventually went to jail due to a series of other burglaries he had committed.

While in jail, God started to convict him and he phoned me (Ken). I forgave him, led him to the Lord, and ministered to him over the next few months. I was able to show mercy, but God had another item on His agenda: He wanted to strengthen the young man through godly justice. God's discipline did not scare him off. Instead the young man found the Lord and the courage to reveal his sin and ask our forgiveness—in the midst of his incarceration.

God had to train me (Ken) to shift from my natural thought patterns so that I could learn how to discipline in love. In my earlier years, I had administered most of my discipline (actually punishment) because my children did things that irritated me. But God doesn't discipline us for making mistakes; He disciplines us for our disobedience.

Mistakes are errors in judgment, not a sign of rebellion. Real authority does not try to force obedience; that is just an exercise of raw power. Real authority and godly covering attracts people to come under and submit because it is profitable for them.

If children are not free to make mistakes, they will always be afraid to attempt anything new. Punishment for mistakes is manipulation; correction for disobedience is training for consequences. We discipline and correct, not for our satisfaction, but, rather, to prepare our children to come under God's rule, which is His Kingdom.

When we warn our children to avoid touching a hot stove, we are not trying to stifle their curiosity; we just want to keep them from getting hurt. If they won't listen, we bring discipline. If they still won't listen and they do it again, the stove will bring discipline. Either way, they will learn: Touch a hot stove and you will get burnt.

BALANCED JUSTICE

Our friends Ron and Brenda were having marital problems many years ago. They were not talking and were unable to find a solution. Ron was also having trouble with lust and had started phoning a 900 number to satisfy his craving.

Ron had carefully stashed the phone bill so his wife wouldn't find out about his activities. God dislikes having sin hidden in the dark, so He arranged to have that phone bill fly out of its hiding spot and land in the garden right where his wife was working. (Remember: God always gives us opportunities to repent and receive mercy. If we refuse the "lesson," then the judgments or consequences come.)

Brenda picked up the bill and realized it was theirs. Once she saw the series of 900 numbers, she stormed back to the house for a showdown.

Ron was sipping coffee, oblivious to his impending doom. The confrontation amounted to a series of accusations, justifications, harsh words, and hurt feelings. After Ron sulked off to work, Brenda retaliated by chopping down all the trees Ron had planted.

Neither party's reactions brought resolution, but God in His mercy used this situation to bring their issues to a head. After much ministry and repentance, Ron was set free from the mind-set that had kept him bound. Today, Ron and Brenda have cemented their relationship and are a strong family. They are good friends of ours and vital to several ministries in the church.

Ron and Brenda shifted their thinking and learned to operate under God's Kingdom—the Kingdom of light.

We enter into this realm of light by covenant. The covenant allows us to become part of the family and to be treated like sons and daughters of God. Like every family, our covenant family has its own relational dynamics, which include certain restrictions and privileges. One of dynamics involves mercy (see 1 Kings 8:23).

Since Kingdom dynamics operate under the law of sowing and reaping, we must show mercy if we want to receive it (see Matt. 5:7). In fact, we are told that God requires of us "...*to do justly, and to love mercy, and to walk humbly with thy God...*" (Mic. 6:8).

In the Kingdom, we can't grant mercy for ourselves and heap judgment upon others. That is a worldly mind-set. Human nature is to justify our actions, but condemn the actions of others.

If I am late for church there was a good reason; the alarm didn't go off, the dog escaped, the car needed gas, the kids lost their shoes, and so on. These are *my* good reasons. But if somebody else is late, there is no good reason. The voice of judgment says: They just don't care; they are always late; they are not committed.

The natural response is to grant grace for ourselves and assign judgment to others. However, that's not how God's covenant works. We need to change the way we think; God always links mercy and truth together (see Ps. 85:10).

MERCY'S COVENANT PLACE

In God's Kingdom, we must take ownership of our own stuff and release other people's stuff. God is angry when we withhold mercy and demand our "pound of flesh" from those who offend us;

Jeanne and I had a situation with a pastor. He was under a lot of pressure. God was dealing with him in a particular wounded area and desired his healing. The pastor resisted God's gentle hand; as a result, every situation God arranged was seen by the pastor as an attack.

One day he showed up at our house with his associate pastor. We were elders in the church and loved this man of God. We appreciated where he had taken us in the Spirit, but we knew that he was struggling in this particular area.

He seemed agitated as he paced back and forth in our living room. I waited for him to explain his reason for visiting. Finally, after about half an hour of small talk, I asked him outright. He exploded and accused us of setting up a meeting to get rid of him. He said he had overheard a conversation and knew this secret meeting was being held at our house.

I was floored. I quickly phoned all the other leaders and discovered that one of the other elder couples were taking a young lady out for coffee that morning. She had received some correction and the elders just wanted to connect with her and show her some love. That was the secret meeting!

The pastor's emotional state was very fragile. He broke down at that point and cried in my arms. As leadership, we were so concerned that we sent him and his wife to Hawaii for a week and arranged for some counseling. We showed him mercy. Because of fear, he had attacked me. I could have been offended and demanded an apology. But that's not what God wanted. He desired to overwhelm the pastor with love and a demonstration of His mercy.

Mercy is not to be separated from justice and truth. That fact is emphasized by the attributes of God's throne. The psalmist wrote: *"Justice and judgment are the habitation of Thy throne: mercy and truth shall go before Thy face"* (Ps. 89:14).

God speaks judgment from the seat of His throne. For ancient Israel, the place of His presence was the Ark of the Covenant. It is important to note that it was topped with the mercy seat (see Exod. 25:22).

UNSANCTIFIED MERCY

God values mercy; therefore, He administers it justly. Mercy without justice would be "cheap" mercy, which is really unsanctified mercy. It is neither God-ordained nor blessed.

One year, our neighbors experienced financial difficulty. The wife shared their problem at a prayer group. One of the women decided to bless them with some food. She bought a bag of groceries and delivered it to the family. The wife was so thrilled with the gift that she decided to host a tea for the generous woman the very next week.

When the donor arrived at our neighbors' home, she was shocked to find that they lived in a very nice, well-furnished house. The tea included expensive food items and was more extravagant than any she had ever experienced. She was angered because she and her husband were struggling themselves, living in their garage while their house was being built.

Natural, human compassion is a poor substitute for a word from God to show mercy. The generous woman and her husband left the church over the tea incident. Their reaction was evidence that their giving was not Spirit-led. Instead, it was fleshly inspired compassion.

Our flesh always gets offended if its original perception is proven wrong. In this case, one couple used manipulation when they had a need; the other used unsanctified mercy when they gave. Both were wrong. God's promptings of mercy may not make natural sense, but they produce better fruit.

We had a friend once who was in need of some money. He had been praying and believing that God would supply. We wanted to be that supply, but felt a check in our spirits to wait. Our friend continued to cry out to God and we continued to pray, but God would not release us to give. Jeanne and I wanted to show mercy, but God knew more than we did and had a bigger plan than just meeting our friend's financial need.

Finally after weeks of prayer, we felt released and went over to give him the money. He graciously accepted and then told us the rest of the story.

He had demanded that God supply the need in a "supernatural way" (what I would call a "spooky" manner). He wanted an angel to come down, but God would not be manipulated by his demands.

No angel came. When the man came to the end of his demanding approach, he told God, "Whomever You send, I will accept." That is when God gave us the release to help.

Our mercy must not be based on need or human compassion but, rather, on the nature and purpose of God. Jesus didn't show mercy to Lazarus. He waited two days before going Bethany, leaving Lazarus' sisters grieving for their dead brother four long days. Jesus then told his disciples, *"I am glad for your sakes that I was not there, to the intent ye may believe…"* (John 11:15).

God had something more in mind than even the healing of Lazarus' sickness. Yet, we know that Jesus' choices around the Lazarus miracle were mystifying to others, because they did not make natural sense.

The power in which Jesus operated is available to us, but we will not walk in it unless we shift out of our natural reasoning and rely totally on the leading of the Spirit—even when it mystifies us.

God reiterated this principle when He said *"...cursed be he that keep(s) back his sword from blood"* (Jer. 48:10). God had ordained Moab to come under judgment so that the nation would change its nature (see Jer. 48:11-12). He is not telling us to go out and kill people but to allow justice to fall when He has ordained it.

Based on the larger picture God showed to Jeremiah (and in the absence of New Covenant options), the prophet warned the nations to bring God's judgment and not show mercy, in obedience to His commands.

God always had in mind the larger picture of Israel's relationship with Him and His plan for them as His people. He desired to extend mercy worldwide, but it had to be balanced with judgment and discipline and had to result, not in more rebellion, but in submission to God.

Unsanctified mercy is just that: unsanctified. It is a work of the flesh and will not produce life. Neither can we assume that God must bring judgment. That, too, is a work of the flesh.

The disciples were guilty of this overreaction when they desired to call fire down on a village that refused to accept Jesus. Jesus called them on their reaction, saying, *"Ye know not what manner of spirit ye are of"* (Luke 9:55). They took secondhand offense for Jesus and only wanted judgment.

Mercy and justice, to be profitable, must come out of the heart of God rather than our soul realm. Any response from the soul realm will be a religious response. Religion is man's attempt to do what only God can do. Since we can't actually do what God demands, we try to sacrifice or substitute for what is really required. Then we hope it will be accepted.

As we learned earlier on, *"...to obey is better than sacrifice..."* (1 Sam. 15:22). God holds mercy and justice in the same category. He said, "...*I will have mercy, and not sacrifice...*" (Matt. 9:13); "*to do justice and judgment is more acceptable...than sacrifice*" (Prov. 21:3).

We need a shift to enter into what God is doing!

WISDOM REQUIRED

Human judgment can be swayed by human fears of other people's reactions. We often fear the consequences of confrontation; in reality, a proper addressing of inappropriate actions and reactions would disarm many lies and prevent many broken relationships and church splits. I learned this lesson at work and was later able to apply it in church and the Kingdom.

I was general foreman on a construction site that had many large, soft potholes. An ironworker (we'll call him *Tom*) was driving a man lift (an aerial work platform), but a large mud hole was in his way.

I warned, "Don't try and drive through there; you'll get stuck. Go around the boom." The long way around the boom would have taken an extra five minutes.

I turned away, but sure enough, Tom decided he knew what was best and proceeded into the mud hole, only to get stuck. I turned and hollered at him for disobeying. He fired a few expletives my way and put the machine in reverse.

Tom managed to back out of the hole but, instead of going around the boom, he took another run at the mud hole and got stuck again. Not having learned about true authority myself, I acted like the boss and reamed him out in front of a dozen other men.

Tom lost his cool and immediately announced that he was quitting. This all happened right at lunchtime. I was mad, so I just waved my arms and turned to go back to the office thinking, "Who cares if you quit!"

Unfortunately, it was not over. My poor leadership and Tom's anger fed into each other. He fumed and fussed about the conflict through lunch and managed to get himself even more riled up than he was before.

After lunch, I walked across the site to go back to work. Tom stepped out of the lunchroom with his tool belt on his shoulder ready to quit and go home. When he saw me, he decided to fire his farewell volley. He started swearing and calling me names and shouting lies about what had transpired. I stopped in my tracks; I felt that I couldn't let his accusations go.

When I turned, Tom exploded, dropped his belt, ripped off his jacket, and stormed toward me. I thought, "I am going to get pounded out." Tom was a fighter and I was not, but God had a strategy to save my hide and to keep Tom's job. The Spirit said, "Don't show fear or anger. Speak truth and show mercy."

When Tom arrived within six inches of my nose, I said, "You don't want to do this Tom. I didn't fire you; you quit. I should not have hollered at you and I apologize. You should have obeyed me and not tried to go through the mud. Turn around, pick up your belt, and go back to work. You are too good of a man to do this, and I value you on this job."

Tom stood there for a few seconds. I don't know if he was weighing his options or if the Holy Spirit was talking to him. He was a Christian, but was a bit of a diamond in the rough. He finally responded and said, "You're right. I should have listened, but you shouldn't have hollered at me."

"I agree; I shouldn't have, and I apologize again."

"OK," he said and turned away and went back to work. The 80 or so men who were watching couldn't believe what they were seeing. They fully expected to witness a fight; Tom had a reputation for fighting, and I had certainly egged him on.

You can see how mercy, truth, and justice must always flow together—and how important it is for true authority to be a blend of justice (what is right and true) and mercy or grace.

I'm not sure whether I showed the mercy or Tom did, but in the end, we became good friends.

PROPER JUDGMENT

Justice is about righteousness. Thirty-five times in the Bible the words *justice* or *judgment* and *right* or *righteous* are linked together.

To link these two concepts in life, we must *"judge not according to the appearance, but judge righteous judgment"* (John 7:24). We are not to judge a book according to its cover. The problem is that judging by appearances is exactly what we tend to do.

The prophet Samuel had a hard time recognizing whom he should anoint king over Israel. Understandably, he at first tried to judge God's selection by natural appearances. God corrected him saying, "[I] *seeth not as man seeth; for man looketh on the outward appearance, but* [I] *looketh on the heart"* (1 Sam. 16:7).

Samuel could only have the discernment to anoint the right king when he learned to see and judge as God did. As a result, he picked the right king—David, who happened to be the "runt" of the litter.

I remember a story, told by a pastor's wife, about how she had sown judgment when she should have sown mercy. She avoided one particular old man in the church because of his slovenly appearance and odor.

At some point, a bad car accident put her in the hospital, where she lingered in a light coma. She was completely aware of her surroundings, though she could not open her eyes or respond in any manner.

Many visitors came, but because the pastor's wife was just lying there, the people visited with each other. They talked about her, not to her, because by all appearances she was not aware. The old man she had worked so hard to avoid was different, however. He came in and talked to her. He read to her, prayed "with" her, and talked to her. While still in her coma, the pastor's wife repented.

Because of his clothes and his odor, she had judged this man to be unworthy of her time. Her judgment had been skewed by her misperceptions. She judged him, but never with righteous judgment, until after her accident.

She cried out to God, promising that when she got out of her situation she was going to hug and love that old man, just as he had shown her love. He had demonstrated his spiritual discernment by recognizing that, even while her body was shut down, her spirit was alive and functioning. When she emerged from her coma, she repented to this man. He became a vital prayer covering for her and her husband.

God has anointed and appointed certain people in the Body to show mercy; God called us to be *"...vessels of mercy..."* (Rom. 9:23). He listed mercy as one of the gifts and explained that it is to be meted out with cheerfulness (see Rom. 12:8).

Mercy is not just letting someone off the hook; mercy is the sowing of spiritual seed. If we sow mercy, we will reap mercy, but we must sow it *"...not grudgingly or under compulsion, for God loves a cheerful giver"* (2 Cor. 9:7 NASB).

DIVIDING HEARTS

Churches are designed to be places not of friction, but of tension, just as families are called to be. Tension is the act of stretching; it is a necessary component of growth. Jesus said *"...I came not to send peace, but a sword. For I am come to set a man at variance against [others].... And a man's foes shall be they of his own household"* (Matt. 10:34-36).

That sounds like war, but war is not the intent. The sword mentioned is actually a knife[3] designed to divide not people, but heart attitudes. The physical family and the spiritual family are to be places where love and intimacy grow. When they do, we let people get closer to us. As a result, others bump against any areas of woundedness in our character, forcing us to judge how we will react.

The Greek word for "judgment" is *krisis*,[4] the root from which our word *crisis* originated. It is also translated *justice*. We must make right, just, merciful decisions in a time of crisis, when we feel stretched.

Our current pastor has displayed a marvelous ability to function in mercy. In one instance, a young man who had been elevated to the position of deacon was too immature for the position and the spiritual attacks that came with it. He did not like the pastor and constantly spoke against what the pastor was trying to do in the church. Yet, our pastor would take him out for coffee and even invited him on a mission's trip with him.

I (Jeanne) warned the pastor about what was happening behind his back, but he wasn't concerned. He continued to show that young man love until the day that he resigned as a deacon and left the church.

The pastor was able to love and show mercy because he wasn't concerned about himself; he was concerned about the young man. By leaving judgment to God and being joyfully merciful, the pastor gained respect and authority and defused a volatile situation.

We need to show mercy to each other so that healthy tension does not become damaging friction. The oil of the Holy Spirit is designed to ease the pain caused by intimacy. We all have wounds in our character. Intimacy reveals these wounds so that the Holy Spirit can bring healing. Once we are healed in these areas, we can get closer to others. Yes, new wounds will occur, but we will be confident of His power to heal us again.

SOUND MOTIVES

This is why we can't judge each other's actions, motives, or reactions. We ought not judge lest we be judged ourselves (see Matt. 7:1). *"But if we judged ourselves rightly, we would not be judged. But when we are judged, we are disciplined…so that we will not be condemned…"* (1 Cor. 11:31-32 NASB). Clearly, we are called to judge ourselves only.

When we judge others, we are actually assigning motives to their actions (most often, inaccurately). When we presume to know the motives of others, we give vent to our own fears: fears of what others may be thinking or saying, planning to do or not planning to do.

If fear is present, love is absent. The two are mutually exclusive (see 1 John 4:18). We cannot judge rightly if we do not love. Another discernment disaster is to judge based on our own selfish motivations. Jesus said His *"...judgment is just; because* [He seeks not His] *own will, but the will of the Father..."* (John 5:30).

Jesus never judged situations based on His emotions. Instead, He appraised them according to His knowledge of the Father's will, a pure and unadulterated standard.

To shift from the natural to the supernatural in ways that align with Christ's ways, we must shift from the standard of our feelings and apply what we know is truth. Then, we can access and operate in God's supernatural wisdom.

I remember trying to make an investment decision at a time when my judgment was distorted by greed and the fear of missing what I thought was a good opportunity. Jeanne prayed and heard from God: this company would overextend itself and create a financial disaster. I then looked at the business plan and told Jeanne that some of the stuff didn't add up.

With her word from God and the checks in my spirit, the decision became a no-brainer: Best thing to do was to stay out of the investment. The problem was, the emotions of greed, and the fear of missing out, still drove me. I took my "authority" and invested a large sum of our money.

My "authority" did not have the power to turn this investment around, so we lost nearly everything that we put into it. Proper judgment is power; distorted judgment is not. In fact, if you *"...do justice and righteousness...* [it will be] *well with* [you]" (Jer. 22:15 NASB).

The proper use of authority is an important issue in the Body of Christ. God has designed us to "...[reconcile] *the world unto* [Him]... [as] *ambassadors for Christ...*" (2 Cor. 5:19-20). As ambassadors, we are to function in both the will and the authority of the One who sent us.

Authority issues can affect every area of church life. We have had several incidences where outside prophetic voices have spoken questionable doctrine or exhibited questionable behavior in our church.

A common overreaction to prophetic missteps is to avoid prophetic ministry altogether. But prophets bring a powerful dimension of the Holy Spirit to the Church. So, while it is true that an off-course prophet can create a mess, we must be careful not to "throw out the baby with the bathwater."

If we want the strength of the prophet, we must be willing to use our discernment and authority to clean up any occasional messes and move on. The Bible says it this way:"...*where no oxen are, the crib is clean: but much increase is by the strength of the ox*" (Prov. 14:4).

Every functional family—including the Church family—has messes. We need to shift our thinking and be willing to judge what prophets say; then we can also receive the benefits the prophet brings to the Body.

Sometimes, as was the case with the prophet who acted inappropriately, bringing judgment and correction is a godly way of showing mercy—both to the prophet who can then repent and be restored and to the congregation caught in the mess.

I earlier told the story of Randy, who stabbed me in the back on two different occasions. God specifically told me to let him do it. God wanted me to show mercy and properly manifest His nature to Randy—and to the spirit realm. God put His nature in us to...

> ...*do good to them that hate you, and pray for them which despitefully use you, and persecute you; that you may be the children of your Father...for He maketh the sun rise on*

the evil and on the good, and sendeth rain on the just and on the unjust (Matthew 5:44-45).

That takes healed, mature disciples who think and walk as Jesus walked.

We need to learn how to properly judge here because eventually we will judge the world and angels (see 1 Cor. 6:2-3). We have to know what is right because we are destined *"to execute vengeance on the nations, and punishments on the peoples...bind their kings...and their nobles...to execute on them the written judgment..."* (Ps. 149:7-9 NKJV). That is a heavy responsibility, but if we know God's heart it will be a joyful assignment.

What is God's heart? He desires for all men to repent and come under His protection. We all deserve judgment, but God sent Jesus to bear the penalty that belonged to us. With justice satisfied, He can now show mercy because *"...mercy rejoiceth* [over] *judgment"* (James 2:13).

Once, when I was in charge of a dragline job, I (Ken) had to fire one of my foremen on the nightshift. One of the apprentices on the shift took exception to my action. He challenged me to step outside the gate to settle things. I told him to shape up his attitude. I could have fired him for his threats right there, but I didn't.

Later that night, I was touring through the hundreds of compartments on the huge machine. I stepped over a bulkhead in a remote compartment and stumbled upon that apprentice. At first I thought he had fallen and gotten hurt, but then I realized he was sleeping. I decided to go get the job steward, so he would be there when I woke up the apprentice and fired him.

I only got about 50 feet before the Holy Spirit arrested me. That verse about mercy rejoicing over judgment (see James 2:13) sprang into my head. I realized my own thoughts were in opposition to what the Spirit was speaking and I needed to make a shift.

I turned around and awakened the apprentice privately. We had a good talk. He asked my forgiveness when he learned what God had done for him in turning me around. My son later told me that this apprentice became a Christian. God loves to marry mercy and justice!

Another time, Jeanne and I were doing marriage counseling with a young couple. The questionnaire they filled out for us indicated that one of their weaknesses was the handling of finances.

Ironically, the counseling, which lasted almost ten hours, was to cost the couple $100. The money was supposed to be paid up front, but they forgot to bring it. At the next session, they came up with another excuse for not paying. The third time we met, the subject never came up.

I realized that the questionnaire was correct; they were immature when it came to money. Jeanne and I decided that showing mercy for their lack of concern over the broken financial agreement was not working. So we brought judgment.

They had yet another excuse for not bringing the money when the fourth session arrived. I suggested they go back to their car and talk about why they didn't think it was important to keep their promise concerning the payment. Once they knew the answer, they could schedule the last session.

They were very embarrassed and apologetic, but I insisted that they leave. It took almost a month before they could face us again, this time with the money. We returned all of the money (because money was never the issue for us) as a wedding present.

As Paul wrote, *"Behold...the goodness and severity of God..."* (Rom. 11:22). God took this couple through His school of finances and they now are doing well. We were simply the instruments God used to expose their weakness and bring them to restoration.

God is good and merciful. He is also just. He used all aspects of His nature in bringing Jesus to the cross. God has also ordained that we walk in authority and power. We must be able shift out of our natural mind-sets to discern what combination of mercy and justice He wants us to administer in each and every situation.

SHIFT INTO PRAYER

God, help us to extend grace and mercy to others. Help us to walk only in Your sanctified mercy and do only what You show us to do. Give us Your love and strategy for every situation that we encounter. In Jesus' name.

ENDNOTES

1. *Webster's New Twentieth Century Dictionary*, s.v. "justice."

2. Zodhaites, Spiros. *The Complete Word Study Dictionary: Old Testament* (Chattanooga: AMG Publishers, 1994), s.v., 2617, 2603.

3. Zodhaites, Spiros. *The Complete Word Study Dictionary: New Testament* (Chattanooga: AMG Publishers, 1992), s.v., 3162.

4. Ibid., s.v., 2920.

Chapter 10

CREATE YOUR OWN UNIVERSE

Declarations

WORDS have power, but only if they are communicated or spoken out. They are designed to illuminate both our minds and our world through the qualities of light and sound.

Both qualities were connected when God uttered the very first declaration over the earth saying, *"Let there be light: and there was light"* (Gen. 1:3).

The literal words spoken were, "Light exist or be."[1] Thus, the first spoken word became light. Light and sound are similar in the fact that both generate waves. Light produces electromagnetic waves; sound, by vibrations, produces mechanical waves.

Light waves have the capacity to move through a vacuum while sound waves cannot; they require something to vibrate. It is interesting that God first spoke the Word, which needs a medium or substance to be heard. That Word then carried the substance of creation within itself, thereby allowing it to be heard.

Using sound and light was how, *"in the beginning God created..."* (Gen. 1:1). The apostle John describes creation by saying: *"In the beginning was the Word...and the Word was God....In Him was life; and the life was the light of men* (John 1:1,4). John went on to say that *"the Word became flesh..."* (John 1:14 NKJV).

God included us in the creative process. Jesus said, *"...the works that I do shall [you] do also; and greater works..."* (John 14:12). Thus, Jesus ordained our creative words to exude light and life. In other words, our words have the divinely imparted "energy" to shift us... others...situations...and outcomes from the natural to the supernatural realm.

Our creative words of life and light are the evidence that we are made in God's image (see Gen. 1:27). God intended our words, containing His power, to bring His Kingdom to the earth. He arranged the Kingdom to work that way; He gave us dominion and commanded us to occupy the earth (see Gen. 1:26; Luke 19:13).

He started, through creation, to lay the groundwork for our faith. He created the animals *"...and brought them unto Adam to see what he would call them..."* (Gen. 2:19). The Hebrew text literally says that God *formed* or molded them[2] and Adam called them forth.

Adam's first creative act was to name or "call out"[3] the animals. He was actively participating in the creation as a partner with God. God formed them and Adam "gave names"[4] (see Gen. 2:20). He called out characteristics for each animal; whatever characteristic Adam gave them, that was how they functioned and lived.

God also called Ezekiel to create with Him. He brought Ezekiel into a *...valley which was full of bones.*

> *"Son of man, can these bones live?"*
>
> *"O Lord God, thou knowest..."*
>
> *"Prophesy upon these bones, and say, ...hear the word of the Lord."*
>
> *So I prophesied as I was commanded: and...there was a noise,...a shaking, and the bones came together,... the sinews and flesh came upon them,...skin covered them... but there was no breath.*

"Prophesy unto the wind…"

So I prophesied… and the breath came into them, and they lived…(Ezekiel 37:1-10).

If God calls us to do something—even to bringing life into inanimate or dead objects—we can do it.

This is why we have dominion over everything on the earth; we, through Adam, were co-creators with God. Our words are designed to give substance and life to ideas, just as Adam's gave function to the animals God had formed. We have lost the concept of using creative words but God is restoring that idea as His Kingdom is being restored on the earth.

In 1862, Harriet Beecher Stowe went to see Abraham Lincoln, pressuring him to speed up the emancipation of the slaves. Stowe's daughter Hattie, who was present at the meeting, reported Lincoln's opening salvo in the conversation: "So you're the little lady who started this Great War."[5]

Stowe's 1852 book *Uncle Tom's Cabin* was the impetus that changed thousands of minds about freeing the slaves in the United States. It was just a story made up of words, but it brought the truth to the light and changed the way people perceived the slavery issue.

DECREES

One Sunday, our church was worshiping and pushing for the glory of the Lord to come. As we moved in the Spirit, a sound came out that had a different ring to it. Our pastor Marc, decreed, "That's the sound of cocaine being destroyed. Keep pushing. We are bringing the hidden things to the light. Activities that have been hidden from the authorities are going to be exposed. They can no longer remain in darkness."

That was a strange declaration to make in the middle of worship. I (Jeanne) thought, "Let's see if this stuff we do is real." Our small city doesn't have much in the way of spectacular crime, so this was a significant declaration.

The next Friday, a major cocaine bust occurred in our city. We experienced the power of that declaration within days of its being broadcast into the atmosphere. This and subsequent declarations are still having an effect in the community.

A week before this manuscript went to the publisher, the local paper reported that the drug trade in our community had been so set back that people now have to go to the neighboring city to obtain their drugs.

When God's truth is declared in faith, it will never *"...return... empty, without accomplishing what* [God desires], *and without succeeding in the matter for which* [He] *sent it"* (Isa. 55:11 NASB).

Job said, *"...Decree a thing, and it shall be established unto thee: and the light shall shine upon thy ways"* (Job 22:28). Kings make decrees because, in their realms of authority, their words are law and they will come to pass. Our problem is that we don't believe that we are kings whose words matter in our realm.

We have to change the way we think if we are to align with Jesus' worldview, which pits two distinct realms against each other: satan's realm of darkness (see Matt. 12:26) and God's *"kingdom of His dear Son"* (Col. 1:13), which is a Kingdom of light. The battle is one of light against darkness.

If God were to fight satan, the battle would not last a nanosecond. However, He does not lower Himself to battle His creation; He has men and angels to do that. The prophet Micaiah saw a vision of the council of heaven. *...the Lord said,*

> *"Who will persuade Ahab, that he may go up and fall at Ramoth-gilead?"*
>
> *There came forth a spirit... and he said, "I will be a lying spirit in the mouth of all his prophets."*

"Thou shalt persuade him and prevail also; go forth, and do so" (1 Kings 22:20-22).

God was not asking for advice; He was offering the hosts of heaven to participate in His judgments.

That is why Jesus *"...was manifested, that He might destroy the works of the devil"* (1 John 3:8). Jesus came, not because God hated satan, but because *"God so loved the world"* (John 3:16). He was delivering us from the death and destruction that satan had wrought.

In Jesus' first encounter with the devil, He countered all the suggestions and lies fired His way with declarations from God's Word (see Matt. 4:4,7,10). Thoughts cannot defeat thoughts; words defeat thoughts. We must shift our thinking and use declarations of God's Word instead of petitions to dislodge the enemy.

If we are to live as Jesus, we also must defeat satan *"...by every word that proceeds from the mouth of God"* (Matt. 4:4 NKJV).

I (Jeanne) recall a time when Ken had just been laid off from a good job. He was upset, but I had been praying (a better course of action). I heard God say that as soon as we were in bed a job offer would appear. Normally, job offers do not come in the evening, but I was so excited at what God was going to do that I insisted we go to bed at 7:30 P.M. that night.

Ken thought this was crazy, but yielded to persuasion (and my expectation) and went to bed early with me. Ten minutes later, the phone rang and a job offer was on the table. I didn't say a thing; I just sat there and smiled.

Words are powerfully connected to things. In fact, the Hebrew word *debar*[6] means both "words" and "things." In the Hebrew mindset, words were things and things gained their substance through being declared. I had, through faith, given substance to the word that God had spoken to me. Hear God; believe Him; declare what He says; then receive it.

The Bible says *"The word is…in your mouth and in your heart, that you may do it"* (Deut. 30:14 NKJV). Why? So that you can create what God speaks.

BELIEVING AND SPEAKING

All of these aspects of faith must be present to create as Jesus and Adam did. The question then begs, if we have this authority, why are we not doing more good and destroying the work of the enemy? (See Acts 10:38.)

The answer obviously lies in the fact that we do not have all the parts of the formula in place, which the Word states we require.

Let's use a chemical experiment—the combining of an acid and a base—as an analogy of our faith in operation. Consider the acid in this experiment to represent our faith and the base to be a situation we have encountered.

If the acid is strong and concentrated, then adding the base will produce a powerful reaction or even an explosion. If the acid is weak (having a pH of 5 or 6), limited bubbling of the mixture may occur. If the acid is diluted further (to a 5 percent solution), then only a minor fizzle will result.

Compare these chemical reactions with our faith.

Suppose I pray for a friend to be healed, but only a fizzle occurs instead of a miracle. I know God's Word says that *"…they shall lay hands on the sick, and they shall recover"* (Mark 16:18). I also know that I had a word from God to pray. I was obedient; I laid hands on the sick person and declared his healing. Yet nothing happened.

What went wrong? At this juncture, we often conclude that it wasn't God's will to heal…or it wasn't the right time…or the person we prayed for didn't have enough faith…or maybe healing really was only for the apostles' day…or I don't have enough faith. We may not even believe in divine healing at all, but may have decided to go through the motions in the hope that something might occur.

We may think that prayer is like some heavenly lottery in which only the lucky ones receive their requests.

We have all spoken or imagined such thoughts when our prayers went unanswered, but the truth is much simpler than any of them. If Jesus said, "*...whatever things you ask when you pray, believe that you receive them, and you will have them*" (Mark 11:24 NKJV), then any defeat we experience in this process must come in either the believing or the speaking.

Our level of belief is equivalent to the strength of the acid in our little experiment. If we did the speaking, yet there was no answer, it may be that we don't truly believe what we say.

Not so with God. God's Word has perfect integrity and God cannot lie. Why not? Because everything He says happens. God's word is His creative force and He has *...angels, that excel in strength, that do His commandments, hearkening unto the voice of His word* (Ps 103:20). In fact, when *...He sends out His command to the earth; His word runs very swiftly* (Ps 147:15 NKJV).

He declares as much in Isaiah 55:11: "*...My word... which goes forth from My mouth...will not return to Me...without accomplishing what I desire...*" (NASB).

Our words are designed to function in a similar manner. If they don't, we must conclude that we don't believe what we are speaking. Why would we not believe our own words? Because we often say things that we don't believe! Consider the following examples of common expressions:

God recently told me (Ken) that I could no longer speak facetiously or sarcastically because these speech patterns declare things that are contrary to the truth. If we consistently say things we really don't believe, our hearts won't respond when we want to believe our words.

It's like the boy in the story who always cried, "Wolf!" when there was no wolf. When there was real danger, nobody believed his cries.

WE SAY:	WE MEAN:
"That's awful" (Literally: "It fills me with awe.")	"That's terrible." (Not awe-filling, but extremely negative in some way)
"I'm getting sick and tired of his attitude." (Literally: "I'm becoming ill...")	"His attitude upsets me."
"I'll kill him if he does that again." (Literally: "I will take his life if...")	"There will be serious consequences for his actions."
"I'll be just a second."	"This won't take long."
"Well, I'll be a monkey's uncle!" (A physical impossibility)	"That would surprise me!"
"That was helpful!" (sarcastically)	"Somebody messed things up."

This constant speaking of falsehoods weakens the effect the tongue has on the heart. Solomon said that *"death and life are in the power of the tongue..."* (Prov. 18:21). That power—the chemical reaction in our analogy—is compromised when we continually say things we don't believe. It is the way in which we weaken our faith "acid."

We also dilute our faith by speaking the opposite of God's revealed will. James 3:11 says, *"...[No spring send[s] forth fresh water and bitter"* (NKJV). Yet we use our mouths to both bless and curse (see James 3:9-10). This indicates two sources of speech within us: the flesh (our carnal nature) and our spirit.

The spirit speaks in agreement with God, but *"the carnal mind... is not subject to...God"* (Rom. 8:7). The more we allow our flesh to speak, the more we dilute the Spirit and our faith. Like the watered down acid, our words become incapable of producing an explosive miracle.

This is a serious issue. Jesus said we would be judged for speaking useless or "idle words" (Matt.12:36) because we are supposed to *"...speak as the oracles of God..."* (1 Pet. 4:11).

We carelessly speak negative words or curses over our lives and other situations. We say things such as:

"Nothing good ever happens to me." (Self-condemnation)

"I always get the short end of the stick." (Self-pity)

"Whatever. I don't care." (Passivity)

"If it's God's will." (Passive/weak faith)

"Holy Moly!" (Invocation of the god *Molech*)

"Holy cow!" (Invocation of Hindu gods)

"I'm getting sick." (Confession of feelings rather than faith)

If we are to act like God, then we must talk like God. Talking like the world will not produce Kingdom results; it will dilute our faith and cancel God's promises. If our faith wavers, the Bible foretells the result: *"...the one who doubts...ought not to expect...anything from the Lord"* (James 1:6-7 NASB).

God wants to bless us, but we must cooperate. We have the words to contain His power, but our words and His words must agree.

WORD SEEDS

We've talked about seed and God's Word. Jesus spoke of words being seeds. He said, *"...the seed is the word of God"* (Luke 8:11). Two laws govern the growth of every seed: the law of sowing and reaping, and the law of increase. If we sow barley we will get barley; if we sow wheat we will get wheat. If we sow one or two bushels per acre, we can expect to reap 30 or 60 or 100 bushels per acre.

These laws work all the time, even for thorns and thistles; that is why they are called *laws.* When I farmed, I noticed that the weeds always matured before the grain. Because they grew faster (and if they were thick enough), the weeds threatened to choke out the grain.

Jesus said that the seeds or words that are sown *"...among the thorns...are choked...and bring no fruit to perfection"* (Luke 8:14). We need to root out our negative speech if we expect to produce anything for the Kingdom.

I (Jeanne) was a people-pleaser when I was younger. I had difficulty saying "No." This caused me to commit to things I was not actually prepared to do.

A pattern began to develop in my life. When I felt overwhelmed with the commitments I had made, a dread of each coming event would rise up within me. Then I would begin to feel sick; I would confess that sickness; and I would soon get sick. Once I was sick, I could get out of my obligation. Unfortunately, I was totally unaware of the fact that I was cooperating with satan.

God eventually exposed this to me as sin and told me that I had to keep my word even to my *"own hurt"* (Ps. 15:4). I am now careful of what I agree to do and I no longer allow the feelings of being overwhelmed to lead me to sickness.

Nor do I use the demonic structure of sickness to get out of commitments. If I gave my word, I must keep it. Now I can get through things I didn't think I could manage, and I am not sick all the time.

Demonic structures, though we may appear to use them, in fact, use us. I could not summon up sickness when it suited me; it arose when it wanted to because I had given it the right to operate in my life. I had to repent of speaking negative words about my health and dismantle the structure of dread so that I could walk in freedom and health.

Now that I understand the power of our words, I speak the opposite of the sicknesses I used to declare. I now say, "I walk in divine health and I have divine healing." This is a declaration of gratitude; it creates an atmosphere in which the seeds of faith can grow.

This is not positive thinking (though I am positive). It is a declaring into the heavenlies of the things God has spoken and wants us to declare. It is a transforming process—a shift that moves us from the natural to the supernatural.

We need to be *"transformed by the renewing of* [our minds] *that* [we] *may prove what is that good, and acceptable, and perfect, will of God"* (Rom. 12:2).

I had to change my thinking to line up with the Word so I could walk in health and not curse my own body.

REALMS OF AUTHORITY

As mentioned earlier, God established specific realms to nations, families, and individuals. Within those realms, He intended us to operate as He does: declare and create. God started with the Word and *"all things came into being through Him* [the Word/Jesus]*"* (John 1:3 NASB).

God stirred up Abraham, who is *"...the father of all who believe..."* (Rom. 4:11 NASB), to speak into his own family realm concerning his descendants. Abraham spoke like God *"...who gives life to the dead and calls into being that which does not exist"* (Rom. 4:17 NASB). As Abraham's children, we should speak the same way. It is the only way we will get the results that Abraham did.

Gideon caught God's vision for victory after he heard the interpretation of a dream one of the Midianites had. God had sent Gideon to the Midianites' camp to encourage his heart before battle (see Judg. 7:10-15).

Gideon returned to his camp and declared to Israel, *"Arise; for the Lord hath delivered into your hand the host of Midian"* (Judg. 7:15). He spoke these words before the battle, as if the battle had already been won.

That is the stance of faith. Hear God speak; believe it; declare it; receive it. The 300 men Gideon had chosen were of the same spirit as Gideon and they believed the word Gideon declared. This company had so much confidence in it that they didn't even make provision to hold a sword to fight. They had a lamp in one hand and a trumpet in the other with their swords stuck in their belts (see Judg. 7:20).

When they shouted, God responded and entered the field of battle on their behalf setting *"...every man's sword against his fellow..."* (Judg. 7:22). That is how battles are to be fought: hear God; believe God; declare God's Word; accompany God in the victory.

We have a friend, Randal, who exercised his faith in a similar manner. He works for a Christian company which had experienced significant problems securing certain contracts. He related his story to me:

> I was praying as I drove to work (I often pray when I drive), and as I was praying, God told me to declare an end to the resistance that was coming against our company and stopping us from getting some major contracts signed.
>
> The contracts had been held up for a few weeks, even though the other party wanted to settle. As I spoke out against the demonic resistance, three companies came to mind, one which I knew we had already lost the bid for. I declared out into the spirit realm an end to the resistance and almost immediately things happened.
>
> As soon as I returned to work, the first and largest company called and settled on the contract for the year. Before the week was up, the second company called and settled. The third company, the one whose bid we lost, called before the week was out to inquire about a different product. God is faithful and able. Let's obey what He asks us to do.[7]

We obtain our righteousness by believing what God says concerning Jesus' finished work. Salvation (being saved from our situations) comes when, after agreeing (believing), we declare what we believe into our realm of authority.

When I (Jeanne) met Ken, I was not a Christian, although I had been searching my whole life. One night, Ken explained to me the Scriptures concerning Jesus.

Although I had always loved God and had prayed consistently, I had not personally encountered Jesus. After Ken left that night,

I prayed and confessed to God all my sins, receiving Jesus as my Savior. As I cried and truly repented, a great peace came over me.

The next Sunday, at church, I publicly declared my salvation. It is not enough just to believe; "...*even the demons believe...*" (James 2:19 NKJV). We must go a step further and "...*with the mouth* [make a] *confession...unto salvation*" (Rom. 10:10).

This confession testifies to a genuine relationship with God—a secure, lasting relationship. When we are insecure in a relationship, we can only *ask for* things that we want; when we are secure, we *confess or declare* the things that we want. That shift of position comes from a shift in our thinking about who we are.

This is why Joshua could command the sun and moon to stay in the sky during the battle with the Canaanite kings. He saw when God "...*confounded* [the Amorites] *before Israel, and He slew them with a great slaughter...pursued them...and struck them...*" (Josh. 10:10 NASB).

God even "...*threw large stones from heaven on them...*[until] *more...died from the hailstones than those...killed with the sword*" (Josh. 10:11 NASB).

Joshua recognized God's purpose in this battle, and because he was secure in his relationship and authority, he could dare to declare what he did. The Bible says "...*Joshua spoke to the Lord...and he said...'O sun, stand still at Gibeon, and O moon in the valley of Aijalon'*" (Josh. 10:12 NASB). The cosmic convergence that was required to stop or reverse the rotation of the earth must have been awesome!

Joshua was speaking into the Lord's realm but, because he knew what God's will was, he could take a faith position and command even that realm. Joshua heard from God before he declared into the heavenlies. Then, when Joshua spoke, God hearkened to Joshua's voice, although the declaration was made directly to the sun and the moon (see Josh. 10:14).

Jesus mirrored the same submission and dominion when he stated, "...*the Son can do nothing of Himself, unless it is something He sees the Father doing...*" (John 5:19 NASB). Yet He could rebuke the wind and calm the waves (see Mark 4:39). Jesus' ability is our ability because our "*...life is hid with Christ...*" (Col. 3:3). Like Him, we can do what the Father is doing. Adam called out the animals. Moses called down hail and darkness; he parted the Red Sea and won battles by holding up his hand (see Ex. 17:11). Joshua stopped the waters of the Jordan; Elijah stopped and started rain, all by declarations.

The Bible is full of the evidence of man's authority found in submitting to God's power to change circumstances.

LIGHT VERSUS DARKNESS

This is part of the conflict between the Kingdom of God and the kingdom of satan. When Jesus rebuked the wind, He spoke as we would with our children.

We don't say to our kids "I rebuke you," when they are doing something they shouldn't. Instead, we command, "Stop that," or "Quit that." Jesus rebuked the wind and sea, essentially commanding:

"Stop that."

"Now settle down."

"Don't be so agitated."

He rebuked the wind because it was causing the waves; He simply calmed the water. He was speaking to it and it obeyed Him. God wants us to shift from asking to commanding, provided we know the will of the Father.

Jesus demonstrated this when he said that He prayed to God "*... because of the people...that they may believe....*[And then]*...cried with a loud voice, Lazarus, come forth*" (John 11:42-43). He was not praying a petition; He prayed to strengthen the people's faith in Him. His fellowship with God allowed His declarations to have power.

A friend, Barry, and I (Jeanne) were ministering at a large conference to a young woman. She began to manifest and rise up as if to strike. I bound the spirit; surprisingly, she immediately froze in her attack position and stayed suspended there for some time.

We continued to minister and the pattern repeated itself several times, with the same result. We did bind the spirit harassing her. She was so deeply wounded that it took several hours before we were able to bring her to a place of freedom and healing. But, as we watched, I was amazed at the authority of the Word of God.

Jesus initiated his attack on the devil's kingdom when He "... *rebuked* [a demon] *saying, Hold thy peace, and come out of him*" (Mark 1:25). Jesus was simply saying, "Shut up and get out of here." The same word *rebuke* was used against the fever attacking Simon Peter's mother-in-law. He "...*rebuked the fever; and it left her...*" (Luke 4:39). "*It left her,*" refers to an entity rather than a condition.

Jesus often treated illnesses as Paul did demons: He cast them out. Paul commanded a demon attached to a slave girl, to "...*come out of her. And he came out that same hour*" (Acts 16:18). Sickness is a result of the Fall and whether sickness is demonic or caused by the demonic, Jesus often treated sickness as an entity and commanded it to stop its activity and leave.

Bob Jones spoke to us of viruses being the lowest level of this demonic activity. One Sunday, a young lady, Devyn, came forward for prayer. She had a hard lump just behind her ear. The doctor was concerned about it; he wanted a specialist to look at the mass for a possibly biopsy. Several people prayed for her and I (Jeanne) felt led to command the lump to disappear.

When I felt behind her ear, it was gone. Her mother took her back to the doctor for confirmation, who after checking her and hearing the story, cancelled the specialist's appointment.

We should attack the kingdom of darkness the same way as Jesus did, because God "...*did predestinate* [us] *to be conformed to the image of His Son, that He might be the firstborn among many brethren*" (Rom. 8:29). Jesus was the first of many just like Him. This prophecy concerning Jesus then applies to us; we also are anointed to preach, heal, deliver, recover, and liberate (see Luke 4:18).

TAKING AUTHORITY

Everything we obtain in the Kingdom depends on our faith: that is, on believing and declaring what God declares. I reiterate *"faith cometh by hearing...the word of God"* (Rom. 10:17).

Faith must be single-minded, for *"a double minded man is unstable in all his ways"* (James 1:8) and will receive nothing from God (see James 1:7). A prayer that says, "If it is Your will, God" is a prayer with no power because it is not of faith. Faith is assertive and knows how to claim what belongs to it.

When Jeanne and I were building a house, I (Ken) encountered a problem obtaining my windows. I had arranged for the windows to be delivered on a Wednesday and be installed on Thursday and Friday. That would allow my dry-wall contractor to begin work on Monday. When the truck didn't show up on Wednesday, I made a phone call. One of the drivers was sick and another had left for a funeral; my windows would not be delivered that week.

I decided to rent a truck and pick them up myself. By the time I got to the warehouse, the dayshift was leaving. I went inside, but was confronted by the manager, who was not sympathetic to my plight. I had prayed and God had told me to go get the windows, so I wasn't about to accept defeat. The manager told me there was no way to get my windows, as there was nobody working that night.

I said, "I was told I could get the windows today; I've spent the money to get a truck and I'm not leaving without my windows." I had already paid for them and they sat only a few feet away. I was not about to be deterred. He protested, "I don't even know which are yours." I finally convinced him to let me go back by the loading dock and sure enough there sat my windows.

I dug in my heels and demanded that my windows be released. Finally, he gave in and found a man in the back who could run the forklift. Twenty minutes later, I was on my way with my precious cargo. Had I wavered or shown the least sign that I could be put off, I would have left empty-handed. God wants us to display tenacity in demanding release of those things that are bound up.

A conscious decision to trust what God has said will spawn a declaration in agreement with God's words. Paul said, "...*we having the same spirit of faith...I believed, and therefore have I spoken*" (2 Cor. 4:13). Without a sure word in your heart, you cannot speak or work the works of God.

If what we declare falls within our realm of authority, it will come to pass. Still, we must believe that we can before we can. God is looking for those who, by their faithful lifestyle declare that "... *they were strangers and pilgrims on the earth. For they that say such things declare plainly that they seek a country...* [in which God]...*hath prepared for them a city*" (Heb. 11:13-14,16).

Abraham's life created an inheritance for his children; condemned evil nations to destruction; created a family, which become a nation; and blessed the entire world through his seed. Did he understand what he was doing? I doubt it.

Abraham had prophetic insight into what was coming; Jesus said as much (see John 8:56). But it is unlikely he saw the complete picture. He just humbly walked with God, even when it seemed he was alone. He was preparing a resting place for God's Spirit and God liked Abraham, the father of faith.

Three religions claim Abraham as their spiritual father. Yet he was just a shepherd. His secret was he was always looking for God and was willing to change his plans to suit the Father's will. His life was a confession of faith and produced supernatural results.

CLASH OF KINGDOMS

Jesus was the seed that Abraham was promised (see Gal. 3:16). He stepped into what Abraham saw "...*afar off...* [and what he]... *embraced...and confessed...*" (Heb. 11:13).

The life of faith often seems contradictory: speaking things we don't see is counterintuitive. So is the idea of winning battles by doing good. Yet, Jesus knew that sickness, sin, demonic oppression, destructive weather, and even death were part of satan's kingdom. He defeated satan by going "...*about doing good...healing all...*" (Acts 10:38). We, too, "...*overcome evil with good*" (Rom. 12:21).

Jesus attacked satan's kingdom wherever he went, suffering rejection (though He had favor); being scorned (though He was worshiped); knowing poverty (though He had abundance) and suffering ridicule (even though He was adored). He was hated by those in power (but loved by the outcasts); had various attempts made on His life (though others would lay down their lives for Him); was lied about (though He knew all the truth) and was killed (though He had assisted even in that and dismissed His own Spirit. Jesus said, ...*I lay down my life... No man taketh it from Me ...I have power to lay it down, and I have power to take it again...*(John 10:17,18)).

Was this a life of contradictions? No, it was the manifestation of two kingdoms: The devil's kingdom in opposition to Him and the Kingdom of God in awe of Him. That is why a Christian's declarations seem so strange; they are in opposition to the logic of the realm in which they are declared.

Our lives also will be marked as Paul's was with open doors of opportunity and great opposition—all at the same time (see 1 Cor. 16:9). If we are going to be effective in the Kingdom, then satan *will* attack us.

Yet, we are not defenseless. I (Jeanne) like to declare the psalms over situations whenever I feel a demonic attack is underway. I will often proclaim, *"No evil will befall you, nor will any plague come near your tent"* (Ps. 91:10 NASB).

I will also parry an attack by declaring Psalms 35:1-9 which begins: *"Plead my cause, O Lord, with them that strive with me: fight against them that fight against me"* (Ps. 35:1). These declarations release angelic hosts into our situations and will bring dramatic breakthroughs.

DECLARATIONS

We need a word of God for every situation in our lives to facilitate the release of angels. The antithesis of this is to speak curses, thereby releasing demons. We can use words to bring either evil or good. Solomon cautioned his readers to *"curse not the king, no not in thy thought; and curse not the rich...for a bird of the air shall carry the voice..."* (Eccles. 10:20).

Jeanne and I had a contract to install some steel in a tar sands extraction plant 500 kilometers north of our home. I had a Christian foreman, Roger, to look after the job and everything was going smoothly.

We had gotten two words concerning our jobs that year: First, I heard that I would not be able to use my own efforts or the force of my will to accomplish the work. I would have to use faith. I (Jeanne) had heard: *"Many are the afflictions of the righteous: but the Lord delivereth him out of them all"* (Ps. 34:19). We recognized from the nature of these words that things would not necessarily go smoothly, but in the end it would all work out.

We had hired two additional men to round the crew of ironworkers we had working up north. Requests for camp rooms and site orientation were sent in on a Wednesday, four days before the new men were to arrive on site. I was well within the 72 hours prior notice that was required—or so I thought.

The man to whom I sent the requests had taken an extra-long weekend and left work on Wednesday. As a result, the forms were never passed along to the camp supervisor or to those in charge of the orientation. At nine o'clock on Sunday night, I got a phone call from my foreman stating that the men were at the gate, but weren't allowed in because they weren't on the list.

I made a quick call to the housing office, only to be informed that there were no rooms, the men were not registered, and they would not be allowed on site. I asked to speak to the supervisor, but was told that would not be possible, Then the person to whom I was speaking hung up the phone.

I made another call to the security gate and a second one back to the camp registration with zero results and no hope of anything more.

Talk about frustrating! Actually *frustration* is far too tame a word; I was livid. I kicked the desk; I threw a book onto the floor; I thrashed and spewed. But I could not make a dent in that fortress 500 kilometers away.

This administrative glitch had huge ramifications for our company. One of the men had traveled over 1500 kilometers just to get to the job. Now, he and the other man would have to backtrack 70 kilometers just to get a hotel room in Fort MacMurray.

Not only that, but there would not be another orientation for three days. The cost to us for their transportation, accommodations, and compensation for loss of wages was going to run in excess of $6,000. Needless to say, I was not a happy camper.

Jeanne looked at me and calmly said, "What did God say to you? Maybe you should repent for your anger and claim the Word. God can open any door."

I was so upset that it took me a minute to calm down, repent for my angry outburst, and finally declare the words that we had received.

We interceded for the situation and claimed access onto that site. I then phoned Roger back and reassured him of God's sovereignty over the situations that we had submitted to Him. I then said, " Start praying and go over to the housing office. I am going to phone again and the supervisor will get the guys a room. God will give you favor and the guard will break the rules to get the guys through."

I hung up and commanded favor for Roger and the two men. Ten minutes later, the phone rang and Roger announced, "We're in. Don't worry about orientation. If we can get through the gate with no papers, indoctrination will be no problem. Have a good night."

With that, Roger hung up. I turned to look at Jeanne. She said, "I knew they would get in. You need to operate in more faith and less anger."

Satan cannot control a peaceful Christian. We are told to cast *"all* [our] *care upon Him; for He careth for* [us]" (1 Pet. 5:7). The Bible says, *"The steps of a good man are ordered by the Lord: and He delighteth in his way"* (Ps. 37:23).

Without those words we received and declared, those guys would never have gotten through the gate. Such is the power of a faith declaration. Remember, hear God; believe what He says; declare it; receive it.

THE OTHER SIDE

Jesus said, *"By your words you will be justified, and by your words you will be condemned"* (Matt. 12:37 NKJV). Our words allow us to create our universe for good or ill.

I (Ken) have been healed of gout in my two big toes, but I still get attacks from the enemy concerning that healing. Some days I wake up and the pain and stiffness are almost unbearable.

If I agree with the symptoms, then my healing will evaporate. So, I aggressively claim what Jesus purchased for me: my healing. Within minutes or hours of speaking life back into my toes, the pain and stiffness disappear. These attacks are only lying wonders. The truth is that *"...with His stripes we are healed"* (Isa. 53:5).

We can use our tongues to serve both kingdoms. Peter declared that Jesus was *"...the Christ, the Son of the Living God"* (Matt. 16:16). Jesus said that revelation was from Heaven (see Matt. 16:17). Moments later, Peter rebuked Jesus and declared He would not die at the hands of the Sanhedrin. Jesus turned and identified the source of that rebuke as satan (see Matt.16:23). We must be careful what we say.

Years ago, in Washington, Jeanne and I attended a conference. The man who set up the conference was an apostle with dozens of churches under his charge in Africa. During the worship that night, he confessed that even though he had authority in Africa, he didn't feel he had any here.

Shortly after that, the worship leader said to the crowd, "We are not going to lead tonight; we are going to accompany you."

I turned to Jeanne and said, "They just gave away all their authority."

Where there is no legitimate authority, illegitimate authority will rule. The problem began with the apostle who believed he lacked authority. Within minutes of the worship leader yielding his authority, the place went nuts.

Flag wavers, dancers, and pseudo-singers (all of whom had a rightful place of worship in their own realms of authority) now descended upon the worship team. I have never seen such a debacle in my life. People actually took the mikes away from the worship team and literally pushed them out of the way. The worship leader lost all control and had to come down and consult with leadership team.

Finally, another apostle, who knew what had happened, took control, shut down the nonsense, and taught on coming under proper authority. Later, the worship was rebooted with the worship team firmly in control.

You will get what you say. When the children of Israel spoke negatively, the Lord chastised them saying, "*...just as you have spoken in My hearing, so I will surely do to you*" (Num. 14:28 NASB). They had wished to die in the wilderness and that is where they died (see Num.14:2,29).

I (Jeanne) spoke a curse over myself just before a prophetic council. I didn't feel worthy to be invited and said to Ken that I didn't know why I was going. I didn't feel prophetic and was I sure I would have nothing to say. When I got there, God did give me revelation, but I felt the words snatched out of my mouth as I tried to express myself. I had to repent of the negative words I had spoken before I again felt fluid in my speech.

James warns us that *"the tongue is a fire, a world of iniquity...that it defiles the whole body, and sets on fire the course of nature; and it is set on fire by hell"* (James 3:6 NKJV). If we can control our tongues, then we can *"...bridle the whole body"* (James 3:2).

The Bible says, *"But those things which proceed out of the mouth come forth from the heart; and they defile the man"* (Matt. 15:18). The problem with the mouth is the condition of the heart.

I remember hearing Corrie ten Boom say that we are like sponges; when we are pushed against a wall, whatever is in us will come out. If we have bitterness, or unforgiveness, or abandonment and rejection, that is what will spew out when we get offended.

The key then to our Christian walk is to get these areas healed. Then, when the *"prince of this world cometh,* [he will find] *nothing in* [us]*"* (John 14:30)—no place for him to sink his hooks into and manipulate us.

THOUGHTS AND WORDS

How then do we get healed? That subject is beyond the scope of this book, but one of the most effective methods is to speak encouragement to your heart. Just as the devil is looking to hook into places of your heart that agree with him, so is God.

Jesus knew the Jews wanted to kill him. He explained to them the reason: *"...because My word hath no place in you"* (John 8:37).

We all have unconverted areas in our hearts that do not agree with the Word. Deep down, we don't really believe our declarations. Therefore, our words are not supported with faith and cannot change the world if we do not believe them in our hearts. We must *"...be filled with the Spirit; speaking...in psalms and hymns and spiritual songs, singing and making melody in your heart to the Lord"* (Eph. 5:18-19).

We know that, when everyone was against him, David *"...encouraged himself in the Lord..."* (1 Sam. 30:6). The psalmist also spoke to his own soul saying, *"Why are you cast down, O my soul?...Hope in God, for I shall yet praise Him..."* (Ps. 42:5 NKJV). David was talking his soul and his heart into believing that God was his help and health.

Satan's only weapon over you is suggestion: negative thoughts. That is how he defeated Eve and how he attacked Jesus. That is how he will attack us. Thoughts do not defeat thoughts; words defeat thoughts. Eve didn't know personally what God had said concerning the tree of the knowledge of good and evil. When she tried repeat the words she got them wrong, therefore those words did not repel the enemy or break off the power of his suggestions. The word says *"...the woman saw"* (Heb-considered, gaze, take heed)[8] *"the tree"* (Gen 3:6). She considered what the devil had spoken and through her fleshly assessment fell under those suggestions and abandoned what God said. Jesus, on the other hand, countered with the Word every thought the devil threw at Him:

Satan said, *"If..."* (Matt. 4:3)

Jesus said, *"It is written..."* (Matt. 4:4)

Satan said, *"If..."* (Matt: 4:6).

Jesus said, *"It is written..."* (Matt. 4:7)

Satan said, *"...if..."* (Matt: 4:9).

Jesus said, *"...it is written..."* (Matt. 4:10).

Jesus did not entertain the thoughts or even argue with satan. He declared the Word, letting it speak to the lies. Even *"Michael the archangel, when contending with the devil...said, 'The Lord rebuke thee'"* (Jude 9).

Our job is to speak God's will and Word—not only to satan, but also to those places within us that are not yet converted. It is not our place to reason or argue. The way we dismantle strongholds is to shine the light into their dark places by declaring the Word of truth.

Friends of ours, Jason and Tangie, were good examples of this principle. Jason had gone to university for several years, had acquired his degree, but had also accumulated a large debt from a student loan. Partway through his schooling, he became very sick. This sickness continued after university, limiting his capacity to work.

The debt from the loan and his reduced income soon put them in a financial bind. They claimed the Word that if they would *"seek... first the Kingdom of God, and His righteousness...all these* [necessary] *things* [would] *be added"* (Matt. 6:33). By faith, they declared the Lord's blessing and provision and often saw God's hand move in mighty ways. Still, they struggled financially.

They persevered for years, desiring to see God's blessing. Still sick, Jason received another word of encouragement from God: *"...I will give thee the treasures...and hidden riches...that thou mayest know that I, the LORD...call thee by thy name..."* (Isa. 45:3).

Jason and Tangie began to call forth the hidden treasures, but saw little change in their financial situation. They continued to struggle, until God opened their eyes to the fact that they were walking in a "poverty mentality."

This stronghold in their minds prevented them from believing the creative words that God had given them. In order to make ends meet, they had withheld tithes, only trusting God to provide their bare necessities. Once they realized how their mind-sets and words had blocked the flow that God wanted to supply, they repented.

First, they asked forgiveness for their lack of faith demonstrated by not tithing and broke off any curses associated with this. Then they declared God's blessing (see Mal. 3:8-12). Next, they repented of agreeing with the lies of the enemy, broke the stronghold, declared the prosperity they had been promised and began tithing.

God's hand began moving in their lives, and shortly afterward, the government of Canada forgave Jason's entire student loan of close to $80,000. Our circumstances, our universes, are shaped by the words we speak.

INVOLVE GOD IN THE SITUATION

God spoke a word to me (Jeanne), saying, *"All thy children shall be taught of the Lord; and great shall be the peace of thy children"* (Isa. 54:13). I had to claim that word often, as all of our boys went through difficult times.

Our son Michael got tied up with four other young men who were pulling him in all the wrong directions. I started to pray for their salvation and felt I was to declare that whatever relationships were not from God would be removed.

Within a month, three of his friends were in jail and the fourth moved up north to avoid the same fate. Now that the evil influences were no longer present, it took only a short time for Michael to turn back to God. Today he owns his own film company and produces documentaries and Christian television. A mother's declarations and prayers cause change!

God hears everybody's words, Christian or not. The Bible says, *"The eyes of the Lord run to and fro throughout the whole earth, to shew Himself strong in the behalf of them whose heart is perfect towards Him..."* (2 Chron. 16:9). At the same time, derogatory comments against His nature can also demand His attention.

God had already appointed Jehu to replace Ahab as king over Israel (see 1 Kings 19:16) when the Syrians insulted the nature of the God. God entered the battle on Ahab's behalf, saying:

> *...Because the Syrians have said, The Lord is God of the hills, but he is not God of the valleys, therefore will I deliver all this great multitude into thine hand...* (1 Kings 20:28).

God heard the Syrians lower Him to the status of a minor deity who only had authority in certain realms. He addressed their words.

Through the centuries, Israel continued to grumble against God. We do the same thing when we complain about our situations instead responding in faith. God later chided the Jews, saying, *"Your words have been stout against Me, (says) the Lord....Ye have said, It is vain to serve God: and what profit is it...?"* (Mal. 3:13-14). This accusation was declared right in the middle of a prophetic word of hope.

God loves us and doesn't ignore us. Our declarations are not just those we publish aloud, they are also those things we have whispered. Whatsoever we *"have spoken in the dark...and...spoken in the ear in inner rooms shall be proclaimed on the housetops"* (Luke 12:3 NKJV). The declarations that come from our hearts do not need to be shouted to be heard.

Our declarations of God's sovereignty and goodness are weapon in the His mighty hand. God designed us to subdue the earth; that mantle of authority is still available to those who are willing to wear it. God told Israel, *"Thou art my battle axe and weapons of war: for with thee will I break in pieces the nations..."* (Jer. 51:20).

God set Jeremiah *"...over the nations and over the kingdoms, to root out, and to pull down, and to destroy, and to throw down, to build, and to plant"* (Jer. 1:10).

In Revelation 19:15, Jesus is depicted as having a sword in his mouth so *"...that with it He should smite the nations: and...rule them...."* Likewise, we are told to keep *"the high praises of God...in* [our mouths], *and a two edged sword...to bind kings...and...nobles...to execute upon them the judgment written..."* (Ps. 149:6, 8-9).

Peter, through revelation, declared Jesus' divinity, which prompted Jesus to hand him the keys of the Kingdom (see Matt. 16:16-19). Those keys are the Spirit-breathed declarations that allow us to *"...bind...and...loose on earth...*[as in] *heaven"* (Matt. 16:19). Jesus only gives the keys to His house and the access to His bank accounts to those He trusts. Like Peter, we need to believe and declare God's words into situations. It is those Spirit-breathed, prophetic declarations that are the keys and will unlock our destinies.

We must shift our thought patterns when we encounter closed doors. Suppose I am trying to unlock a door but the key doesn't seem to be working. If I know I have the right key, I will keep trying until it works. If I am not sure, I will give up, thinking I have the wrong key. That is why we need a sure word from the Lord; so we will persist until the door opens.

You may be reading and thinking, "I haven't experienced these things in my walk; therefore, these biblical examples must not mean exactly what they say." The Word has perfect integrity; it is true regardless of any of our experiences.

When we base our doctrine on things that happen or don't happen in our lives, we will never believe the Word. If we can repent and *"be transformed by the renewing of* [our minds], *so that* [we] *may prove what the will of God is..."* (Rom. 12:2 NASB), then we can reign with Him. God wants our wills so molded to His that the two are identical. Jesus could say *"...he that hath seen Me hath seen the Father..."* (John 14:9). God wants us to manifest Him in the world.

If we believe it and speak it, we can do as Jesus did: We will open a door in Heaven that allows the Kingdom of God to displace the kingdom of darkness wherever we go. Jesus functioned in the power of the Spirit, and whenever He spoke, a force went out from Him that overpowered the enemy, no matter how he had manifested himself. The Word documents the divine response to the manifestations of evil:

> To sickness: *"Say the word, and My servant will be healed"* (Luke 7:7 NKJV).
>
> To demons: *"What word this is!...He commands...spirits, and they come out"* (Luke 4:36 NKJV).
>
> To death: *"...He said...Arise....And he that was dead sat up..."* (Luke 7:14-15).
>
> *"Peter...said, Tabitha, arise.... And he...presented her alive"* (Acts 9:40,41).

To the elements: "...He commandeth...winds and water, and they obey Him" (Luke 8:25).

To lack: "...At Thy word I will let down the net. And... they inclosed a great multitude of fishes..." (Luke 5:5-6).

To opposition: "...He said...I am He, they went backward, and fell to the ground" (John 18:6).

To sickness: "...According to the saying of the man of God: and his flesh came again...and he was clean" (2 Kings 5:14).

To demonic possession: "...Paul...said to the spirit. I command thee...to come out.... And he came out..." (Acts 16:18).

To weather: "Elijah...a man with a nature like ours... prayed...and it did not rain.... And he prayed again, and the heaven gave rain..." (James 5:17-18 NKJV).

To the economy: "Elisha said...to morrow... shall... fine flour...be sold for a shekel... in the gate of Samaria" (2 Kings 7:1).

To enemies: "Elijah answered...Let fire come down from heaven.... And there came down fire..." (2 Kings 1:10).

Jesus told His disciples that He would *"...give* [them] *a mouth and wisdom, which all of* [their] *adversaries* [would] *not be able to gainsay nor resist"* (Luke 21:15).

Words! They are the creative force of the universe. But remember, both God *and* satan want to use our words. Satan wants our words because he has no power of his own in this realm. He subverts the authority we have, manipulating us to speak curses and unbelief into our lives and realms of authority.

God uses our words because He has chosen to work through men in this world. He trusts the nature of Jesus in us so completely that He declared, *"...Concerning the work of My hands command ye Me"* (Isa. 45:11). We need to shift our thinking so we can pull the power of the supernatural into this natural realm.

If we believe the Word and our authority in this realm, we will call God's power down to dispel the darkness. It is not necessary to rebuke the darkness. It's only necessary to declare the light. We rebuke the enemy wherever we find him but the enemy is not the darkness; the enemy dwells in the darkness.

SHIFT INTO PRAYER

Lord, change our speech so that our words line up with Your words. Give us a stronger awareness of our power over darkness as we make declarations of health and healing. We declare now that we live in the light and have Your life in us! In Jesus' name.

ENDNOTES

1. Zodhaites, Spiros. *The Complete Word Study Dictionary: Old Testament* (Chattanooga: AMG Publishers, 1994), s.v., 216, 1961.

2. Ibid., s.v., 216, 3335.

3. Ibid., s.v., 216, 7121.

4. Ibid.

5. "Harriet Beecher Stowe's Life & Time," *Harriet Beecher Stowe Center,* http://www.harrietbeecherstowecenter.org/life/#war (accessed May 27, 2009).

6. Young, Robert. *Analytical Concordance to the Holy Bible* (London: United Society for Christian Literature, 1973). Thing, page 975/Word, page 1068.

7. Gillet, Randal. Manager, Spruceland Millworks Inc., personal e-mail, January 2009.

8. Zodhaites, Spiros. *The Complete Word Study Dictionary: Old Testament,* s.v., 559.

Chapter 11

WHERE ARE WE?

Wisdom and Knowledge

KNOWLEDGE is power! That concept is well known and accepted in the business world. If we had access to tomorrow's newspapers, we would be empowered to accumulate vast amounts of wealth, avoid adverse situations, and avail ourselves of beneficial opportunities.

We would appear to others to be knowledgeable and astute, people whom even governments would seek out for savvy insights. We would make instant decisions with courage and conviction while others agonize over choices for days or weeks.

In short, we would be seen as the new "Solomons" of the earth—and all because we had knowledge unavailable to others.

"Through wisdom a house is built...by knowledge the rooms are filled..." (Prov. 24:3-4 NKJV). Knowledge enables us to navigate, even in unfamiliar or unknown circumstances, with an ease that belies our professed ignorance.

Imagine you are planning a trip into the woods. You will need two things: a topographical map and a compass. The map (which tells us where we are in relation to our destination) will be of no use in our navigation unless we can read it. The compass will be useless as well, unless we are able to assess how its indicated directions relate to the map we are using.

God has equipped us for life: He has given us both a map and a compass—and just to be on the safe side He also laid out a trail. The Bible is our map; the Holy Spirit is our compass; and Jesus left His footprints for us to follow. This chapter is designed to help you shift your thinking in order to use the supernatural equipment God has provided.

In fact, Jesus' *"...divine power hath given unto us all things that pertain unto life and godliness, through the knowledge of Him..."* (2 Pet. 1:3). He is the Word, the anointed One; He is and our guide as we walk through this life. If we know Him, we are wise, for He is *"...made unto us wisdom...righteousness...sanctification, and redemption"* (1 Cor. 1:30).

During World War II, the Allied Forces ferried the planes needed at the front to islands in the Pacific Ocean. There was sometimes no radar or radio communication on these islands. The planes flew over the cloud cover to avoid enemy detection and then dropped down through the clouds, at the designated distance, hoping to find the small atolls so they could refuel.

If they couldn't see the islands when they came out of the cloud cover, they had a problem: Which way to turn? Even if the information they had was correct, the pilots may have deviated slightly from the course. Those deviations, over thousands of miles, could have put them 20 or 30 miles off course—but which way? Were the islands to the right or left? Did they overshoot or come out of the clouds too soon? With limited flying range, a wrong turn now could cost planes and lives.

The ferry pilots overcame this potential disaster by veering off course a set amount that would always bring the planes to the left of the desired targets. That way, even if they were off slightly, the pilots still knew which way to turn.

Knowing where you are in relation to where you want to go is vital for survival. Unlike these pilots, we have a destination, the Father, who is in touch and actively guiding us from Heaven.

THE MAP

The Bible is our map, but to use it, we must read it. It only takes 90 hours to read through the Word; 15 minutes a day will get you through the entire Bible in a year.

We believe there are several reasons why most of us don't read the Bible: we fear we won't understand it; we've tried a couple of times and found it dry and lifeless; we don't really believe that God cares enough to speak to us personally; or we aren't truly in love with God and His Word.

All these reasons come from fleshly mind, which *"...does not receive the things of the Spirit...for they are foolishness to him..."* (1 Cor. 2:14 NKJV). When we come to God, we do so not with intellect, but in faith. It is the only way we can receive anything from Him.

Since the Garden, satan has tried to ban the Word, burn the Word, and bury the Word in insignificance. He knows how important the Word is to our ability to walk in authority. We also need to recognize its importance to us.

I (Jeanne) had an unsaved woman come to me, looking a word from God. A Scripture popped into my mind as I looked at her: *"Before I formed you in the womb I knew you..."* (Jer. 1:5 NASB). I immediately said to her, "You weren't a mistake; you weren't an accident. God wanted you to be born."

The woman started to cry. I continued to pray for her and explain God's love and plan of salvation for her life. She was willing to pray to receive Christ because the word she heard was alive, speaking into the very wound that was troubling her. She had always felt that she was a mistake and unwanted by her parents. God saw the wound and gave me the right Scripture to heal it. The Word also opened my insight, enabling me to get to the heart of her hurt so that she could be healed and drawn to God.

When we drive in a big city like Los Angeles, I (Ken) both drive and navigate. Some people don't understand maps very well; Jeanne is one of them. She has a hard time figuring out where we are on the map. She likes to navigate by landmarks, things she can actually see, rather than by their representations on a sheet of paper.

Jesus said of Himself, *"I am the way, the truth, and the life: no man cometh unto the Father, but by Me"* (John 14:6). He is the map, the compass, and the path. His life is what we can follow, even when we don't understand all the doctrines or directions.

I sat beside a couple who were doing prophetic evangelism at an outreach in the marketplace. They were uncomplicated people who loved Jesus but lacked some of the skills I thought necessary to bring people to the Lord.

As I listened to them guide the person to whom they were ministering, I winced. I said to myself, "You can't say that." A minute later, as they led a repentant soul to the Lord, I whispered, "Then again, I guess you can." If you know Jesus, you know the way, and the truth, and the life.

What actually transpires when we become Christians? What changes? What doesn't? To answer these questions I am going to sketch a topographical map—of us. If you are a visual person, like Jeanne, you will appreciate a topographical map that includes landmarks like rivers and lakes and indicates the varying elevations of hills and valleys.

Below is a schematic; it shows how our body, soul, and spirit interact, and it will help us understand just where we are in relation to God.

God originally intended all three realms to act in concert and harmony. When Adam fell, all three aspects of his nature fell, and all were separated from God. Adam was originally *"a living soul"* (1

BODY, SOUL, SPIRIT SCHEMATIC

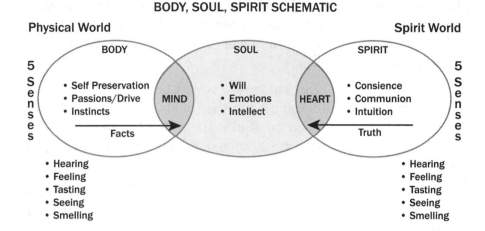

Cor. 15:45). This was his main realm of functioning: he walked in the natural, but was connected to the spiritual.

Because he was both in the spiritual and physical realms at the same time, he could see God, experience God, and have communion with Him. Adam's three parts acted as one unit in perfect harmony. In this aspect, he was the image of God, whose three personalities: Father, Son, and Holy Spirit are one in thought, word, and deed.

When Adam fell, the oneness within himself was shattered. With the breaking of his communion with God, he lost his perspective on the spiritual realm. His physical eyes became veiled to the presence of God. Isaiah said it this way: *"...your sins have hid His face from you..."* (Isa. 59:2).

At his creation, Adam had wisdom but no knowledge. Knowledge comes from accumulating information and storing it in our memories. Adam had no memories because he had no experiences: he had no history; he was created, not born. He operated in wisdom, which came out of his spirit, through his heart, to his soul.

After the Fall, that direct connection was lost and he began to draw on his soul, which now filtered information from his five senses through his mind. All of humanity, since Adam, has been limited to this low level of existence. The spirit still functions, but because it is not directly connected to God, it becomes subservient to the soul. When we become Christians and trust God, Jesus reestablishes that spirit connection to Him.

The three parts of our nature are connected by two interfaces. The interface between the spirit and the soul is the heart. The interface between the body and the soul is the mind. Because the interfaces cross over two aspects of our nature, their function also has two natures.

Take the mind: If I ask, "What is two plus two?" the mechanical or bodily function answers, "Four." The intellect or soulish side of the brain comes into play when it gets an "idea." The mind assimilates and sorts all the information from both the body and the soul, and presents it to the will to decide on a course of action.

The heart functions in a similar capacity between the spirit and the soul. It must analyze and sort the information that comes through the spirit and the soul, likewise submitting it to the will to decide on a course of action. The larger the interface on either side, the greater is the flow of information to the soul.

The capacity of the mind is determined largely by our DNA, though that can be altered depending upon whether we have a closed or open mind. The capacity of the heart depends on whether or not the spirit is allowed to control (see the following diagram).

Just as the capacity of our mind determines our intellectual abilities, the Word says we can "...*run the way of Thy commandments, when Thou shalt enlarge* [our hearts]" (Ps. 119:32). Our hearts enlarge as we allow the Spirit to gain more access to the soul, as the circles indicate.

Becoming born again, or receiving salvation, dramatically changes the makeup of our nature. Our spirit becomes the container to hold the Holy Spirit. From that moment on, there is a shift from the soul functioning as the main control center to the spirit taking over.

CARNAL CHRISTIAN

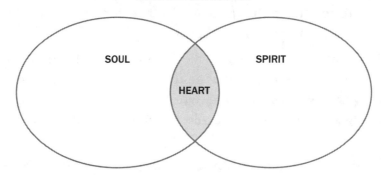

SPIRIT LED (CONTROLLED) CHRISTIAN

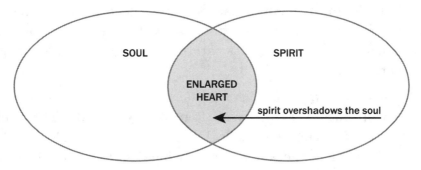

Our part in receiving God's salvation is to acknowledge our sinful state, ask forgiveness, repent of our sins, acknowledge that Jesus' sacrifice on the cross paid for those sins, and receive Him personally as "[our] *Lord and* [our] *God*" (John 20:28).

God's part of this divine exchange is to bear the cost of our sins and indwell us with His Spirit. It's not what you believe, but who you receive that puts you in right standing with God. The Bible says, "*If any man have not the Spirit of Christ, he is none of His*" (Rom. 8:9). God's putting His Spirit in our spirit is the first step in our salvation.

The children of Israel experienced the Passover (the type of salvation) as the first step in their journey to the Promised Land. The object of our salvation is not just gaining access to Heaven; God wants to restore us to the purposes He had for Adam—fellowship with God and dominion on the earth.

That goal will be realized when we conform to the image of Christ. We apprehend this change in increments, usually initiated in our everyday lives: at home, work, school, and play. These are the testing grounds where our old thoughts hold sway and resist change.

I (Ken) was looking over a set of prints, preparing to bid on a job. Normally, I do a quick overview, to get a feel of the scope of the project. Then I look at the specifics to do my bid. As I was running through the civil part of the job (which is not normally in our scope), I felt drawn to a particular detail. As I looked at this connection detail, I realized that it was part of our scope, but that it would not work.

Something in my spirit set off an alarm in my brain. I am the type of guy who grabs every bit of work that I can, even if I don't have the capacity to do it. This time I knew I didn't want anything to do with any of the work connected to this drawing detail. I started investigating a couple of other details and felt the same thing. I like to say, "The devil is in the details," but this time God was in the details.

I pulled all the work connected with these drawings out of my bid. The total value of this work was close to $80,000. In the end, all of the work proved to be a nightmare, but as we did it on a cost-plus basis, I could joke, saying, "Chaos is cash."

Had I bid those aspects of the job, we would have lost thousands of dollars. (A cost-plus bid is a bid that covers all your costs—labor, equipment, and materials plus 10 percent profit. If the work takes longer, you actually make more.) My spirit, not my "superior" intelligence, alerted me. I had to make a shift from following my mind to obeying the promptings of the Spirit to avoid disaster. Thank You, God, for Your Spirit's leading!

THE COMPASS

The Holy Spirit was given to allow us to walk with God in power. Jesus told the disciples, *"Ye shall receive power, after that the Holy Ghost is come upon you..."* (Acts 1:8). They received power because the Spirit became resident in them.

The original *Pentecost* (meaning "fifty" in the Greek)[1] occurred 50 days after Passover and was highlighted by the giving of the law. God said He would make *"...a new covenant...I will put My law in their inward parts, and write it in their hearts...and they shall be My people. And...they shall all know Me..."* (Jer. 31:31, 33-34).

Today, the law is no longer meant to be a set of rules that we filter through our minds, deciding how or what we will obey. Instead, through salvation, it becomes part of our nature, residing in our hearts so that we instinctively obey.

Peter called for all, on the day of Pentecost, to receive *"...the gift of the Holy Ghost"* (Acts 2:38). We receive the actual person of the Holy Spirit, meaning all His nature and power. Included in this are manifestations of wisdom and knowledge (see 1 Cor. 12:8). Jesus, who is the baptizer, revealed that *"...your heavenly Father* [gives] *the Holy Spirit to them that ask Him..."* (Luke 11:13).

This indwelling of the Spirit represents a dramatic shift in how we receive and process information. Where all information previously came through the mind from the five senses, we can now perceive with the heart information gained through the spirit.

To function in this manner, we must be *"...transformed by the renewing of* [our minds]*..."* (Rom. 12:2).

Jeanne and I used to get into arguments when I would logically lay out a course of action, only to have her say, "I don't feel we are to do that."

"What's your reason?" I would ask.

"I just feel something is wrong," she would reply.

That would exasperate me to no end. I was functioning out of my soul; she was functioning out of her spirit. Because I didn't understand that concept, I thought that she was just fearful.

You'll remember that when we were considering an investment I really wanted to be involved in, Jeanne prayed and said, "They will overextend themselves and lose our money. We should stay out of this."

I decided to ignore her and made the investment. You know the rest: We lost the investment. Jeanne drew her knowledge and her wisdom from the prophetic gifting that operated through her spirit. I have since shifted my thinking about her wisdom in hearing from God. I now listen to her, after years of ignoring warnings she garnered from the Spirit. I have also made a shift to listening to the Spirit for myself.

God alerted my spirit to the strange behavior of a renter whom we were helping to move. Two of our sons and I were helping to unload their furniture off their truck. We were willing to take it into the appropriate rooms, but they insisted that we put all of it in the garage. I found that peculiar.

Jeanne and I prayed; we felt that they were not going to pay the rent. God prompted me to prepare all the pertinent documents that would enable me to evict them. Sure enough, when the rent was due, there was no money. I served notice on the spot. The man was shocked and tried to play both on my sympathies and my compassion as a Christian. I told him that God had warned me and I had obeyed. I said, "If you come up with the full rent before the end of the month I will rip up the eviction notice."

He appeared offended that I didn't trust him and accused me of being something less than a Christian, but because I had a word, I wouldn't budge. The fact that all the utility companies later called looking for this couple told me that they had skipped out on them also. My own nature would have given the man many chances, but God warned me and gave me supernatural wisdom in dealing with him.

The discerning process went like this:

God gave revelation (we saw): *Stuff going into the garage.*

God gave knowledge (truth): *We knew they were going to skip out.*

God gave wisdom (strategy): *We prepared the eviction notice and presented it immediately upon nonpayment.*

The following schematic further illustrates this process and the progressive nature of God's wisdom.

Graham Cooke talked[2] about four tiers that reveal God's purposes. As in the previous story, these include revelation, knowledge, and wisdom. The fourth stratum is best called mysteries, or secrets.

Revelation comes from reveal, which means "to uncover or disclose,"[3] from the Latin *revelatus*, meaning "to draw away, as in pulling back a curtain."[4] Most prophecy and prayers are initiated from this level. God pulls back the curtain on something or someone and lets us see. God has told me to neither prophesy nor pray my revelation until I have understanding, as 90 percent of what we see will appear to be negative or, at best incomplete.

LAYERS IN GOD'S PURPOSES

REVELATION — Dig Here:

X

TRUTH — Knowledge

STRATEGY — Wisdom

MYSTERIES

Paul said, "...*now we see...darkly...*[we] *know in part...*" (1 Cor. 13:12). We also see the world through the filters of our experiences, character, fears, and personal preferences. These color and warp the view of revelation.

A revelation may be true and accurate, but can still be misinterpreted by our flesh. Although revelation is what we see in the Spirit, we often mix it with what we see and hear in the physical realm. We may know some of the facts; we may have seen some situations, or believed a rumor. Mixing these with true revelation results in suspicion instead of truth. God wants us to move beyond revelation into the larger truth.

I (Jeanne) was ministering to a friend. When I laid my hands on her, I received an electric shock. In the Spirit, I saw an electric eel, but I didn't know what it meant. Not wanting to go on only the revelation, I decided to dig deeper. I left her in the living room and opened an encyclopedia to gain some insight about the picture of the eel that I had seen. I discovered that these eels live in South America and immobilize their victims by shocking them.

Now I understood what my revelation meant. This woman's husband was in South America and had taken up with another woman, who happened to be into witchcraft. My friend was totally immobilized, in fear and panicked by this turn of events in her life. I was able to pray a release for her because I had insight into her problem. The revelation alerted me about where to dig for the truth.

Truth is always deeper, buried somewhere under revelation. Jesus came before Pilate and said He came to "...*bear witness unto the truth...*" (John 18:37). Pilate sneered and demanded, "*What is truth?*" (John 18:38). That is still the response of people today: they believe truth is unattainable and unknowable.

Everybody has his or her own version of the truth. *The* truth is Jesus is truth. He said, "...*Everyone that is of the truth heareth My voice*" (John 18:37). True prophecy and prayer are rooted in the hearing of Jesus' voice. This truth is powerful; the Word says it "...*shall make you free*" (John 8:32).

Revelation is the sign or the X that marks the spot on our map and says, "Dig here." Revelation was Moses' burning bush; it was Paul's Damascus road experience; it was Jacob's glimpse of a ladder protruding into Heaven. It was even Peter's declaration of who Jesus was.

Revelation is a sudden opening of our eyes, with little or no understanding of what we just saw. Moses argued with God and tried to dodge the assignment God was giving him to do (see Exod. 3:11–4:14).

Paul asked, *"Who art Thou, Lord?"* (Acts 9:5) and was blind for three days before he received back his sight. Jacob took more than 20 years before he returned to the spot where his revelation occurred. It took Jacob wrestling with an angel (see Gen. 32:2) before he could change his name and his walk to enter into the original revelation (see Gen. 28). Right after his prophetic insight, Peter's next words were a rebuke of Jesus (see Matt. 16:23) because he didn't have a clue what his revelation would entail.

Truth is the root from which revelation emerges. It is knowledge, buried beneath the soil, veiled under the flesh, hidden from sight and memory. Without an uncovering by Jesus, the truth or root of the situation cannot be known. Truth brings hidden things to light.

When we started ministering to our friend Ron, he had no idea why he was feeling rejected. We asked the usual questions about his family and other things in his past, but to no avail. Everything seemed normal enough, as far as he could remember. So we told him to pray and ask Jesus to reveal something that would point to a root. He prayed and said that all he got was a memory about falling and breaking a plate, but he was blank about any significance concerning it.

I (Jeanne) seized onto the picture and started praying about the truth behind the plate incident. Immediately, Ron started crying as he slowly unraveled the truth about the broken plate story. He had hidden, from himself, the memories about his schizophrenic mother who was unable to look after all the responsibilities of raising a family. Ron had taken the brunt of the abuse and the work, constantly picking up what his mother could not carry. He had buried those memories to protect himself from the pain they brought up. The revelation was a broken plate; the truth was a broken mother. Truth can be devastating.

Even when we know the truth, we often don't know what to do with that knowledge. Truth deals with what is or what was. It is the spot on the map proclaiming, "You are here."

That affirmation of our location is invaluable when we are looking for a store in a strange mall. If we know where we are, we can develop a strategy to get to where we are going. Wisdom is that strategy that enables us to discover our destiny and deal with our present circumstances.

I (Ken) was trying to be a good witness at work, one having the right attitudes and actions. God opened up a Scripture one morning before work that allowed me to deal with a potentially volatile situation. The Word said:

> *He will not allow your foot to be moved; He who keeps you will not slumber…. The Lord is your keeper…. The Lord shall preserve you from all evil; He shall preserve your soul* (Psalms 121:3,5,7 NKJV).

We were erecting some steel inside a powerhouse where a crane could not navigate. Since we couldn't unload it with a crane, we dumped the trailer carrying the iron in the bay we were erecting.

Stan, my foreman, and I now faced a large, tangled mess of beams and channels to sort through. We were using tuggers (small, air-powered drums with cables) and snatch blocks to hoist the load. Trying to save time, we sent up two or three pieces of steel at the same time, all connected together, one above another.

We worked for an hour or so pulling apart the steel, finding the right pieces and sending them up to be connected by the crew working above us. The tugger operator was on the third floor, so he could see both the ground and the ironworkers above.

We had just sent up a lift of three pieces, when we noticed that the bottom one was upside down. We signaled the operator to stop hoisting and send the lift back down, so we could turn over the bottom beam. Because we had been randomly pulling out steel, the pile resembled a game of pick-up sticks. Stan and I could not really move without falling or breaking an ankle, so we just stayed under the load as the operator stopped the lift.

It was at that point that tragedy almost struck. The operator had stopped the lift and kicked the tugger out of gear to start coming down. He had failed, however, to put on the brake, so when he took the tugger out of hoist mode, the entire load rocketed down in free wheel. We were jammed in the steel down below, as 3,000 pounds of iron crashed into the pile. It careened around Stan and me as we ducked, fully expecting injury or death to slam us.

Seconds later, when the dust settled, we looked at each other in disbelief: no broken bones, no severed limbs, nothing but relief. God then reminded me of the Scripture which He had given me that morning. He had revealed a truth about Himself saying He would preserve us.

The operator rushed down, expecting the worst, only to find us dusting ourselves off in relief as we climbed out of the pile. He now expected to be on the receiving end of my wrath, but instead, I was able to share with him the goodness and faithfulness of God.

Without that Scripture rising up within me, I would have lost my cool and attacked that operator, who almost killed us. God had spared our lives and kept me from ruining my witness on the job. God's wisdom in situations is always tied to His love.

Beneath wisdom lie the mysteries and secrets of God. These only get opened up when their time has come. Jesus told His disciples, *"Unto you it is given to know the mysteries of the kingdom...but to others in parables; that...they might not understand"* (Luke 8:10). Jesus called these mysteries *"...things...kept secret from the foundation of the world"* (Matt. 13:35).

There are mysteries still kept secret. Daniel was not given to understand *"...the words...closed up and sealed till the time of the end"* (Dan. 12:9). Paul heard *"...unspeakable words, which it is not lawful for a man to utter"* (2 Cor. 12:4). John was told to *"seal up those things which the seven thunders uttered, and write them not"* (Rev. 10:4).

Other mysteries have been opened: Paul was able to reveal and expound the *"...mystery...which is Christ in* [us], *the hope of glory"* (Col. 1:27).

THE PATH

Jesus said, *"I am the way, the truth, and the life: no man cometh unto the Father, but by Me"* (John 14:6). He came to demonstrate how to walk this earth in the light of eternity. While here, He refused to use any of His divine powers, relying instead on the Holy Spirit to manifest the Kingdom through Him. That way, He could challenge us to do *"greater works"* (John 14:12) than He did, because we have both, the Holy Spirit and the Son.

Jesus walked as He did because He had *"...the spirit...of the fear of the Lord"* (Isa. 11:2) resting upon Him. *"The fear of the Lord is the beginning of wisdom..."* (Prov. 9:10); it is also the hatred of evil (see Prov. 8:13). (We are not tempted to do things we hate.)

I do not smoke because I hate the smell and taste of tobacco. Refraining from smoking does not demonstrate any willpower or great discipline on my part; nor does it indicate holiness or superiority. It simply says that smoking has no power over me because it has no place in my affections.

It can be the same with all sins: when we displace them with the love of God, they lose their power.

Jesus dealt with His flesh by using this principle. He knew he was *"...equal with God: but made Himself of no reputation"* (Phil. 2:6-7). Even as a man *"...He humbled Himself, and became obedient unto death..."* (Phil. 2:8). His fleshly nature loved exaltation just as ours does, so He went out of his way to discipline it by humbling Himself. When people wanted *"...to make Him a king, He departed...alone"* (John 6:15) because He was only willing to let God exalt Him (see Phil. 2:9).

We have a hard time acting the same way because we don't fully believe that God loves us. We don't believe that truth because our parents, who may have loved us, still did things that hurt us. We learned earlier that, as a result, we developed structures of disappointment, rejection, and self-pity to protect ourselves.

These structures, though they were designed to insulate us from further wounds, actually lock us into the level of wounding we already have. They also block us from receiving love because they create mind-sets portraying us as unlovable.

You'll remember that I (Ken) had a structure like that. I thought my only value was in whatever work I could do. This allowed me to have an attitude of a servant which was good, but prevented me from believing I could be a friend—to God or anyone else.

Jesus, on the other hand, knew *"...He was a Son..."* (Heb. 5:8 NKJV). Therefore He could take *"...upon Him the form of a servant..."* (Phil. 2:7) without creating inner conflict about His appointed roles.

His mind-set of being a beloved Son *allowed* him to be a servant; my mind-set of being a servant prevented me from being a beloved son. If we are going to be like Jesus, we must think like Jesus, which means we must also believe that God loves us!

Our wounds are the main hindrances preventing us from walking like Jesus. I have a large scar on my right wrist, which I received when a grinding blade cut me to the bone. That accident happened 37 years ago. The scar doesn't hurt; it's not bleeding; and it's a long way from my heart. It's completely healed and most of the time I don't even notice it.

There is one problem, however; the scar tissue blocked the regrowth of the nerves that were severed in the accident. As a result,

I lack some feeling in my hand. Sometimes, I burn myself and don't even realize it until later.

Our woundings have a similar effect on us. They interfere with the signals that God wants to send, such as, "I love you." When our wounds filter out these signals, we respond inappropriately. We may push away the ones God has sent and embrace those we should shun.

There is only one solution: Get healed. Jesus spent 40 percent of His ministry healing people; He is the same today. My scar was necessary for the initial healing of my wrist, but it prevented proper functioning later on. That scar tissue needs to be removed to restore full function. Likewise, we must shift out from under our self-protecting scars to enter into the realms God has for us.

Emotional woundings prevent us from functioning in the truth. The Bible says truth makes us free (see John 8:32). If it is freedom we want, then we need to make a decision to embrace truth.

When we want to know the truth about a situation in the world, we grab a newspaper or watch the news on TV. When we are wounded, we don't get the straight news story; we get an emotional editorial—*our* editorial.

We then base our responses on this slanted version of reality—a distortion that is not the truth. Jesus said, *"Thy Word is truth"* (John 17:17). The truth is in the Word of God, not in what we feel, and not in what we see.

I (Ken) bid on a job a few years back. It looked like a sure thing. I had done my homework and the numbers looked OK—not great, but OK. I had a good crew and was getting lots of support from the steel supplier. Several things about this job appeared to make it a divine opportunity.

First, I got a call from the steel fabricator asking me if I would like to erect steel buildings for them. God had blessed them with so much work they needed some experienced manpower to assist them. I had prayed for the owner several years before and had always thought it would be nice to work with him. So when this call came, I took serious notice.

Next, I dreamt about an exceptional ironworker, Wayne, about whom I hadn't thought for a few years. Two days later, he phoned me wondering what I was doing and whether I had any work.

Now I was getting excited; things were coming together. I had the open door: I had the dream about my potential foreman, the phone call that corresponded to the dream, the finances to do the job, and the desire to do it. I was ready to launch.

Jeanne was not so sure. I showed her the numbers and said, "Nothing can go wrong." Well nothing could be further from the truth. Jeanne said, "I think you should ask God again. He knows things you don't know and I won't feel right about this until you ask God if you should proceed." I sent up a cursory prayer, then I gave Jeanne my "editorial."

The truth was, I could not control the weather.

We started the job at the end of September. Traditionally in Alberta, the weather turns cold and the ground starts to freeze about that time, but not that year. It started to rain and didn't let up for two months. We were in a brand-new development, which had no roads and poor drainage.

For the next two months, we pulled trailers and cranes and trucks out of knee-deep mud. The steel got covered, the equipment got covered, and the guys got covered with that mud. One of the trucks even had its frame bent trying to negotiate the ruts.

The truth was I lost $30,000 on that one building. Except for the generosity of the fabricator and some help from the union, the losses would have been even bigger. God knew the unexpected thing would happen. Jeanne had a sense of it; but I was oblivious because I filtered it all through my "working wounds." I chose to believe what I could reason and see the facts. But facts are not truth: the Word of God is the truth (see John 17:17).

God is looking at our hearts, not our actions. When we get our hearts right, our actions flow out of them. The Word says, *"Keep thy heart with all diligence; for out of it are the issues of life"* (Prov. 4:23).

God called David *"...a man after His own heart..."* (1 Sam. 13:14), yet David murdered, committed adultery, and was a lousy father who tolerated incest, murder, and competition within his own family. He had at least eight wives and dozens of concubines; and he built palaces for himself with the billions of dollars he possessed. Would you want him as your spiritual leader?

We talked about God's regard for David in Chapter 3. David became the plumb line by which future kings would be measured—despite his obvious faults.

God loved the purity of David's heart. David was willing to repent and take responsibility for his sin. When he numbered the people and brought down judgment upon them, he said, *"...I have sinned, and I have done wickedly: but these sheep, what have they done?..."* (2 Sam. 24:17).

That heart attitude also fostered David's prophetic gifting, as the Word says *"...the pure in heart...shall see..."* (Matt. 5:8).

David never doubted God's love, justice, or mercy. He could pen these words:

> Yea, though I walk through the valley of the shadow of death, I will fear no evil: for Thou art with me...Surely goodness and mercy shall follow me all the days of my life: and I will dwell in the house of the Lord forever (Psalms 23:4,6).

David could have said, as Jesus did: *"Into Thine hand I commit My spirit.... My times are in Thy hand..."* (Ps. 31:5,15). God could be merciful, because David was willing to *"...fall...into the hand of the Lord..."* (2 Sam. 24:14).

Unlike his predecessor, King Saul, David was willing to let God decide his fate. Saul was determined to control his own destiny.

When Samuel spoke a judgment on Saul and turned to go, Saul tried to prevent him and ripped his robe. This prompted Samuel to repeat the judgment of the loss of the kingdom, citing the ripping as a prophetic act (see 1 Sam. 15:27-28).

Saul revealed his true heart when he replied to Samuel, *"I have sinned: yet honor me...before...people..."* (1 Sam. 15:30). This was his true desire, not to stand before the Lord, but before the people. He had just lost the kingdom (though he refused to accept the loss); yet his only interest was in appearance. He was not concerned with humbling himself or repenting. In fact, he had no intention of letting God rule with whom He saw fit.

Conversely, David, when threatened with the loss of the kingdom and fleeing, refused to take the ark with Him even though it was the symbol of God's authority. David said, *"Carry back the ark ...if I shall find favor in the eyes of the Lord, he will bring me again ...let Him do to me as seem(s) good unto Him"* (2 Sam 15:25,26). David saw God as who he was: God! He saw himself as insignificant and totally dependent on God's favor.

Saul fought for his position as king; David was satisfied with God's favor. Saul actually fought against God as he struggled to hang onto his position.

David sought God's favor through repentance and received the position Saul strove to keep. Therefore, David's sons inherited the kingdom, not on their own merits, but on the merit of their father.

That is where we stand today: trusting that the favor Jesus has with the Father has been assigned to us. The Word says, *"Set your affection on things above.... For...your life is hid with Christ in God. When Christ...shall appear, then shall ye also appear with Him in glory"* (Col. 3:2-4).

We are in Him; loved by Him; seated with Him in the heavenlies (see Eph. 2:6). We are destined to *"...reign with Him..."* (Rev. 20:6).

He has invested us with all that He is and in Him *"...are hid all the treasures of wisdom and knowledge"* (Col. 2:3).

He has prepared for us everything we will ever need or desire in Him. Now, all we have to do is *shift* our ways of thinking—and we will receive!

SHIFT INTO PRAYER

> Lord, I pray that, as You lead us by Your Spirit, we will see and hear what You are doing and saying. Sharpen our discernment to know clearly what is of You and what is of us. Cause us to hear and follow Your still, small voice. Give us Your wisdom and knowledge to make us victorious in this life. In Jesus' name.

ENDNOTES

1. Zodhaites, Spiros. *The Complete Word Study Dictionary: New Testament* (Chattanooga: AMG Publishers, 1992), s.v., 4005.

2.. Cooke, Graham. Eyes and Wings conference, Kelowna, British Columbia, 2001.

3. *Webster's New Twentieth Century Dictionary*, s.v. "reveal."

4. *Webster's New Twentieth Century Dictionary*, s.v. "revelation."

CONCLUSION

I (Ken) had a dream that was I driving down a road, late at night. There was no moon and the headlights did not illuminate the ditches because of the high windrows of snow that had been thrown up by a plow.

As I drove, a deer appeared on the road ahead. It turned, startled and blinded by the headlamps, and began to bound ahead of me down the tunnel of light. I slowed down so as not to hit it, hoping it would vault the snow banks and return to the safety of the woods flanking both sides of the road.

Although the deer had just come out from those trees, it could no longer see them because of the brightness of the headlights. Therefore, it chose to stay with the only thing it could see: the road.

As I inched closer, panic set in and the deer became frantic, dashing back and forth, looking for an escape. Finally, in one last desperate effort, it leapt over a drift and escaped into the bush.

That's when I woke up.

God started to speak concerning the dream, saying, "The Church is like that deer. We have drifted into territory we were never designed to inhabit. When the enemy appeared and applied pressure on us, we panicked and started to move in the only direction we could see...down the road. We were blinded by that realm of sight and unable to discern our place of safety, which was beyond the grid of that natural road and over in the supernatural.

Like the deer, if we stay with what we can see, we will die. It will only be a leap of faith into the unseen realm that will take us to where the enemy can no longer harass us. We were designed to live beyond the road of this plane: off the grid of natural human reasoning and experience.

The enemy is not our problem; we were created in the presence of an enemy: the snake was in the Garden. Our mind-sets and thought patterns are the elements that betray us when the enemy oppresses. That's when we panic and resort to reason, instead of hearing a word from God.

Still, He comes behind and says, *"This is the way, walk...in it..."* (Isa. 30:21). But His gentle voice of direction is too often lost in the consuming glare of our situations.

We were designed for dominion, but have chosen to live in survival mode. We were designed to operate like God, the Creator of the world who is not controlled by the world.

He does not have a plan *B*. His original plan is still operating. It is to have *"...the earth...filled with the glory of the Lord"* (Num.14:21). Jesus' Kingdom is not based on the political/economic structures of this world. It is based on His power and His will.

Storms raging across the oceans of the earth do not affect the tranquility of an orbiting spaceship. Even though our bodies are down here in the storm, we *"...are not in the flesh, but in the Spirit..."* (Rom. 8:9).

I listened to an apostle from Zimbabwe, Tudor Bismarck, speaking in Edmonton, Alberta, Canada. He stated that even though the economy of Zimbabwe was imploding, his church was not suffering.

The inflation rate within his country rose to an astronomical 231,000,000 percent in July 2008[1] and the official exchange rate devalued the Zimbabwean dollar (ZWD) from par with the U.S. dollar all the way down to where US$1 equaled 669 billion ZWD on November 8, 2008.[2] Combine this with an average wage for a laborer of 200 billion ZWD (US 60 cents)[3] per month and you have a disaster of gigantic proportions.

Yet Tudor Bismarck said, "We don't need your money. The financial principles of the Kingdom of God work in Zimbabwe the same as they do in Canada. They don't depend on the economy of the country to work."[4]

He said that his church has 80 percent employment while the rest of the country suffers from 80 percent unemployment. They are able to walk in abundance while the rest of the country struggles in lack. The main things he was asking for from the North American Church were Bible teachers. The Church in Zimbabwe has been forced to take their eyes off the problem and place it on the promise that says we will not see *"...the righteous forsaken, nor his seed begging bread"* (Ps. 37:25).

God is the God of the impossible. He delights in doing what the world says can't be done; having slaves defeat the strongest army in the world; parting the Red Sea; feeding millions in the desert for years (see the Book of Exodus).

Yet the generations that left Egypt *"could not enter in because of unbelief"* (Heb. 3:19).

We are called to be *"the sons of God...*[if we] *believe on His name"* (John 1:12). To do this we must be *"...led by the Spirit..."* (Rom. 8:14). This is our calling, not to just survive in this world, but to have dominion over the whole earth (see Gen. 1:26). The whole of *"... creation eagerly waits for the revealing of the sons of God. [For then it]... will be delivered from the bondage of corruption into the glorious liberty of the children of God"* (Rom. 8:19,21 NKJV).

It is our job, through the power of the Spirit, to change the course of nature. First, we need to change our mind-sets, our beliefs, and our doctrines to conform to God's. He has declared that He is going to do it. He said we are His appointed, anointed emissaries through which He will accomplish this. If we cannot change our slave mentality of unbelief and operate in faith, trusting what He says, then God will not be pleased (see Heb. 11:6). He will pass us by and take the next generation that *will* believe to usher in the next phase of the Kingdom.

We wrote this book to challenge you. Don't be like the deer and get caught in the headlights of this world. Instead, *shift from the natural to the supernatural* and take that leap into your destiny in God's purposes.

Go ahead! Get "out of your mind" and into your spirit where God dwells. He loves you and has been waiting for you to join Him in His realm of glory. Jesus showed us the way and invites us to pick up our cross and follow Him through the veil (see Heb. 6:19-20).

The first leap may be frightening, but once you are off the grid, you will experience the peace and joy you been longing for.

> I pray that we, as a Church, begin to shift into a mindset of hope and faith. I ask that You prepare us for the great harvest that is to come, our minds hearing Your will and following after it. I pray that we would be a part of the army of God, rescuing people from the kingdom of darkness and ushering them into in the Kingdom of light. I pray that faith is imparted to every reader to receive more of You in Christ—knowing they are precious and important to the Kingdom of God.

> Lord, release faith that moves Your people out of the natural and into the supernatural, that they might

experience a mighty, vibrant life in Christ. In Jesus' mighty name.

ENDNOTES

1. http://en.wikipedia.org/wiki/Zimbabwean_dollar (Hyperinflation).

2. http://en.wikipedia.org/wiki/Zimbabwean_dollar (Exchange rate).

3. http://en.wikipedia.org/wiki/Economy_of_Zimbabwe (2006-2008).

4. Bismarck, Tudor. End-Times Handmaiden Conference, Edmonton, Alberta, Canada, July 2007.

TREASURE CHEST MINISTRIES

www.treasurechestministies.ca

MINISTRY CONTACT:

Brenda G. Smith—Treasure Chest Ministries
Box 3458
180 Century Road
Spruce Grove, AB T7X 3A7

780-962-5699

info@treasurechestministries.ca

WORKSHOPS/SEMINARS:

Breaking Generational Curses and Enacting Your Blessings
Healing Toxic Thought Patterns
Stirring up the Prophetic
Character: The Door to your Destiny

RESOURCES:

www.treasurechestministries.ca

Additional copies of this book and other
book titles from Destiny Image are
available at your local bookstore.

Call toll-free: 1-800-722-6774.

Send a request for a catalog to:

Destiny Image® Publishers, Inc.
P.O. Box 310
Shippensburg, PA 17257-0310

*"Speaking to the Purposes of God for This
Generation and for the Generations to Come."*

**For a complete list of our titles,
visit us at www.destinyimage.com.**